"The Way to Jerusalem"- Exposition of the Gospel of Luke

Written by Samantha Davidova (

The gospel of Luke is most famously
that in contrast to Matthew's gospel in
to the lost sheep of Israel only in Luke
envisaged with Jesus having taken the
reasoning from the Scriptures that it h

the Gentiles through him he giving the examples of Elijah having been sent only to
the Sidonian widow of Sarepta (or Zarephath) to resurrect her son and of Elisha his
successor having been instrumental in the cleansing of Naaman the Leper from his
leprosy when there had been many lepers in Israel itself at that time in Luke 4:26-
27, God's concern for those outside of Israel being manifestly stressed in Luke as
compared with Matthew's Israel-centric view of things. And so it is in harmony with
this general outlook of Luke's gospel that in its very preface it is addressed to a
Gentile dignitary at its outset, for Luke addresses himself to the most excellent
Theophilus (i.e. a Greek name meaning "loved by God" or possibly "friend of God")
in writing his account of those things which had most surely been believed among
them such as had been delivered unto them from those who were from the beginning
eye-witnesses and ministers of the word (i.e. Christ if "Logos Λόγος" here translated
"word" is a title as it appears to relate to the physical man Jesus in John 1:14; 1st
John 1:1 and in Revelation 19:13 "His name is the word of God." And so Luke
begins his account to the "most excellent Theophilus" in verse 5 by setting the scene
there that it came to pass in the days of king Herod the Great that there had been a
certain priest whose name had been Zacharias of the order of Abiathar in fact, that
notable priest in the Old Testament Histories who had been a contemporary and
confidante of king David and it so transpired at that time that Zacharias' wife
Elizabeth had been barren like her ancestress Sarah Abraham's wife before her,
having become well-stricken in years but they were nevertheless "both
righteous before God, walking in all the commandments and ordinances of the
Lord blameless" in verse 6.

Then in verse 8 Luke tells us that it came to pass upon a certain day that it fell by lot
for Zacharias to execute the duties of his priesthood's office in going into the temple
to burn incense before the Lord from the altar of incense located in the outer
sanctuary of God's temple and while he were so doing the whole multitude of all the
people stood outside praying. Now it came to pass at this time as Zacharias offered
up the incense that an angel sent by God appeared to him standing upon the right
side of the altar of incense and Zacharias being much perturbed at the sight of him is
instructed by this angelic personage not to fear and to take courage in so much as his
prayer had been heard and Elizabeth his wife would indeed bear a son whom they
were to name "John" meaning "God Answers or is Gracious" in whom they were to
have joy and gladness with many rejoicing at his birth. It would appear in verse 15
that the child would follow the Nazarite vow in Numbers 6:1-8, 12-13 including not
eating strong drink or wine as implied by the Hebrew "Nazirיִ ׁ ִ ,נ " as referring to a

separated one or the verbal form "lehazir יר ִ ֶה ַל " meaning to be separated (i.e. for divine service) as also expressed by the noun "nizer ר ֵ ֶנ " (i.e. separation) and by way of enabling this the child would be full of God's Holy Spirit from his mother's womb and so in this endeavour he would turn many of the children of Israel to the Lord their God. Verse 17 referring back to both Isaiah 40:3-4 and Malachi 4:5-6 then foretells that the child would fulfill an Elijah-like role in relation to the coming of the Messiah as that ancient prophet was expected to immediately precede his advent in bringing about a national reformation to make the people fit to receive him at his coming and so he would "go before him in the spirit and power of Elias, to turn the hearts of the fathers to the children, and the disobedient to the wisdom of the just; to make ready a people prepared for the Lord." Zacharias appearing spellbound by these glad tidings from the angel who announces his name as Gabriel (i.e. "God is my strength" (or "strong man")) in verse 19 (as appearing also in Daniel 8:16; 9:21) who had come forth from God's very presence is now rebuked like Abraham and Sarah before him for doubting the angel's word in esteeming he and his wife to be too old and stricken in years, Zacharias being struck dumb for his disbelief until the angel's words should be fulfilled. Thus Zacharias emerging from the temple is forced to gesticulate to the people who understood that he must have seen a vision to be so afflicted and having departed to his own house he remained dumb until such time that the child was born, Elizabeth herself becoming pregnant and hiding herself for a full five months declaring of how the Lord had "taken away her reproach from among men" by granting her this child.

After this the narrative then shifts to Mary the soon to be mother of Jesus residing in Nazareth in Galilee, in the sixth month the angel Gabriel being sent there to announce to her her son's birth in similar fashion but with one notable difference in that Mary was still betrothed to Joseph her future husband and had therefore not known a man in verse 34 her pregnancy therefore established from the outset as being "miraculous" in that "the Holy Spirit would come upon her, and the power of the Highest would overshadow her so that that which should be born of her would be called the Son of God" God himself supernaturally causing Mary to conceive by his Holy Spirit or power upon her to create the fetus in her womb. Thus the angel began by declaring "Hail, thou that art highly favoured, the Lord is with thee: blessed art thou among women" and quelling her fear instructed her to call her coming child "Jesus" (i.e. "God Saves") in so much as he would not only fulfill God's promises to her ancestor David to sit upon his throne forever and restore the kingdom of Israel that had divided after David's immediate son, heir and successor Solomon but moreover he would save God's people Israel from their sins as implied by his name Jesus. Thus having delivered this good news to Mary and the angel having departed from her Mary lost no time in going to see her cousin Elizabeth in the hill country of Judah to inquire after her as the angel had described her that had been barren to have now been in her sixth month of pregnancy. Indeed upon Mary's arrival at the house of Zacharias the baby literally leapt in Elizabeth's womb and Elizabeth being inspired by God's Holy Spirit declared Mary blessed among women and blessed the fruit of her womb esteeming it such a great thing that the mother of her Lord (although not yet born as in Psalms 110:1) should come to her in verse 45 Mary being blessed particularly in her belief that God would do what the angel had

2

promised for without "belief" nothing would be possible Mary replying how her soul (i.e. her being) magnified the Lord and of how her spirit now rejoiced in God her Saviour who had so regarded her low estate as his handmaiden for from thenceforth all generations would call her blessed. The remainder of Mary's speech then from verses 49 to 55 concentrates on God's mercy throughout all generations, how the arrogant and mighty had been or would be put down with the lowly exalted, the hungry filled, the rich sent away empty handed and especially here God had helped or was to help his servant Israel in remembrance of his mercy as he had spoken to Abraham and his descendants forever, the Israel-centric emphasis in Mary's speech likely to make this a genuine recollection of her words in a gospel whose original material if such exists is clearly angled towards the Gentiles' participation in Israel's heritage rather than God helping his servant Israel exclusively.

Verse 56 then informs us that Mary abode with Elizabeth for three months before returning north to Galilee and her house, her departure around about the time of the son's birth in verse 57, Elizabeth's neighbours and cousins being spoken of as rejoicing with her in perceiving how God had shown great mercy upon her in granting her this child when she had been "old" and "stricken in age." Then in verses 59 to 64 upon the occasion of the child's circumcision on the eighth day they wished to call him Zacharias after his father but Zacharias in accordance with the angel's instruction overruled this writing that his name was to be John and having done so his mouth was opened and his tongue loosed so that he could speak and praise God for his great mercy upon them that day in having so granted them the child when he and his wife had well nigh given up hope. In verse 65 a Godly fear fell upon all who witnessed these things and word of the "semi-miraculous" birth spread throughout all the hill country of Judaea people considering what manner of child it would be and God's hand was accordingly with the boy in verse 66. The remainder of this chapter then consists of Zacharias' long speech occupying from verse 67 to 79 the principal themes of which are that he prophesied by God's Holy Spirit of how God had visited his people to redeem them in the current events anticipating the further birth of Mary's child in the next chapter of Luke doubtless, more precisely in verse 69 he had "raised up a horn of salvation for them in the house of God's servant David," the "horn" figure being used for political powers in Daniel 7:7-8, 20, 24; 7:3-12; 20-24, Revelation 17:12-14 etc and doubtless associates Mary's child with the coming kingdom of God to supersede all human kingdoms in the apocalyptic visions of Daniel and Revelation, thus in verse 70 these things had been foretold by God's prophets since the world began that they should be saved from all their enemies as God had spoken of it in his holy covenant made with their forefathers, especially Abraham, in verse 73 to whom God swore an oath concerning it (i.e. Genesis 22:17 cf. 1st Corinthians 15:24-28) the forthcoming deliverance particularly enabling them to serve God freely without fear in the constraints placed upon them by their enemies being cast off, Zacharias' words recalling not only the current Roman subjugation of their nation but the even more restrictive Babylonian captivity and Egyptian dominance of their nation that had so hitherto marked their history.

Thus in verse 75 Zacharias articulates his people's dream to serve God freely "in holiness and righteousness before him all the days of their lives" after which he directs his attention to his newly born son whom he declares would be called "the prophet of the highest" now in steadfast belief of the angel Gabriel's words to him for it would be John's role to go before the face of the Lord (i.e. by manifestation in his Messiah as he had previously done so through the angels who had possessed the Cherubic "faces") to prepare the Lord's (i.e. in his indwelling in his Messiah) ways before him quoting again from Isaiah 40:3-4 and in this discharge of his heraldic role John would give the knowledge of salvation unto God's people whereby their sins might be remitted the entire thing having been orchestrated through the tender mercy of their God whereby the dayspring from on high had "visited them,"

"dayspring" translating the Greek "anatole ἀνατολή " (used of the eastern star seen by the wise men in Matthew 2:2, 9 and here appearing to refer to the sunrise) but possibly alluding back to the prophecy of Isaiah 11:1 concerning a branch springing forth (the other meaning of "anatole" as covering "shoot" or "branch" in the Greek Septuagint also in Jeremiah 23:5, Zechariah 3:8; 6:12) or "rising up" upon the stem of Jesse (i.e. of king David, Jesse's son's lineage and in Zechariah 6:12 "the man

whose name is the Branch," the Hebrew "netzer נֵצֶר " translated "branch" in Isaiah (but not in Zechariah) also signifying a separated or cut off one (compare Isaiah 22:25) or crown (i.e. kingship in Exodus 29:6; 39:30, Leviticus 8:9; 21:12, Proverbs 27:24, Zechariah 9:16) as in the Nazarite vow and implying this branch from the Davidic tree or ancestry was also to be "separated" from it or "cut off" from it as well as being a king for which the anointing, consecration or crown was upon his head, he being "separated" or "cut off" perhaps both in the circumstances of Christ's virgin birth and in the circumstances of his death as far as superseding the kingship was concerned he would have to be "cut off" as a broken branch before so doing. The dayspring being from "on high" then (compare Isaiah 4:2 "the branch of the Lord") not only relates to the circumstances of Jesus' birth by the Holy Spirit which would also have been instrumental in John's conception (but to a more limited extent in enabling Zacharias and Elizabeth to copulate successfully in spite of their old age) but also it refers to the fact that God would thereafter come down and "tabernacle" in Christ by his Spirit being present there inspiring him to speak his words in John 3:34; 7:16; 12:49-50; 14:10, 24; 17:8 and show forth his character in John 14:9 described as manifesting or declaring his "name" in John 17:6, 26 in so much as the expression of God's name was a declaration of his moral character in Exodus 33:17-19; 34:5-7. Thus the dayspring like a morning star (compare Isaiah 14:12) was "to give light unto them who sat in darkness and the shadow of death (quoted from Psalms 107:10 but similarly used in Isaiah 9:1-2 compared with Isaiah 60:2 concerning the enlightening of the Gentiles) and to guide their feet in the way of peace" (Christ making peace through his crucified body on the cross between Jew and Gentile to give them mutual access to God in Ephesians 2:11-19). Then in the final verse of the chapter, verse 80, Zacharias' speech having concluded Luke returns to the historical narrative briefly to report how "the child grew, and waxed strong in spirit, and was in the deserts till the day of his shewing unto Israel."

Luke Chapter 2

4

The second chapter of Luke then recounts the birth of Jesus, the angels' appearance to the lowly shepherds in contrast to Matthew's majestic magi, their visiting the baby Christ in the manger, Jesus' day of circumcision and subsequent presentation in the temple where the devout Simeon and the aged Anna give their blessings upon the child and finally in this chapter is recorded the event of Jesus' tarrying behind in the temple when he was twelve years old to discuss with the doctors of the Law about such sublime subjects that appertained to it, they being astonished at his understanding and answers at that young and tender age. Thus the chapter commences with recall of the decree that was issued from Caesar Augustus that all the world be taxed Luke writing for a Gentile readership making reference to the secular history of the time with which they would have been familiar and moreover noting that such taxation had first been enforced at that time when Cyrenius had been governor of Syria and so it came to pass that all men went to be taxed each one to his own city. And so because Joseph was of the lineage of David it required him to go up from Judaea to the city of David, namely Bethlehem where David's father Jesse had resided with his sons in 1st Samuel 16:1 as the ancient inheritance of that particular family line in Israel but it was a cumbersome journey for his wife Mary who was by then heavy with child drawing near to the time of her delivery but nevertheless because of the Roman mandate they were compelled to make the trip. Verses 6 and 7 of Luke chapter 2 then describe the birth of the child that Mary gave birth to Jesus her firstborn son whilst at Bethlehem in a manger as it so transpired upon account of there having been no room for them at the inn and so in this humble setting she wrapped the infant Jesus in swaddling clothes and laid him down there amid we imagine from the Christmas nativities the animals and hay.

After this in verses 8- 20 the story of the shepherds is recounted they being out in the fields keeping watch over their flock by night which detail is unlikely to support the Catholic dating of Christmas as the birth of Christ as in the mid-winter time the region is susceptible to snow and not suitable for keeping one's flock out at night it not being recorded in fact in the Bible the precise time of year when Jesus was born but the Christian date is more than likely to be a Christianized takeover of the old Roman celebration of the mid-winter solstice or longest night of the year we now accurately knowing to be upon the 23rd December but we may allow a couple of days difference for such an enormous time gap as two thousand years from modern times as well as the difficulties in precisely counting the minutes of the night in those ancient times. Nevertheless that dark night that had enclosed the shepherds is suddenly pierced by the dramatic appearance of the angel of the Lord to them and God's glory as a dazzling light shining all around them to make them sore afraid but the angel bade them not to fear in verse 10 for he had been sent with good tidings of great joy for all God's people in so much as that in the city of David that day a child had been born who would be their Saviour, namely Christ the Lord, and they would recognize the babe as being found within the humble environs of a manger enwrapped in swaddling clothes. No sooner then had the angel given this sign to the shepherds by which they might recognize the child than with him appeared a multitude of the heavenly host praising God and declaring "Glory to God in the highest, and on earth peace, good will toward men." Then the angels having finished this heavenly chorus and returned by the way they had come down back into heaven the shepherds resolved to seek out the child in Bethlehem as they had been instructed and finding the baby Jesus in the manger lost no time in imparting to the boy's parents such incredible things that the angel had told them concerning the child's destiny so that all that heard these things wondered at that which was told them by the shepherds Mary pondering them within her heart as to what would become of her child. And then the story of the shepherds' visit by divine revelation and instruction to the manger concludes in verse 20 with word of their going their way glorifying and praising God for all the things that they had heard and seen precisely as it had been revealed unto them.

And then after eight days in verse 21 it required for Mary and Joseph to have the child circumcised as according to the Law of Moses in Genesis 17:9-14, a procedure to be performed upon the eighth day in verse 12 there (and in Leviticus 12:3). And the child was officially named "Jesus" (i.e. "God saves") as according to the angel Gabriel's instruction before he had even been conceived in Mary's womb. And then when Mary had fulfilled the days of her purification after the birth as laid down in Leviticus chapter 12 they presented the newly born child at Jerusalem verse 23 quoting from Exodus 13:2 (also referred to in Exodus 13:12-15; 22:29; 34:19, Numbers 3:13; 8:16-17) concerning every "firstborn" male that opened the womb being holy to the Lord, the reason being because of the Passover so long ago in the nation's history when God's angel of death had slain all the firstborn in Egypt but had "passed over" the Hebrew homes there whose doors had been protected by the blood of the Passover Lamb smeared and daubed upon the threshold, lintels and doorposts but nevertheless such were "given to God" in so much as they should have ordinarily died along with the Egyptian firstborn that night if God had not provided a means of atonement for them and later in Numbers 3:11-13 it was agreed that the Levites or priesthood were "given to God" instead of the natural firstborn so that in Ezekiel 44:15, 28 they do not have an allotted inheritance like the other tribes territorially in so much as God is their inheritance (also mentioned in Numbers 18:23-24, Deuteronomy 10:9; 12:12; 14:27; 18:1-2, Joshua 13:33; 14:3; 18:7). Nevertheless in verse 24 of Luke chapter 2 it still required that Mary redeem her firstborn son with an offering according to the Mosaic legislation of a pair of turtledoves or two young pigeons this being prescribed in Leviticus 12.6-8 in the event that the cleansed mother did not have the financial resources to attain to the offering of a lamb laid down for the richer offerers there.

Then next in Luke chapter 2 we have the account of Simeon's blessing upon the child from verses 25 to 35 introduced as a just and devout man who awaited the consolation of Israel and to whom it had been revealed by God's Holy Spirit that he would not see death until he had seen the Lord's anointed (i.e. Christ) and being directed by God's Holy Spirit to enter the temple at that exact moment when Mary and Joseph brought in the baby Jesus to do to him after the custom of the Law Simeon took up the child in his arms blessing God for showing him his salvation (i.e. for all men) so that he might now depart in peace having seen the Lord's anointed or future king of the world whom God had prepared before the face of all people and not just the Jews alone so that in verse 32 the child would be "a light to lighten the Gentiles, and the glory of thy people Israel" together Simeon referring back to the words of Isaiah 60:2; 9:1-2. And so it was in verse 33 that Joseph and Jesus' mother Mary marvelled at such things that were being spoken of their child Simeon continuing by inspiration to speak of the more imminent future concerning him that he was set for the fall and rise of many in Israel with the current hierarchy and Jewish leadership set to reject Christ when the moment arrived whereas others of a more humble demeanour than these religious leaders consumed by their own self-righteousness would have the humility to accept Christ as their Saviour but in respect of his first coming before his kingship it involved sacrificial death that men might be saved from their sins to subsequently be able to participate in his kingdom and so with regard to this Simeon foretold by the Holy Spirit that a sword would pierce through Mary's own soul too that the thoughts of many hearts might be revealed men being judged by the word Christ spoke in John 12:47-48 which was like a two edged sword "piercing even to the dividing asunder of soul and spirit, and of the joints and marrow, and is a discerner of the thoughts and intents of the heart" in Hebrews 4:12.

Then after Simeon whose name means "he who hears" from the Hebrew verb "shamaשָׁמַע " to hear we have three verses concerning Anna (Hannah) the prophetess (from the Hebrew "channahחַנָּה " meaning "grace" or "favour") who was also present there in the temple that day to see the child, introduced as of great age, having been a widow for eighty four years in addition to having lived with her husband for seven years from her virginity making her ninety one but even this figure does not include her life preceding her marriage which would have presumably included another sixteen years making her well over a hundred. She is also mentioned as having been a prophetess, the daughter of Phanuel of the tribe of Asher (i.e. "Happy" being the exclamation of Leah when her child was born in Genesis 30:13) and it had been Anna's custom not to depart from the temple but served God there night and day with fastings and prayers and so it came to pass in verse 38 that she too coming in that instance "gave thanks likewise unto the Lord and spoke of him (i.e. Jesus) to all them that looked for the redemption of Israel." After this in verse 39 the family returned to Nazareth but of Jesus it is said that "the child grew, and waxed strong in spirit, filled with wisdom: and the grace of God was upon him."

Finally then in this chapter from verses 41 to the end (although the final verse consists of another general observation concerning Jesus' spiritual development as the previous chapter had ended with a similar statement concerning John) we have the account of an incident that occurred when Jesus was twelve years old Mary and Joseph going up as was the custom to Jerusalem at Passover time in order that they might keep the feast and it so transpired that the feast having ended they returned a day's journey to go back to Nazareth assuming that the boy Jesus was in the company but having sought him among their kinsfolk and acquaintances and not found him they were compelled to return again to Jerusalem seeking what had become of him. And indeed after three days they found him in the temple (this figure probably being introduced in so much as according to John 2:19-21 Jesus' crucified body became a future dwelling place of God or "temple" forever in the flesh "upon the third day"). Thus to their surprise Jesus was sitting in the midst of the doctors of the Law hearing them and asking them questions they being astonished at his understanding and answers for he was but a lad of twelve years old but Jesus' mother reproved him for dealing so thoughtlessly with them in so far as they had been sick with worry looking for him. Nevertheless Jesus replies to them that they need not have sought him anywhere else but in his Father's house for they should have known said he that he must be about his Father's business. But not understanding the thing that he said to them they took him in tow back to Nazareth he complying with their wish that he accompany them home but of Mary it is said that "she kept all these sayings in her heart." Thus the chapter concludes with Luke's observation that during his formative years so it was that "Jesus increased in wisdom and stature, and in favour with God and man."

Luke Chapter 3

Luke chapter 3 then is largely concerned with the ministry of John the Baptist within the wilderness of Judaea and his introducing Christ as the Messiah and his own role as Christ's forerunner. John now having come of age we are told that it was in the fifteenth year of the reign of Tiberius Caesar when Pontius Pilate was governor of Judaea, Herod Antipas Tetrarch of Galilee and his brother Philip Tetrarch of Ituraea and of the region of Trachonitis and Lysanias the Tetrarch of Abilene Herod the Great's kingdom having been divided up by the Romans into four Tetrarchs or quarters over whom his son Herod Antipas who features most notably in the gospels in the story of John the Baptist held the authority over one such quarter. Philip the Tetrarch of Ituraea and Trachonitis is not to be confused with Philip Herod II to whom Herod's wife Herodias had previously been married and who still lived for which cause she is rebuked by John the Baptist and he subsequently imprisoned for this was a different Philip although both sons of Herod but through different wives Philip the Tetrarch (20 BC to 34 AD) having been the son of Herod the Great and Cleopatra of Jerusalem whereas Philip Herod II had been the son of Herod the Great and Mariamne II (circa 27 BC to 33/34 AD). The reason for John reproving Herod for marrying his brother Philip's wife in verses 19 and 20 of this chapter was because it was written in Deuteronomy 25:5 that one should only marry one's brother's wife to raise up offspring for him after his death and doubtless under the instigation of Herodias herself Herod locked him up in prison (for Mark 6:20 indicates Herod Antipas had a measure of respect for John whom he feared as "a just and holy man" and liked to hear him gladly and moreover in Mark 6:26 was "grievously sorry" when his hand was forced in the matter of John's execution because of his foolish oath before his dinner guests that he would give Herodias' dancing daughter Salome anything she desired being prompted by her mother to ask for John the Baptist's head in the story in Mark not found in Luke's gospel except alluded to in Luke 9:7-9).

Then moreover at the time of John's ministry in verse 3 of chapter 3 Annas and Caiaphas were high priests it appearing that Annas was still regarded as high priest while he was alive although Caiaphas had succeeded him to the office for according to the original instruction in Numbers 35:28, Joshua 20:6, repeated in Hebrews 7:23

a high priest was consecrated to serve for life. And so John the son of Zacharias having retreated to the wilderness received the word of God there and commenced to preach his baptism of repentance for the forgiveness of sins drawing a large crowd of people who came forth to be baptized by him in verse 7. As it was foretold by the angel Gabriel to Elizabeth John's mother that he would go before the Messiah "in the spirit and power of Elijah" in Luke 1:17 so John is introduced as the Messiah's forerunner by the recitation once again of the words of Isaiah 40:3-5 that he was "the voice of one crying in the wilderness, Prepare ye the way of the Lord, make his paths straight. Every valley shall be filled, and every mountain and hill shall be brought low; and the crooked shall be made straight, and the rough ways shall be made smooth; And all flesh shall see the salvation of God" the geological and geometrical figures in this passage indicating world-shattering and transformative events would result from this coming one's imminent ministry even though the effects would not be immediately noticeable as the prophecy anticipates for Christ's second coming will doubtless be accompanied by such seismic disturbances that the prophecy indicates as in Zechariah 14:4 it is written concerning the Messiah that "in that day his feet shall stand upon the mount of Olives, which is before Jerusalem on the east, and the mount of Olives shall cleave in the midst thereof toward the east and toward the west, and there shall be a very great valley; and half of the mountain shall remove toward the north, and half of it toward the south" and again in Ezekiel 38:19-20 "Surely in that day there shall be a great shaking in the land of Israel; So that the fishes of the sea, and the fowls of the heaven, and the beasts of the field, and all creeping things that creep upon the earth, and all the men that are upon the face of the earth, shall shake at my presence, and the mountains shall be thrown down, and the steep places shall fall, and every wall shall fall to the ground." But the idea of "making the Lord's paths straight" in verse 4 undoubtedly speaks of the moral reformation of the nation to become "a people prepared for the Lord" the expressions therefore doubtless having a figurative meaning with regard to this and it is of course in this sense that John's ministry is to resemble that foretold for Elijah as in the closing two verses of the prophecy of Malachi he is to "turn the heart of the fathers to the children, and the heart of the children to their fathers" when he is sent before "the coming of the great and dreadful day of the Lord" as the Messiah's forerunner if in person then requiring his resurrection as indeed it appears he was so upon the occasion of Christ's Transfiguration in our gospel accounts alongside Moses but yet to play a greater role as heralding Christ's second coming by being raised again to fulfill the role of forerunner if Malachi 4:5-6 is to have any kind of literal fulfillment other than John the Baptist's fulfilling the role of Elijah at least in his calling upon the people to repent upon the occasion of Christ's first advent.

But regarding the Baptist's ministry itself now in verse 7 he appears to speak to the multitude generally declaring them to be a generation of vipers as far as their inward orientation was after the "serpentine mind" who as a brute beast of the field made by God in Genesis 3:1 was unable to reflect God's moral character having not been made in his image like the man and therefore the product of its "carnal" reasoning (Romans 7:14-15; 8:6-7, James 3:15) was to "falsely accuse" God of having lied about the effect of their eating of the fruit this mentality having been instilled in our human forefathers thereafter and transmitted to all their progeny so that in John 8:44

Christ had similarly declared the Jews to be the children of the false accuser who had been a murderer from the beginning (i.e. the serpent personified who had been the original false accuser of God whose character they had been exhibiting being "carnally" minded in Romans 8:6 like the one who had brought death upon the human race it being figuratively the "serpent" in them as it were. Indeed these very words of John the Baptist are applied to the Pharisees and Sadducees particularly in Matthew 4:7 as "the generation of vipers" addressed by him pinpointing the Jewish religious leadership as being particularly infected with this serpentine strain that Christ crucified its power to kill him forever upon the cross in Hebrews 2:14 by dying unjustly from it having committed no sin in Hebrews 4:15 requiring the intervention of God within the physical laws of sin and death to rectify the injustice in Christ's resurrection. That the Jewish leaders are addressed particularly in Luke chapter 3 is further evinced by verse 8's call upon them by the Baptist to "bring forth fruits worthy of repentance, and begin not to say within yourselves, We have Abraham to our father: for I say unto you, That God is able of these stones to raise up children unto Abraham" for it was precisely concerning the contentious issue that they the Jewish elite were guaranteed their salvation by being Abraham's natural offspring (as it seemed regardless of their failing morality) in John chapter 8 that Jesus is led to call them conversely the children of the false accuser in 8:44 (erroneously translated "Devil" as though a proper name) in that they were the genetic progeny of "sin in the flesh" (Romans 8:3) and "the lusts of their figurative father they did" in John 8:44.

Then regarding this claim to Israelite genetic inheritance as a guarantee of national salvation John went on to say that this "stock" was of no guarantee whatsoever to that end in the absence of moral reformation for even now he said "the axe was laid unto the root of the trees" and "every tree which brought not forth good fruit was to be hewn down and thrown into the fire," the fire motif applying to God's destructive judgement upon the wicked as in Jude 7 Sodom and Gomorrah "are set forth as examples suffering the vengeance of eternal fire" in so much as it totally destroyed them because of their poor morality, the punishment of immoral thinking and behaviour having been decreed to be "eternal destruction from the presence of the Lord" in 2nd Thessalonians 1:9 upon that day when "the Lord Jesus shall be revealed from heaven with his mighty angels, In flaming fire taking vengeance on them that know not God, and that obey not the gospel of our Lord Jesus Christ" in verses 7 and 8 there. Although these descriptions relate to the post-resurrectional judgement John is saying to the immoral Jews that came to him if it were only that they were consumed by the sin of self-righteousness but also most likely of social exploitation in using their positions as the religious leaders of the people to oppress them (for example in the practice of "Corban" in Mark 7:9-13) that Christ's imminent appearance among them would decide their fate thereafter and certainly as regards the fire motif their subsequent rejection of him would trigger those events that came to pass in 70 AD when God's magnificent temple in Jerusalem came to an inglorious and ignoble end in the Roman holocaust whereby it was burnt with fire and razed to the ground upon the temple mount making it "a burnt mountain" in Jeremiah 51:25. Thus with regard to the inevitable and most necessary reformation of the nation John foretold in verses 16 and 17 of this chapter when the people questioned as to whether he himself might be the Christ that he indeed baptized them with water (as a "washing away of their sins" in Acts 22:16, 1st Peter 3:21, Hebrews 10:22) but one mightier than him were coming whose shoe latchets he were not worthy to untie and that one "would baptize them with Holy Spirit and with fire" (in the sense most probably that "their faith would be tried by fire like gold that perishes" in 1st Peter 1:7 in their coming through "the furnace of affliction" (Isaiah 48:10) to be purified often involving their proving their faith through martyrdom to follow Christ unto death in Luke 9:23-25, Revelation 2:10) but for some of them this "fire" would be ultimately destructive in their not being found worthy of Christ and so John went on in verse 17 concerning the coming one who would "purify the sons of Levi as with fire" in Malachi 3:2-3 that "his fan was in his hand, and he would thoroughly purge his floor, and gather the wheat into his garner, but the chaff (i.e. the rejected of them) he would burn with unquenchable fire," it being unquenchable in relation to the subject of its operation until it had consumed it entirely in its total destruction as for example Jeremiah 17:27 had spoken of God kindling a fire in the gates of Jerusalem to devour its palaces and it never being quenched but in fact it did go out when they were completely destroyed so that only in relation to them as the subjects of the fire's operation it was never quenched until it had accomplished its objective in their complete destruction but with regard to the rest of the world it carried on after these buildings had been eradicated from the earth it being written ultimately that this land would be consecrated to God in Jeremiah 31:40 when that which had hitherto occupied it had been completely destroyed. We have a similar figure of speech in Ezekiel 21:3-5 where God says that his sword would go forth against all nations and no more return (i.e. to its sheath) it being evident that God "would not always be angry" and that ultimately his loving compassion would prevail over his judicial judgements and his sword would finally return to its sheath but of course against the subject of its operations it no more returned until it had totally destroyed them from the earth so that if there is any literal sense to the phrase it is only in relation to them until they are destroyed for they will know nothing else but the sword or fire until they can know no more in their being totally destroyed by them forever.

Returning to Luke chapter 3 the remaining details in this chapter may be briefly summarized with practical illustrations being elicited from the Baptist concerning what the people should do to repent from verses 10 to 14 including sharing one's clothes and food when one had a surplus, the tax-collectors not exacting more tax than required (i.e. to put away secretly in their pockets), the soldiers doing no untoward violence, neither falsely accusing and needing to be content with their wages, in verses 21 to 22 Jesus himself finally coming to John to be baptized (although he did not need it having committed "no sin" in 2nd Corinthians 5:21, 1st Peter 2:22, Hebrews 4:15 submitting to John's baptism as an act of humility signifying his "humbling himself unto death" in Philippians 2:8 although he had done nothing deserving death having committed no sin) the descent of the Holy Spirit upon Jesus after he had been baptized as a "dove" in appearance to John (John 1:32) empowering him for his subsequent ministry for it "abode" on him in the John verse and the acclamation of the heavenly voice that Jesus was God's beloved son in whom he was well pleased being in itself a figurative picture of Jesus' subsequent ministry and its assured outcome for God's Spirit would "strengthen Jesus" (Luke 22:43) to do all things to God's glory and not for his own culminating in his "humbling himself unto death" to fulfill God's will for him in his only Son given as a Saviour and redeemer of mankind through his own self-willed sacrificial death to that body in which he could have enjoyed the temporary and ephemeral pleasures of sin had he chosen to go the other way but the presence of God's Spirit with him strengthened him against his natural temptations (Hebrews 2:18; 4:15) as vouchsafed from his baptism done figuratively to represent his death "fulfilling all righteousness" thereafter in Matthew 3:15 (i.e. that God was righteous to destroy the sin-prone body (in Christ's case on the cross) and that he was also righteous not to exact "eternal" death in the case of one who had not sinned (albeit empowered by God's Spirit not to do so in Luke 1:35, John 3:34), Jesus' death showing God's righteousness or justice in two important ways therefore.

Luke chapter 3 then concludes in the final sixteen verses with the record of Jesus' genealogy traced back through David in verse 31, Jacob, Isaac and Abraham in verse 34 and finally all the way back to Enosh, Seth and Adam in verse 38 by way of showing particularly his Davidic descent (although physically through his mother Mary for Joseph was only "supposed" to be his father) and therefore his lineage qualifying him to be the Messiah as the long awaited "Son of David" and therefore "king" of the Davidic line.

Luke Chapter 4

Luke chapter 4 then contains the account of Jesus' being tested in the wilderness for forty days by an angel dispatched by God for the purpose, his speech in the synagogue at Nazareth and pro-Gentile rhetoric driving the congregation into a frenzy to try to cast him off the cliff upon which their city was built and then finally his healings miraculously performed upon the man with an unclean spirit in the synagogue at Capernaum, Peter's mother-in-law and various other sundry ones as the sun was setting there at Capernaum Jesus' finally being found at a desert place on the morrow where the people resorted to him there to be healed. Thus firstly as regards the temptation account ("tempt" coming in the KJV from the Greek "peirazomai πειράζομαι" which is the same word used in the Septuagint Greek recension of the Old Testament for God tempted or tested Abraham in Genesis 22:1 "test" being the modern equivalent of the 1611 translators' "tempt") having been led into the wilderness by God's Spirit for the purpose showing that the situation was indeed engineered by God one of God's angels who are recorded in the Bible as conversing in his council such as Genesis 1:26's "Let us make man in our image" and in 3:22 "The man has become like one of us to know good and evil" having proposed before him as in the previous case of Job who was similarly tested "Does Jesus fear God for nought? Only make him suffer and see if his faith still holds" in Job 1:9, 11 is subsequently called Jesus' "false accuser" erroneously translated "Devil" in the plain text as though a proper name in so much as the proposition that Jesus' faith would break and he would misuse God's newly bestowed Spirit-power to his own end and for his own benefit proved false, this false accusation being why the angel is so styled "the false accuser" within the account. Thus having been in the desert forty days and nights after the manner of Moses upon Mount Sinai in Exodus

34:28 the first test from the angelic personage who appears to Jesus was to turn the stone into bread that he might satisfy his hunger after having so miraculously survived without food or sustenance thus using God's power to satisfy his own craving and not for God's glory but Jesus passed the test in rebuking the angel with a quotation from Deuteronomy 8:3 that man did not live on bread alone but upon every word that proceeded forth from the mouth of the Lord did he live.

The second temptation or test involved the accuser miraculously transporting the weak and starving Jesus to the peak of a very high mountain reminding him in the words of Hebrews 2:5 and the general tenour of the first two chapters of Hebrews that the kingdoms of this world were now "given" to the angels to invisibly control as in the case of the invisible activities of the angels behind the scenes in manipulating world political events in the book of Daniel and now the angel propositions that he would give them to Jesus such that God had given him authority over as one of his angels if he did but bow down and worship him but Jesus sensing the test that the angel could not as obeying God alone (Hebrews 1:14) either fulfill the proposition or indeed be worshipped in God's stead again rebuked him as his adversary in this test declaring that it were necessary to worship God alone and serve only him in the words of Deuteronomy 6:13; 10:20. The final test in verses 9 to 12 to ensure that Jesus would not misuse the miraculous power given to him from his baptism onwards when that Spirit or power had descended visibly upon him with the appearance as of a dove then involved the false accusing angel who would be found in Jesus' case and as in the case of Job before him to be falsely accusing or slandering Jesus in propositioning that he could disobey God in misusing his power for his own benefit then involved the angel miraculously taking him skyward to the pinnacle of the temple in Jerusalem where he bade Jesus throw himself down to see if God's angels would come and take care of him quoting the words of Psalms 91:11-12 "He shall give his angels charge over thee, to keep thee: And in their hands they shall bear thee up, lest at any time thou dash thy foot against a stone" Jesus replying with the words of Deuteronomy 6:16 "Thou shalt not tempt or test the Lord your God" ("tempt" in Greek invariably covering the sense of the Hebrew "nasa נ,ס,ה ") after which Jesus having proven himself a wholly righteous man like Job before him who feared God the false accuser having been shown up as "a false accuser" within God's heavenly council regarding the matter departed from Jesus back to God having accordingly tested him at least "for a season" until such angelically engineered fresh tests might ensure Jesus fulfilled his destiny to die at Jerusalem they as such being designed to point him in the right direction of sacrificial death to fulfill God's will rather than his own and Jesus' temptation in the wilderness was really a preliminary test preparing the ground for his greater testing to misuse God's power throughout his ministry and ultimately in the crisis of the cross to come down from it "if he were the Son of God" in Matthew 27:40, the phrase "if you are the Son of God" do this or that forming the basis of the temptations that would have led Jesus away from fulfilling God's will to look after himself Jesus recognizing the bigger picture that his own life was of no value ultimately if it were not given for God's service. Jesus then returning "in the Spirit" into Galilee his fame spread abroad in that region doubtless first and foremostly because he had survived forty days in the wilderness without nourishment besides any unrecorded miracles that he might have done at that time (i.e. upon his return to

Galilee to testify to the fact that God had sent him being their primary purpose) and in verse 15 Jesus taught in their synagogues being glorified by all.

There then follows his negative reception at the synagogue in Nazareth his home town he being given the scroll of the prophet Isaiah to read upon the Sabbath Day of assembly there reading from Isaiah 61:1-2 concerning God's servant who had declared "the Spirit of the Lord is upon me, because he hath anointed me to preach the gospel to the poor; he hath sent me to heal the brokenhearted, to preach deliverance to the captives, and recovering of sight to the blind, to set at liberty them that are bruised, To preach the acceptable year of the Lord" Jesus closing the scroll and declaring to the congregation that that Scripture which he had just read had indeed been fulfilled in their ears upon that very day with regard to his healing miracles that he must surely have been performing that day and first of all in verse 22 all bore witness to him wondering at the gracious words from his mouth declaring among themselves were he not indeed Joseph's son but their reception of him soon turned sour when Jesus sensing their doubts with regard to his upbringing and paternity declared concerning miracles already wrought in Capernaum that they should ask him to heal himself (i.e. again the test misusing God's power for his own benefit) doing as a physician what he had done in Capernaum there in his own town he declaring in verse 24 that no prophet was ever acceptable in his own country among those people whom he had grown up with but nevertheless with regard to their unbelief he contrasted it to two Old Testament figures before him, Elijah and Elisha, who had bypassed disbelieving Israelites to help non-Israelites in the case of Elijah with the widow of Sarepta's (or Zarephath) son whom he raised and Elisha with the Syrian commander Naaman being cured of his leprosy in spite of there already having been many lepers in Israel and widows. The people's reaction to Jesus' words was one of fury being convinced of Israel's superiority over the Gentiles as they were as a special people chosen by God in Exodus 19:5-6, Amos 3:2 and rising up cast Jesus forth from the city forcing him unto the brow of the hill whereupon their city was built that they might cast him down headlong from it but Jesus passing through the midst of them "went his way" for it was a "way" that would eventually lead to his God-appointed death at Jerusalem at the right and proper time, this theme of Jesus' "going his way" dominating the gospel as in Luke chapter 9 after Moses and Elijah having been raised for the occasion had spoken of

Jesus' "Exodus ἔξοδος" or "way out" (i.e. from sin and death) that he was about to accomplish at Jerusalem in verse 31 (see Greek) and in 51 following in that chapter "it came to pass, when the time was come that he should be received up, he stedfastly set his face to go to Jerusalem" it being there that his destiny lay so that in chapter 4 God supernaturally enables Jesus to evade his enemies at Nazareth to subsequently be found at Capernaum, another city of Galilee where the man who would become his leading disciple, Simon Peter, lived. There he taught the people upon the Sabbath Days who were astonished at his teaching for his word had power

(or "authority" in Greek "exousia ἐξουσία").

From verses 33 to 37 the story of how Jesus healed a man with the spirit of an unclean demon in the Capernuam synagogue is told for as Saul had been afflicted by "an evil spirit from the Lord" in 1st Samuel 16:14; 18:10; 19:9 and the Egyptians by "evil angels sent by God" in Psalms 78:49 KJV so too here one of God's angels was behind the individual's suffering for "whom the Lord loveth he chasteneth" in Hebrews 12:6 quoting Proverbs 3:12 all suffering, illness and death being instituted to perfect men's characters so that as in the case of Job their faith may be tested to the upmost even to the point and end of premature death in some cases in their faith not breaking in their cursing God they passing the test in being grateful to God for such as they had as long as the breath of life remained in them he disciplining them to make them grateful even for life itself as Job had said that "naked he had come forth from his mother's womb and naked he would return there" in counting all but loss for the surpassing joy of knowing God who had given and taken as he wished. And so it is with all human suffering that God gave and then took away in bringing the suffering upon one to strengthen their faith in the face of it and so too with regard to this man possessed by a "demon" answering in the Old Testament to one of God's "intermediary beings" (i.e. the meaning of the Greek "daimonia δαιμόνια") his affliction was of God's so called "evil angels" in Psalms 78:49 (i.e. evil in relation to man from his own perspective in bringing suffering upon him from God) whom Jesus in having been given "authority" over the angels in the first two chapters of Hebrews commands to leave the man exercising his authority over it prematurely or "before the time" when the angels would be properly subject to man in Hebrews and particularly to Christ who is only said to be officially given authority over the angels post-resurrectionally in Matthew 28:18, the angel obeying Christ in this instance knowing he was "the holy one of God" who would supersede their role ultimately as the then invisible rulers of this world and so as they were both serving God then of course acquiesced to his request to depart from the man coming out of him and taking care not to hurt him further in verse 35 after he had convulsed the man in the midst of them one last time. The people's reaction was one of amazement they declaring "Who was this?" that could command the spirit-beings and they heard and obeyed him in this fashion his fame going out to every place of the surrounding countryside round about.

Verses 38 to 41 then describe further miraculous curings of Jesus notably in Simon Peter's house of his mother-in-law who had been taken with a great fever and beseeching Jesus upon account of her he healed her so that the fever left her and she served them it so transpiring in verse 40 that at sunset they brought to Jesus many afflicted with different diseases and ailments and Jesus using his God-given authority over God's angels prematurely healed them after he had laid his hands upon them the angels in possession recognizing immediately that Jesus was the Christ, the Son of God, and that they were obliged to obey him but since under inspiration it seems the confession came forth through the mouths of those ones they possessed Jesus rebuked them so that the truth might not be known that he was the Christ, the Son of God, at least at that juncture. And when it was day in verse 42 Jesus departed from there and went to a desert place doubtless seeking solitude there but the people nevertheless sought him out in that lonely place coming and staying with him and willing that he not depart from them. Nevertheless Jesus replied to them that it behoved him to go to other cities also to preach the glad tidings of the "possibly" imminent kingdom of God pending Israel's acceptance of him in Matthew 23:39, Romans 11:15 for he had been sent for this purpose and so it was verse 44 concludes the chapter that he preached in the synagogues of Galilee.

Luke Chapter 5

Luke chapter 5 contains the account of the miraculous haul of fish accompanying the calling of the first disciples, the healings of the leper and paralytic, the calling of Levi or Matthew and the criticisms of Jesus and his disciples in Matthew's house which leads to Jesus giving his mini-parables of the torn garment and burst wine bottles to express that he is inaugurating a completely new system of religion which the Pharisees will not easily be able to accept in the required new garment and new bottles that must necessarily replace the old broken ones. Thus far is the general summary of the chapter, as regards the minute details the setting is set for this fishing miracle in verse 1 of chapter 5 where Jesus stood by the lake of Gennesaret (or "Cinnereth," i.e. from the Hebrew "Chinnereth" in Joshua 19:35 signifying "a harp" due to the harp like shape of the sea of Galilee when seen from above) and there there were two ships, the fishermen had gone out in them and were presently washing their nets. But Jesus entering into one of the ships which was Simon Peter's bade him thrust the boat further out from the shore so that he might teach the crowds that thronged the shoreline from the safety of the boat. But in verse 4 Jesus instructs Simon Peter to launch the boat further out from the land Peter protesting that they had toiled all through the night and caught nothing whatsoever but nevertheless in accordance with Jesus' instruction he would let down the nets. The resulting draught then consisted of a great multitude of fishes of such enormous weight and quantity that their nets inevitably broke it requiring their partners in the other ship to come and help them with both boats starting to sink once they had been filled with fish. Peter's reaction to this obviously miraculous haul was to fall down at Jesus' knees confessing himself to be a sinful man not worthy of his presence but Jesus reassured him not to fear for henceforth he and his partners James and John the sons of Zebedee in the neighbouring boat would catch men. Thus coming to land they forsook all and followed him, the miracle of the miraculous haul not being recorded in Matthew and Mark's gospels but their unhesitatingly following Jesus upon the occasion of his calling them in Matthew 4:18-22 and Mark 1:16-20 is to be explained by the unnarrated miracle that Luke now records that converted them so unquestionably to believe in him for although the miracle is omitted both accounts still retain the detail that they were mending their nets (see KJV) at that precise moment when they were called and why were they mending them? Because they had just been broken in the miracle otherwise their willingness to follow Jesus immediately without hesitation or question is difficult to explain in Matthew and Mark's accounts unless some great unrecorded miracle had persuaded them that Jesus were truly and undoubtedly God-sent. A separate miraculous haul of fish miracle is recorded in John's twenty first chapter as part of the sequence of post-resurrectional appearances of Christ to his disciples there but this miracle involves the catching of precisely 153 fish commonly equated with either the number of ancient nations in Genesis chapter 10, the numerical value of God's name or even that of Mary Magdalene's as a significant figure within the narrative in John but to offer comments upon that miracle is not within our present purpose of writing.

And so taking up the text in Luke chapter 5 at verse 12 we have next a miracle recorded concerning a "man full of leprosy" who approaches Jesus in a certain city where he was and falling down before him on his face besought him that he might cleanse him if it were his will Jesus answering in the affirmative in verse 13 (for the man had shown faith in him) and cleansed him charging him in 14 to tell no man but to go present himself before the priests and offer the prescribed sacrifices according to Moses' Law being "two he-lambs without blemish, one ewe lamb of the first year, three tenth deals of fine flour, mingled with oil and one log of oil" for richer offerers and "one lamb, two turtle-doves, two young pigeons, one tenth deal of fine flour mingled with oil and a log of oil" for poorer in Leviticus 14:10, 22 regarding the offering appointed for a leper upon the occasion of his having been declared clean from his leprosy. Thus it was to be a testimony unto the priests that the man was orderly and kept the Law lest Jesus be quickly considered to be a law-breaker who had healed him although we suspect Christ did not even want the man to divulge the manner of his curing even to them and perhaps especially to them for Jesus was clearly fearing the authorities at this time in having gathered quite a following in those towns and cities where he had been preaching and performed his miracles so that now it required him to be more circumspect. But Jesus' best efforts were to no avail in this respect for verse 15 informs us that "so much the more went there a fame abroad of him: and great multitudes came together to hear, and to be healed by him of their infirmities" he being obliged to withdraw from them into the wilderness in verse 16 where he might pray alone.

Verse 17 then presents a new setting for the account of the healing of the paralytic with Jesus sitting in a certain house which was filled with people to hear him including of course by this time the Pharisees and doctors of the Law sitting by for they had come out of every town of Galilee and Judaea and even Jerusalem and of Jesus it is said that the power of the Lord was present with him to heal them. And there was there a certain paralytic, bed-bound whom they sought to bring to Jesus but being unable because of the multitude they devised a scheme whereby they removed part of the roof and lowered the man down to Jesus upon his bed through it Jesus being impressed by their faith to go to such extremities to get the man to him declaring the man's sins therefore to be forgiven him. This leads to a negative reaction from those Scribes and Pharisees present who reason that Jesus must be blaspheming for God alone had the power to forgive sins but nevertheless in proof of his divine credentials Jesus commands the paralytic to get up, roll up his bed and walk, he thus departing before them to his own house to the amazement of all who accordingly glorify God declaring that they had seen strange things that day in verse 26.

Then after this in 27 Jesus went forth and saw the tax-collector Levi sitting at his booth where he received the custom (the man being named as "Matthew" in the parallel account in Matthew 9:9) and Jesus again as with the fishermen invited him to follow him for which cause he arose and followed him at once for which reason we may suspect another hidden miracle in the account here to convince Matthew unless he were present in the house but whatever the case he promptly invites Jesus to his own house in verse 29 (Matthew 9:10 (KJV) has "the house" instead of "his house" presumably because Matthew himself is the author and would naturally not wish to advertise his house or write "my house") and there Levi made a great feast with many tax-collectors and others present including the Scribes and Pharisees who must have followed from the house where the paralytic was healed for they would not ordinarily choose to eat in a tax-collector's house not being a reputable profession in their eyes and moreover if so the probability increases that Levi (or Matthew) might have been present there too before returning to his tax booth and it had been that miracle precisely that had converted him. There then follows in this section of Levi's feast two critiques, the first against Jesus specifically for eating with those despised members of society in Pharisaic eyes described as tax-collectors and sinners Jesus answering them with the simple maxim or motto "they that are whole need not a physician; but they that are sick" for was it not really their responsibility too to restore these gone astray ones in their approximation back to God as their spiritual guides and yet it seemed at that moment that Jesus was doing their job for them. Then the second critique was directed against Jesus' disciples it being reasoned that the disciples of John and the Pharisees fasted as befitting their religious solemnity but Christ's disciples ate and drank in an almost carefree fashion. Jesus replied to this by contrasting the banquet to a wedding feast arguing that the guests or "children of the bridechamber" indicating something more profound than simply guests but members of a particular "family" "called" to the wedding could not possibly fast while the bridegroom was still with them but indeed the days were coming when the bridegroom would be taken away from them and in those days they would fast Jesus later using the same argument concerning Mary of Bethany's lavishing of the precious ointment upon him that it was no waste for she was preparing his body for burial and whereas they would always have the poor they would not always have him and so there would be time enough for fasting and charity after Jesus' departure firstly in death and then subsequently in his removal from them into heaven until such time he would return as the bridegroom to awake his sleeping dead as in Christ's parable of the Ten Virgins in Matthew chapter 25. Moreover a further point about "fasting publicly" could be made here that Jesus taught his disciples in Matthew 6:16-18 that when they fasted they were not to be like the hypocrites who deliberately disfigured their faces so that men might know it but they were rather to keep it to themselves as a private action not performed before men to impress them with one's apparent religious piety but before God alone.

Finally then Luke chapter 5 concludes with Jesus' mini-parables of the torn garment and burst wine-bottles reading "And he spake also a parable unto them; "No man putteth new wine into old bottles; else the new wine will burst the bottles, and be spilled, and the bottles shall perish. But new wine must be put into new bottles; and both are preserved. No man also having drunk old wine straightway desireth new: for he saith, The old is better."" The point of these simple illustrations from everyday life was that the new teaching Jesus was bringing was something quite dynamic and radically different to what the people and particularly the Scribes and Pharisees present had been accustomed to and required a complete readjustment of their entire religious mindset to receive it whereas Jesus' teaching had no part in the old Pharisaic system of legalism to which they were accustomed and from which they positively thrived as the religious leaders of the people (i.e. the old wine which suited them very well) for it required now that they stopped pursuing the works of the Law not absolutely in descending into immorality and disorder (Romans 6:1-2) but at least as a means to the end of salvation for salvation could not come in this way none of them being perfect but all human and inevitably fallible and so it required now that men be justified by faith in "believing" in Jesus and especially in the redemption that would come in his blood (i.e. "the blood of the "new" covenant" in Matthew 26:28, Mark 14:24, Luke 22:20, 1st Corinthians 11:25) which the Jewish leaders were not at all disposed to do in pursuing legalism as a means to salvation. Thus not only did the wine at Jesus' Last Supper with his disciples fulfill the figure of "the new wine" that was now required for Law-abiding Jewry to now truly be saved by faith which the Law should have led them to as "a schoolmaster" in Galatians 3:24 in highlighting the impossibility of their keeping it to be saved when they endeavoured to do so and inevitably failed but moreover as regards the new garment they needed to "clothe themselves" with, it also did not fit their old system of religion a patch of that garment even destroying it because in "putting on" Christ in baptism in Galatians 3:27 in his fleeced slain lamb covering (1st Peter 1:19-20, Revelation 13:8) fulfilling the "covering for sins" provided by God in type in Genesis 3:21, Psalms 32:1, Romans 4:8 through the spilling of blood of the morally "perfect" man (as a lamb "without spot or blemish") it was a declaration of faith that the Law in which the Pharisees trusted could not save them without the necessary human sacrifice upon the moral plane, in other words Christ's sacrifice rendered the Law "useless"as the torn garment or burst wine-bottles in so far as its being used as "a covering" for sin but nevertheless it remained as "a schoolmaster to bring them to Christ" in Galatians 3:24 but having done its job would not give ultimate salvation.

Luke Chapter 6

Luke chapter 6 then continues to describe Jesus' conflicts with the Pharisees over their stringent application of the Sabbath Laws and his Sermon on the Plain being a condensed form of the equivalent Sermon on the Mount in Matthew's gospel in which Christ sets forth his ethical teaching. Dealing first then with the chapter's first half focusing upon the question of breaking the Sabbath and what relation the Sabbath Law had in relation to Christ who declares himself to be "Lord of the Sabbath" in verse 5 the scene is set upon the second Sabbath after the one presumably with which the month had commenced (or else referring back to the synagogue reading in Luke 4:16 on the Sabbath Day) it coming to pass that Jesus and his disciples were passing through the cornfields and they being hungry plucked at the ears of corn rubbing them in their hands this being construed as "reaping" and an infringement upon the Sabbath prohibition against work by the Pharisees Jesus reminding them of what David had done when he and his men with him had been hungry when they fled from before Saul in 1st Samuel 21:1-6 how they had gone into the house of God at Nob where the sanctuary of the Lord had been installed in those times to eat of the shewbread from Ahimelech the priest which it was only lawful for the priests to eat, both he and his men doing so for their greater need of physical nourishment in the absence of any other source of food available to them was a greater priority than the observance of the Law regarding the shewbread upon this occasion as in Matthew 12:5 the priests performed circumcision upon the eighth

19

day of the boy's life and were "blameless" in so much as the Law of circumcision overrode the Sabbath Law and so too did the need to eat override the Sabbath Law in so much as it was a basic human need and the Sabbath was made for man and not man for the Sabbath in Mark 2:27 as a day of rest by which he might be replenished through rest not as a day burdensome to him that he could not gratify his basic human needs upon that day for the day was designed for his benefit rather than he being like a slave who served the Sabbath personified in obeying all those laws that appertained to the day mindlessly for that was not what the spirit of the Sabbath was all about but rather the contrary for it had originally been instituted for man's benefit. But there was another sense in which "the Son of man was Lord of the Sabbath"in verse 5 for of course Hebrews 4:9-10 states "there remaineth therefore a rest to the people of God. For he that is entered into his rest, he also hath ceased from his own works, as God did from his" so that through Christ as the Lord of the Sabbath in whom the meaning of the Sabbath Day had its fulfillment men could rest from the Pharisaic system of legal justification by works for justification before God (by which "no man could be justified" in Romans 3:20, Galatians 2:16) for now salvation in Christ was to be through "grace" and not by "working" to accrue legalistic credit and this too was a kind of resting from one's labours. Hence Christ had declared in Matthew 11:28-30 with regard to God's day of rest having its ultimate fulfillment in him "Come unto me, all ye that labour and are heavy laden, and I will give you rest. Take my yoke upon you, and learn of me; for I am meek and lowly in heart: and ye shall find rest unto your souls. For my yoke is easy, and my burden is light" just as Paul declared the Law including the keeping of the Sabbath laws had been "a heavy burden which neither they nor their fathers could bear" in Acts 15:10 Jesus therefore promising "freedom from the Law" (in Galatians 4:8- 5:12) or "the yoke of bondage" (Galatians 2:4; 5:1) in offering them rest from the endless labouring to accumulate legalistic credit with God in thus embodying the purpose of the original Sabbath Day as a day of rest for all people.

Then in verses 6 to 11 of this chapter Jesus is presented with a man with a withered hand upon yet another Sabbath presumably in the synagogue at Capernaum the Pharisees watching him to see if he would break the Sabbath Day by performing the cure but Jesus knowing their thoughts again announced the greater importance of human compassion overriding the Sabbath Law of abstinence from work in which case as he had reminded them in Matthew 12:11-12 that they would not have hesitated to retrieve their lost and wandering sheep from the pit into which it had fallen although this in itself would have been a work on their part and of how much greater value was a man than an animal Jesus had argued so that therefore it was lawful to do well upon the Sabbath Day saving life rather than destroying it in using the Law as a tool for social exploitation as the Pharisees appeared to be doing. Hence having restored the man's hand the Pharisees are filled with madness in verse 11 communing with one another what they might do to Jesus.

Verses 12 to 16 then recount Jesus' withdrawal to be alone ascending into a mountain to pray and continuing all night after which Jesus called unto him his disciples of which he chose twelve particularly their names being here given as "Simon (whom he also named Peter,) and Andrew his brother, James and John,

Philip and Bartholomew (corresponding to Nathanael in John 1:45-51 who is there likewise associated with Philip) Matthew and Thomas (replacing Lebbaeus whose surname was Thaddaeus in Matthew 10:3) James the son of Alphaeus, and Simon called Zelotes (replacing Simon the Canaanite in Matthew 10:4). And Judas the brother of James, and Judas Iscariot, which also was the traitor." After this from verse 17 onwards Jesus having come down stood upon the plain with his disciples and a great multitude came out to him there from all Judaea and Jerusalem, the sea coast of Tyre and Sidon coming to hear him and be healed of their diseases so that those who were vexed with so called "unclean spirits" using the contemporary medical language of the day were healed. Thus in this setting Jesus began his "Sermon on the Plain" in verse 20 appearing to address his disciples primarily and such who would have been in earshot of him declaring firstly a series of four beatitudes in contrast to Matthew's nine in his chapter five, Jesus declaring blessed were the poor for theirs was the kingdom of heaven, blessed were they that hungered for they would be filled, blessed were they that wept for they would laugh and finally in verses 22 and 23 they were to be blessed when they were socially excluded and hated by men particularly for Jesus as the Son of man's sake for they should rejoice in that day rather than sorrow for it for so their forefathers had wrongly treated the prophets but it was a surety for them that their reward was great in heaven when they were persecuted which reward of immortality would be brought unto them to be conferred post-resurrectionally at the second coming of Christ in Matthew 16:27, Philippians 3:20-21, 1st Peter 1:4, 13, Revelation 22:12 being presently "reserved in heaven" (1st Peter 1:4) before its being dispensed upon earth at Christ's return. But in verse 24 the rich had already received their consolation in contrast to the poor ones set to inherit the kingdom they enjoying their inferior "reward" in their present lives as it were and similar inversions follow in verses 25 to 26 with the full set to hunger, and those who laughed to mourn and weep it being woe to them if men spoke well of them as their fathers had done the false prophets before them Christ teaching "social exclusion" as part of the suffering of persecution that bearing his name would bring upon them.

It was therefore necessary for them to love their enemies doing good and lending hoping for nothing in return, blessing those that cured them, praying for them that spitefully used them and to he that smote their one cheek offering him the other also to so strike and should he seek to take one's cloak it required that one offer him one's coat also and so on not fighting evil but submitting to it, for God had said that vengeance was his and he would repay in Romans 12:19, Deuteronomy 32:35 so that in helping one's enemy one would heap "burning coals upon his head" in Romans 12:20, Proverbs 25:22 in terms of having faith in God's ultimate justice prevailing in that post-resurrectional judgement (Acts 17:31, 2nd Corinthians 5:10). Thus they had to submit to evil not being selective in their philanthropy and benevolent acts for sinners also did good only to those who did good to them, lent only to those whom they knew could repay them but now Jesus was telling them that they must love their enemies and do good to those that hated them in order that they might prove themselves to be "children of the Highest" for God was kind unto the unthankful and evil and he expected those who claimed to share that family trait to do likewise. Thus in emulating his character they were to be merciful as their heavenly father was merciful, not judging so that they would not be judged, not condemning so that they would not be condemned, forgiving so that they would be forgiven Jesus having declared that one must forgive one's brother not seven times but seventy seven times in Matthew 18:21-22. Verse 38 then lays down the principle that it would be as with the measure that they had meted out upon their fellow men that would be returned again to them by God in like measure although here unlike in Matthew 7:2 where a negative judgement of one's brother will return a negative judgement of God upon one a positive action is spoken of as we have a positive action back to one from God so that Jesus declares "Give and it shall be given unto you; good measure, pressed down, and shaken together, and running over, shall men give into your bosom. For with the same measure that ye mete withal it shall be measured to you again."

Then in verse 39 further sayings follow Jesus speaking of the blind leading the blind causing them both to fall into the ditch together as is so obviously true with all necessarily "false religions" that the blindness spreads to those they convert in their stead Jesus describing the Pharisees as "blind leaders of the blind" in Matthew 15:14 and in Matthew 23:16, 24 as "blind guides" or in verses 17 and 26 simply "blind." In verse 40 the disciple is not above his master it being the most that he can do to be as his master in becoming equal to him in attaining to perfection, in verses 41 to 42 the carpenter's similitude is used as in Matthew 7:3-5 for one judging one's brother when one was much more in the wrong with the famous image of one spraining to remove a speck of sawdust in one's brother's eye when one had a mighty beam of wood in one's own eye blocking one's vision and making the action impossible to extract the speck from one's brother's eye although one might endeavour to do so to one's own grief as well as one's brother. In terms of "knowing a man by his fruits" (Matthew 7:16) Jesus went on that a good tree could not bring forth corrupt fruit just as much as a corrupt tree could not bring forth good fruit and in verse 44 everyone's character was to be known by his fruits or actions (or even words) it not being possible to gather figs from thorns nor grapes from a bramble bush. Thus a good man would naturally bring forth good from the treasure of his heart whereas an evil man contrariwise for Jesus said that out of the abundance of the heart the mouth spoke in view of the evil nature of men's hearts it being advised in Matthew 5:37 that one should answer only "yea" or "nay" with anything else coming from evil and indeed the tongue is although a "little member" a "fire," a "world of iniquity" in James 3:5-6 (Proverbs 25:23 has "backbiting tongue") capable of defiling our whole body and setting on fire the course of nature, being set on fire of hell (i.e. gehenna γέεννα) and Jesus concurs with James here that it is preferable to say nothing at all in so much that "the tongue can no man tame" being "an unruly evil full of deadly poison" in verse 8 there in so much as man's inward thought not guided by God's revealed moral principles is inherently evil by nature in Jeremiah 17:9, Matthew 15:18-20, Galatians 5:19-21. Finally then the chapter concludes in Luke with Jesus' stressing the futility and pointlessness of one calling him "Lord, Lord" and not doing what he said for it was like he said building a house on quicksand that would be quickly swept away by the storm and accompanying torrent of water whereas the one who followed Christ's word or teaching is like one who built the foundation of his house into the hard and solid rock rather than the soft earth so that when it was visited by the tempestuous weather and flood it withstood the brunt of the storm having been founded upon the rock in its builder having followed those divine building instructions precisely and proving itself unshakable and immovable having been built to withstand the test of time whereas shoddy work built regardless of God's instructions would have no such lasting durability to finally see the light of day when the judgement came.

Luke Chapter 7

Luke chapter 7 then has Jesus entering Capernaum after he had made an end of all these sayings to the people and there was there a certain centurion's servant who was very precious to him who lay at the point of death he beseeching Jesus via the elders of the Jews to come and heal his servant. And when they besought Jesus upon his behalf they told him that this man was worthy that he should come and heal his servant in so much as he loved their nation and had built for them their synagogue. And so Jesus accompanying them drew near to the centurion's house at which point he intercepts them sending forth friends who relay them of his message of his feeling of utter unworthiness to have anything done for him by Jesus, not even esteeming himself worthy enough to come to Jesus in person but he need only say the word for his servant to be healed the Roman centurion considering himself as a man under authority under whom he had soldiers of one of whom he might say "go" and he went and to another "come" and he came and to his servant he commanded that it be done and it was so. And so the man was under the authority of Caesar as "emperor supreme" in 1st Peter 2:13 (RV) and under him were soldiers of lesser rank who obeyed his commands he expressing his faith in Christ as being like him in the first place under the authority of God instead of Caesar for the centurion began "I am also a man under authority" (in verse 8 expressing the parallelism of his situation compared with that of Jesus but as with Jesus he had others under his authority in turn for what the man was expressing was the fact that Jesus controlled God's invisible angelic "legions" (Luke 8:30) as set to have authority over them in Hebrews 2:5, Matthew 28:18 and using it prematurely (i.e. "before the time" in Matthew 8:29) in his then present miracles whereby he commanded the so called "evil angels" sent by God (Psalms 78:49 KJV) or "evil spirit from the Lord" in 1st Samuel 16:14; 18:10; 19:9 to vacate the object of their operations by reducing their hold upon the man to make him so suffer and die according to which men's faith was strengthened in experiencing the reality of suffering, illness and death within their personal experience and not losing trust in God in the light of it. But in this instance like the centurion with his soldiers Jesus commands the angels and one goes recognizing his being over-authorized by one who was "the Son of God" and "Holy One of God" set to exercise authority over the angels in the coming age in Hebrews chapters 1 and 2 who now exercised it prematurely in performing this miracle in Hebrews 6:5 Jesus using "the powers of the world or age to come" in performing the cure even from a distance. Thus in verse 9 Jesus marvelled at the Roman centurion's faith in this pro-Gentile gospel it being specifically pointed out here that it exceeded any such faith that Jesus could find in Israel itself among the natural Jews in so far as the centurion recognized Christ's status as being given authority over God's angels upon the supernatural level as still exercising this authority or power as subject to God and not for his own use which fact of course would result in Jesus' sacrificial death being an effective one in his offering himself up as a wholly sinless man as having been perfectly obedient to God in his own life which "atonement" would have been the natural implication of the centurion's faith. And so the centurion's story concludes in verse 10 with the servant being found well and quite recovered from his sickness in accordance with his great faith in Christ that he had shown and all that it implied.

Then in verses 11 to 17 of this chapter we have the account of the raising of the widow of Nain's son Jesus approaching the city with his disciples and a large crowd of people in tow who followed him upon account of his miracles and teaching. And it came to pass as they drew near to the gate of the city that there was a certain dead man carried forth upon the bier who had been the only son of his mother who was moreover a widow and left very much alone by his son's premature death although again a large crowd accompanied her at this particular moment it presumably having been some kind of funeral procession out of the city en route to the cemetery. Jesus seeing her was moved with compassion for her and having exhorted her to cease her weeping he touched the bier causing it to stand still after which he commanded the young man to arise, the dead one sitting up and beginning to speak in verse 15. Thus Jesus resurrected the man restoring him to his mother and causing great fear and wonder to fall upon the bystanders so that the rumour of the miracle quickly spread throughout all Judaea and throughout all the region roundabout, it being declared that a great prophet had risen up among them and that God had truly visited his people.

After this attention in the narrative turns to John the Baptist who naturally hears the report of those incredible things that Jesus was doing and so calling two of his disciples sent them to Jesus inquiring whether indeed he were the one (i.e. the Messiah foretold whom he had fore-announced) or whether they should look for another there appearing to be some displacement in the chronology here compared with Matthew 4:14-17, John 1:29-37 in so much as John is not presented with the same certainty regarding Jesus that he is depicted as having at the time he baptized him in the gospels although in Luke 3:21-22 the Baptist's faith in Jesus at the time he baptized him is not expressed in the plain text as it is expressed in the other gospels making it more a problem with the comparative study of the gospels than in Luke itself that John might have lost his faith in Jesus for some reason. Jesus then replies to John's messengers in verse 22 of Luke chapter 7 by drawing their attention to his miraculous works wrought among them at that very moment which testified so clearly to whom he was in so much as the blind saw, the lame walked, the lepers were cleansed, the deaf heard, the dead were raised and the gospel was preached to the poor although not miraculous the last action being the most important of all so far as ultimate salvation was concerned. Thus in verse 23 the one who took no offence in Christ was truly blessed. Then in verses 24 to 28 after John's messengers had departed back to him Jesus paused to discuss concerning John asking the people what they had gone out into the wilderness to see, hardly a reed shaken by the wind, nor a man clothed in soft raiment for those so delicately attired lived comfortably in king's houses for it was evident that John was a prophet and more than a prophet in so much as he had and was fulfilling that prophecy of Isaiah 40:3-5 of that messenger sent before the Messiah's face to prepare his way before him identified as

Elijah in Malachi 6:5-6. After this we have one of those cryptic sayings of Christ regarding John the Baptist in verse 28 Jesus declaring to them that "among those that are born of women there is not a greater prophet than John the Baptist: but he that is least in the kingdom of God is greater than he" John the Baptist being truly great as the last of the prophets but Christ exceeded him in greatness in that he humbled himself unto death (i.e. the least in the kingdom of God meaning his act of "humility" in submission unto death) whereby he was greatly exalted in Philippians 2:5-9 just as Mary his mother had foretold in Luke 1:52 that the child was set for the putting down of the mighty from their seats and the exalting of those of low degree it requiring the "humility" of character first after Christ's perfect example before one may be exalted in his kingdom.

In verses 29 to 30 the people who had heard Jesus and the tax-collectors there present justified God in having been baptized with John's baptism of repentance before coming to him but the Pharisees and Lawyers' rejected the counsel of God against themselves having not been baptized by John, their lack of spiritual insight concerning him being highlighted by Jesus in verses 31 to 35 following he declaring of them that they were like children sitting in the marketplace calling to one another that they had piped to them and they had not danced and mourned to them and they had not weeped in so much as they had criticized John in his solemnity coming neither eating bread nor drinking wine accusing him of having a "demon" according to their own apostate superstitious understanding of the word and yet the Son of man (i.e. Jesus) did the opposite and their reaction to him was "a gluttonous man, and a winebibber, a friend of publicans (i.e. tax-collectors) and sinners" it appearing that they would inevitably criticize Jesus whatever he did whether one extreme or the other just in so much as they were motivated by their own inner natural orientation to seek to regard themselves as superior to him not being able to exercise the spirit of humility that would have enabled them to accept Jesus and subsequently be exalted to become "great" in his kingdom for they had no "mind" for this, thinking too much of themselves in the present life and for this cause they inevitably opposed Jesus whatever he did seeking to assert their superiority over him by their natural orientation to do it wishing to exalt themselves in their relation to him contrary to the way of salvation that he would ultimately show them in the manner of his death. But nevertheless in verse 35 "wisdom was justified by all her children" who were wise enough not to have this superiority attitude towards Jesus to set themselves up as his judges as though in God's place and as if contrary to Christ's maxim that he that was greatest in the kingdom of God would get there by being "great" in the present life rather than the least which involved a non-judgmental attitude, submission to evil to show one's faith in God in his rectifying right and wrong in the afterlife and finally humility unto death as might inevitably come to one who followed this path but the Jewish leaders had no "wisdom" as far as these things were concerned.

Luke chapter 7 then concludes in verses 36 to 50 with Jesus' being invited to dine by Simon the Pharisee in whose house there was a woman of the city who was a known sinner but nevertheless being present in the house and whilst they sat at meat she stood at his feet behind him weeping and washing them with her tears and wiping them with her hair and finally anointing them from an alabaster box of ointment Simon the Pharisee condemning Jesus in his heart for if he had been a prophet he should have known what manner of woman was touching him. Nevertheless Jesus being aware of his thoughts in verses 40 to 43 asked him to consider two debtors one owing a hundred pence (Greek "denaria δηνάρια") and the other only fifty and then in their Lord forgiving their debt Jesus asked which one of them would love him more Simon the Pharisee correctly answering the one whom he forgave the bigger debt and so Jesus then compares his rather cold reception of him giving him no water, kiss or anointing with the woman's devotions who had done it all in abundance declaring that she was forgiven more her great number of sins in ratio to the fact that she had loved more compared to the "Pharisaic" Simon who had not shown such love, Jesus' mention of his forgiving the woman's sins again attracting the hostility of his fellow-diners in verse 49 who reasoned who could forgive sins but God alone as in Luke 5:21. However Jesus' authority to forgive sins lay in his alignment to God's will so that he did so upon God's behalf as his spokesman there and then as it were, a necessity as regards his exercising of God's power at the same time which involved the forgiveness of sins to be manifested as occurred in Luke 5:24 the paralytic only being able to rise up and take his bed away in his sins having been dismissed through the process of the miracle for the miracles exercised the powers of the future world when sin and death would be suppressed in Hebrews 6:5 and did not really belong to the time of Jesus' first advent when sin and death was rampant upon earth. And then finally on this chapter in verse 50 Jesus said to the woman that her faith had saved her (i.e. Christ's miracle being likewise "salvific" in so much as it was only through the subject's faith that they could be effectively performed and their sins forgiven) and moreover she was now to go in peace in so much as the process of salvation involved making "peace" between God and man ultimately, a feat which was only attainable through the forgiveness of one's sins which in turn was only possible through one's faith in Christ as the Saviour there being no independent way of making peace with God through the works of the Law but rather through the one who had shown them much love (i.e. in his death) they might return that love in gratitude to him by washing his feet as a token of their adoration for him

Luke Chapter 8

Luke chapter 8 primarily consists of three distinct sections that might be described as the parable of the Sower, the Healing of the Demoniac and the Raising of Jairus' Daughter with such other material that the chapter contains connecting these three sections together into some kind of coherent whole. The chapter opens with recollection of Jesus' preaching circuit at that time throughout every city and village accompanied by his twelve disciples and others including certain women whom he had healed of various infirmities including Mary Magdalene out of whom he had cast seven demons often identified as the woman who was a sinner in the previous chapter and the seven demons although alluding to a troop of seven angels that had had the dominance over her preceding Christ's overriding their authority in the way that he did traditionally associated with the seven deadly sins regarded as pride, greed, wrath, envy, lust, gluttony and sloth (perhaps based upon the works of the flesh listed in Galatians 5:19-21). And also among the company that followed Christ there is mentioned Joanna (i.e. God is gracious יה (yah), the shortened name of the Lord suffixed by the verb חנן (chanan)) the wife of Chuza Herod's steward; Susanna (based upon "Shoshana" in Hebrew meaning "lily" (i.e. "shoshan שׁוּשַׁן ")) and many others that ministered unto Jesus from their substance. And when a large crowd of people had gathered around Jesus coming forth from all the nearby cities he spoke unto them the parable of the Sower at an undisclosed location here describing how the sower went out to to sow, some of the seed falling by the wayside and being devoured by the birds as presumably being left exposed upon the open ground without any protection of covering of earth, hence it was also trodden down by those who travelled that rough uncultivated land, other seed falling upon the rock but withering away for lack of moisture after an initial optimistic springing up in the shallow soil there, others falling among thorns sprang up to be choked by them and only that which fell upon the good ground sprang up to bear fruit a hundredfold Jesus calling upon the assembled crowd that he among them that had ears (i.e. "spiritual insight" as in 1st Corinthians 2:14) let him hear the meaning of this parable. But the disciples asked Jesus privately about its interpretation in verse 9 Jesus replying to them quoting the words of Isaiah 6:9-10 that to them it was given to know the mysteries of the kingdom of God but for everyone without all things were in parables that seeing they might not see and hearing they might not understand.

In verses 11 to 15 Jesus subsequently therefore interprets the parable for them declaring that the success of the seed represents the responses of various kinds of men to the gospel message it standing for the word of God as articulated by Jesus so that those fallen by the wayside hear but the false accuser or "sin in the flesh" comparing Romans 8:3 with Hebrews 2:14 steals it away what is sown "in" them referring to the false accusing principle embedded in our natural propensities inherited by birth that instinctively makes us sin and declare God's word articulated to us to be a lie (i.e. "a false accusation" against God as Adam and Eve first did in first cultivating this "serpentine" animal-like mind under the serpent's natural carnal reasoning, which became subsequently instilled within them and transmitted to all their offspring by heredity). In Judas' case however there may be reference to the activity of God's angel again called "a false accuser" in John 13:2 in so much as the angel prompted Judas to do precisely that falsely accusing Jesus before the world for the sake of thirty pieces of silver in order to fulfill God's purpose but the action of the false accusation undoubtedly having its origin in God here as is generally true of the existence of sin and evil in the world in general having been created by God (Isaiah 45:7; Job 42:11, Amos 3:6 (all KJV) to achieve a greater good intrinsically related to its existence and impossible without it. Then the seed that fell upon the rock is interpreted as those who have no solid root to persevere in the truth although originally having received God's word with joy falling away in time of temptation referring to such "wanton sins unto death" that 1st John 5:16 refers to perhaps for which there is "no more atonement for sin but a certain expectation of judgement" for wantonly sinning in Hebrews 10:26-27. Those who are sown among thorns have a fall from grace that is not quite so sudden and dramatic but slowly have the Christian life choked out of them by smaller minor sins accumulating and bad habits developing described as "cares and riches and pleasures of this life" in verse 14 not being able to bring forth fruit to perfection. Finally the seed sown upon the good ground are those who with a good and honest heart having well heard the word keep if effectively to bring forth fruit with patience in their spiritual growth not being hindered by materialism as an addiction (equating with those sown and slowly choked among thorns) or sexual sins (equating with those whose spiritual growth is cut short with a sudden and unexpected fall from "grace") or so we may envisage the meaning of Jesus' allegory.

Then in verse 16 the importance of openly promoting God's word to let one's light shine before men as it were in Matthew 5:16 is laid down by Jesus in verse 16 "No man, when he hath lighted a candle, covereth it with a vessel, or putteth it under a bed; but setteth it on a candlestick, that they which enter in may see the light," he moreover declaring concerning the certainty of judgement and exposure by God of those who attempt to hide the word God gives them to preach recalling Jesus' later parable of the Pounds (in Luke 19:11-27 or "Talents" in Matthew 25:14-30) that "nothing is secret, that shall not be made manifest; neither any thing hid, that shall not be known and come abroad. Take heed therefore how ye hear: for whosoever hath, to him shall be given; and whosoever hath not, from him shall be taken even that which he seemeth to have" the appearance of being Christian and a member of Christ's church of no avail without real action arising from one's conviction. In verses 19 to 22 Jesus then appears to disown his natural mother and brethren who come looking for him (as he so speaks to them roughly in John 2:4; 7:3-10 although at least by Acts 1:14 they are recorded as having finally come to believe in him wholeheartedly) Jesus declaring to the crowd when they sought to reach him through the press that what counted for God was one's spiritual family rather than one's natural who might not necessarily share one's faith. After this Jesus crossed the Sea of Galilee upon another day perhaps by way of evading the crowds who sought him for quite possibly the wrong reason as much as wishing to preach upon the other side and there in the midst of the sea the boat came near to capsizing in a sudden storm but Jesus having been awaken by them and rebuked the wind and raging water so that there was a great calm subsequently reprimanded them for their lack of faith in that they had not trusted in God's providential care for them at that moment and they are left questioning what manner of man Jesus was that the winds and water obey him but the truth was these things were angelically controlled as in Psalms 104:4 "He maketh his angels winds" and in Psalms 148:8 "Stormy wind fulfilling his word" so that the whole situation had been angelically engineered to test their faith and Jesus was using in advance of the proper time when nature's control of man bringing organic decay and death would be subverted to man's control of nature (or of the angels the forces behind nature in Hebrews 1 and 2) prematurely in his being the singular man preeminently who had been promised that mastery over the elements and the powers behind them in Hebrews 2:5.

This then brings us to their arrival in the country of the Gadarenes in verse 26 upon the other side of the sea meaning "a troop of lions" in Hebrew (i.e. "Gadדּ‎גּ " troop plus "ariʸ‎ רִ‎אַ " lion) with reference to a whole legion of angels as implied by the fierce "lion" face of the Cherubim that stood as corporate symbols for them in the Old Testament and so here not surprisingly they meet a fierce man like a wild, enraged lion who tells them that his name was "Legion" upon account of such a troop or legion of angels having entered into him to induce his ferocious lion-like behaviour, the selection of the word "legion" recalling the centurion's confession that Christ had authority over such angelic "legions" using the Roman word for a military detachment as he had over his human troops that were under his authority and now it required that Jesus show this authority in action in healing the "Demoniac" who lived naked among the tombs and could not be retained by chains and fetters breaking them in pieces and being driven by the false accuser or angelic stimulus upon his carnal nature into the wilderness for the occasion of this miracle to be performed by Christ as a testimony to him and his power over God's angelic legions (as in Matthew 26:53 Jesus had said to Peter in the crisis of Gethsemane that he could call upon more than twelve legions of angels if it had been his Father's will but how then could the Scriptures have been fulfilled, he nevertheless being angelically strengthened in Gethsemane in Luke 22:43 as "good" and "evil" angels all serving God similarly interact with each other in the original Passover in Exodus 12:23 that foretold the "hour" of Christ's death). But in verse 28 of Luke chapter 8 in the madman's statement "What have I to do with thee, Jesus, thou Son of God most high? I beseech thee, torment (i.e. judicially inflict) me not" the pronoun appears to shift between the possessed man and the angelic host behind him at least in so much as he is inspired to declare that Jesus was the Son of God (as with Peter in Matthew 16:16-17) but "judicially inflict me" ("before the time" in Matthew 8:29) as in Revelation 20:10 implies the man's judgement post-resurrectionally and applies to the man not the angels he speaking of himself for a moment and even in one clause "My name is Legion for we are many" in Mark 5:9 his identity is blurred with the angels speaking through him switching erratically between the two speakers which angelic legion Christ now commands as Peter had wanted him to do in Gethsemane instructing them to go into the swine which were illegally grazing nearby (eating pork being forbidden by Moses' Law in Leviticus 11:7; Deuteronomy 14:8) who are consequently drowned in a stampede down the escarpment in the angels exhausting their power in them, the local farmers and people subsequently begging Christ to depart from their coasts not only because of their loss of the livestock and profit it brought them but more acutely because they were afraid as the disciples had been in the boat concerning what manner of man could do these things seeing the madman restored to sanity sitting clothed in his right mind at Jesus' feet whom Christ commands to return to his home city as a testimony to his own people that they might believe in Christ through the miracle that had been wrought upon him.

After this Jesus having returned to the other side of the sea once again with the people gladly receiving him there there came among them a man named Jairus (name from "Yairיָאִ֫יר," i.e. "He who enlightens" in Hebrew) who was a ruler of the synagogue of the Jews he falling at Jesus' feet beseeching him to come and save his young daughter from dying. En route to the house Jesus is enthronged by the crowd and one bold woman who had had an unstoppable bleeding twelve years and wasted all her money upon physicians none of whom could heal her manages to catch hold of the hem of Jesus' garment behind him as he walked pressed by the crowd and her bleeding is accordingly immediately stanched through the power of her faith in Jesus to heal her. Jesus then sensing that "virtue" had gone out of him in verse 45 turns around to seek out that person whom he had cured and the woman seeing that she could not be hidden confesses with Jesus declaring "Daughter, be of good comfort: thy faith hath made thee whole; go in peace" in verse 48. After this attention returns in the narrative to the crisis of Jairus' dying daughter with a messenger coming from his house to inform him that it was now too late and his daughter was already dead so that Jesus could be of no further use to him but Jesus exhorting him to have greater faith than this took him, his three closest disciples Peter, James and John, and the girl's mother into the room where she lay with him not being put off or discouraged by the peoples outside's laughing at him for saying that the girl was only sleeping and having put them all out and grasping the girl by the hand Jesus called to her declaring "Maid, arise" so that she revived, her spirit coming into her at once enabling her to sit bolt upright and arise to the amazement of all present with Jesus commanding them to give her something to eat and warning them to tell no man of what had been done (as indeed after Christ's raising of Lazarus in John's eleventh chapter it led directly to the Jewish council convening a major meeting in which it was resolved under the high priest's instigation and by popular consent that Jesus must be put to death for doing such things or else as the inevitable leader of a popular uprising with such powers he would bring down the full force of the Roman Empire upon them in response and destroy their nation).

Luke Chapter 9

Luke chapter 9 largely consists of six main subsections which we may roughly identify as the disciples being sent out before Christ on their mission, the Feeding of the Five Thousand, Peter's confession, the Transfiguration, the Healing of the Epileptic Boy followed by a final section of random sayings much concerning Christ's going up to Jerusalem and the cost of discipleship. As concerns section one we are told in the first verse that Jesus gave his twelve disciples power and authority over the demons (i.e. "evil angels" controlled by God in Psalms 78:49) as further anticipating the requirements of the first two chapters of Hebrews in the angels ultimately becoming subject to men with which such empowerment Jesus' disciples could heal the sick as a testimony to the powers of the kingdom of God which was "at hand" in the person of Jesus (Luke 17:20-21) if they could but receive him (Matthew 23:39; Romans 11:15). In verse 3 Jesus furthermore elaborated that they should take nothing for their journey, neither staves, nor scrips (i.e. shepherd's skin bag), neither bread nor money, neither having more than one coat apiece for this was a mission in which they were expected to rely upon God to provide for their needs in trusting in God's providence their faith therefore that "the Lord would provide" (Genesis 22:8, 14) testifying to the sincerity of their belief and truth of their message. In verse 4 they were to abide in whatsoever houses that received them for a limited time before moving on further afield but in the case of any cities that did not receive them they were to perform the action of pious Jews upon reentering the land of Israel from heathen territories in physically scraping the very dust of those lands from their feet thus declaring such cities as no better than the pagans by such a symbolic act as indeed Paul and Barnabas do the like in Acts 13:51 after they had been rejected at Antioch to declare the city out of bounds as far as God's salvation was concerned. Verse 6 then recollects that the disciples did according to as they had been instructed after which verses 7 to 9 digress onto Herod's reaction upon hearing all that was done by Jesus and it being thought that John the Baptist whom he had beheaded had risen from the dead (in Luke there is no account of John's beheading told retrospectively here as it appears in Matthew 14:1-12 and Mark 6:14-27) or else Herod heard that it was believed Jesus was Elijah or one of the prophets of old risen from the dead but he himself desired to see Jesus to ascertain the truth of the matter.

Then upon the apostles he had sent out's return and their report back to Jesus concerning all that they had done it is written in verse 10 that Jesus took them aside to a desert place within the vicinity of the city of Bethsaida (i.e. House of Fishing) and when the people knew of it they followed him there where he spoke to them of the kingdom of God and healed such as who had need of healing. But when the day began to decline the disciples called upon Jesus to send the people away that they might get lodgings and victuals in the settlements round about for the day was far spend and they were there in a desert place. Jesus however called upon them to give them something to eat they reported back to him that they had only five loaves and two small fishes but what would they be among so many for there were about five thousand men besides women and children. Nevertheless Jesus invited them all to sit down by fifties (having been the standard military unit in ancient Israel in 2nd Samuel 15:1 and 2nd Kings 1:9-15 which is probably why in John's gospel after this miracle the people came and tried to take Jesus by force to make him a king in 6:15). And Jesus having taken the five loaves and two fishes looked up to heaven and blessed and broke them as he would do over the Eucharistic bread and wine at his Last Supper with his disciples so that we should see Eucharistic significance in this miracle of Christ's in that it foretold his sacrificial death to feed the great multitude of the redeemed by it unto eternal life and so it came to pass that the bread was miraculously multiplied so that all ate and were filled such as who followed Christ. And the disciples having gathered up the fragments into twelve baskets, one for each disciple, in that those crumbs that the Jewish children let fall from their table in Matthew 15:26-28 (in not everyone of them who had partaken being worthy of the gift) must needs be preserved for the Gentile believers thereafter who would also eat of this "true bread from heaven" in John 6:32, 51, 58 after the type of the manna provided by God to the wandering Israelites in the wilderness of which an "omer" as the ancient Hebrew measurement was preserved for all generations "before the Lord" in Exodus 16:32-34 implying this future usage of the bread for other eaters not there present.

After this in verse 18 in Luke Jesus is alone praying but upon his disciples coming to him he propounds the question to them concerning whom men thought he were with the popular answers being relayed to him by the Twelve that some said he was John the Baptist (i.e. risen from the dead), others Elijah and still others one of the old prophets risen again but upon Christ being insistent upon the question asking them directly what they themselves thought concerning him Peter replied that he was the Christ (it appearing in Luke's gospel that the supernatural element to Peter's confession that Jesus was not only the Christ, Messiah or anointed one (which he might have worked out from their having all been commanded to sit in fifties during the food miracle) but also the Son of God being inspired by God's Holy Spirit to be able to see this is omitted, the confession being as much as Peter's natural reasoning could have led him in Luke without the supernatural element that it receives in Matthew particularly in which Peter is to be considered to be "begotten by God's Spirit" in making the additional confession that he were also the Son of God as "the son of the dove" (i.e. "Simon bar Jonah" in Matthew 16:17) this appearing to reflect much of Paul's teaching upon spiritual rebirth thereafter embedded in Matthew's gospel at this point). Then in Luke in verse 21 Jesus warned them not to make him known by this title lest the zealots among them get politically oriented to establish God's kingdom there and then by force of arms (as Peter was minded to do so in Gethsemane) it naturally following that Jesus then endeavoured to impress upon them contrary to this that the true nature of his mission was self-sacrifice as according to God's purpose and not only this but some of his followers far from being triumphant in some kind of Jewish insurrection against the Romans would suffer martyrdoms of their own in following him likewise to death but nevertheless their "soul" or "life" although "lost" in natural death would be found again in its being restored by resurrection thereafter whereas those who tried to save their natural lives would lose it forever in being annihilated in following the natural thinking of the flesh particularly for self-preservation in a world where sin was king and therefore set to be destroyed with all that thrived in it by God's determinate fore-plan and counsel in 1st John 2:16-17. Thus Jesus declared in verses 22 to 26 concerning the true reality of what his mission involved that rather than leading a popular revolt "the Son of man must suffer many things, and be rejected of the elders and chief priests and scribes, and be slain, and be raised the third day" and further "If any man will come after me, let him deny himself, and take up his cross daily, and follow me. For whosoever will save his life shall lose it: but whosoever will lose his life for my sake, the same shall save it. For what is a man advantaged, if he gain the whole world, and lose himself, or be cast away? For whosoever shall be ashamed of me and of my words, of him shall the Son of man be ashamed, when he shall come in his own glory, and in his Father's, and of the holy angels" it appearing in the last verse that those who took the call to follow Christ lightly would not escape being publicly put to shame by Christ at his coming Jesus saying as much as a forewarning to them

After this in Luke chapter 9 we have Luke's Transfiguration account it being introduced as in all the Synoptic gospels with Jesus' words that there were some standing there (i.e. Peter, James and John) who would not taste of death until they saw the kingdom of God, the verse doubtless originally referring to the early Christian belief that Jesus would return in their lifetimes as for example in 1st Corinthians 15:51-52, 1st Thessalonians 4:13-18 but with the addition of verse 26 just before which speaks of Christ's coming again with his holy angels (i.e. to resurrect the dead) the meaning of verse 27 here is obviously here intended to be fulfilled in the event of the Transfiguration as a vision of the kingdom as much as that were possible and the "not tasting of death" accordingly understood as Peter, James and John's surviving the appearance of God's Shekinah glory that appeared as a luminous light (as indeed Jesus' countenance was altered up the mountain as after the manner of Moses "and his raiment white and glistering") but nevertheless accompanied by the cloud in Exodus 40:34, 1st Kings 8:10-12 that overshadowed the three men Christ took up the mountain in verse 34 that presumably somewhat served

32

to dampen its effect lest direct exposure to God's glory kill them instantly as God's angelic manifestation had warned Moses in Exodus 33:20. As concerns the other details of the Transfiguration account in Luke the mention of the "eighth day" in verse 28 chimes in with the day of Jesus' resurrection when he would be subsequently "glorified," Moses and Elijah appear to have been physically resurrected for the occasion to "appear with Christ in glory" (Colossians 3:4) for this is tenable upon the basis of Matthew 27:52-53 which records the rising of many bodies of saints of old at the moment of Christ's death who went into the holy city and appeared to many and the fact that all men had sinned and died without exception having "fallen short of the glory of God" in Romans 3:23; 5:12 which as a universal statement would have included Elijah and Moses who had been as much under sin as anyone else but in their association with Jesus they are allowed to live again briefly and speak of his coming "Exodus" (i.e. "death" or "departure") that he was about to accomplish at Jerusalem they being physically present with him at that time therefore and the whole thing not being a mere vision of future things without them really there in person for indeed Peter recognizes them as being physically present in seeking to build three tabernacles for Jesus, Moses and Elijah for he recognized this appearance of God's glory as the day of atonement that appeared upon that day (i.e. Jesus' decease at Jerusalem in verse 31 being the key to his kingdom) and invited them to keep the feast of tabernacles that immediately followed Yom Kipper or the Day of Atonement the following week- such was Peter's understanding at that moment that he must have surely understood that it required Jesus to die at Jerusalem).

Then in verse 35 after the cloud had passed over them and the heavenly voice like thunder upon the mountain as in Exodus 19:16-19; 20:18-19 (the Hebrew word "קוֹל kol" meaning both "voice" and "thunder"), John 12:28-30 (possibly being an indirect allusion to the Transfiguration in John) had acknowledged Jesus as his beloved son to whom they must hearken then the cloud having passed they were left alone upon the mountain with Jesus and descending the mountain keeping what they had seen to themselves they meet with a crowd of people at the base of it (as after the story of Moses descending from God) and the other disciples who had remained there are found to have been unable to cure the epileptic boy whose father brought him to Jesus, the spirit in the boy tearing at him so that he foamed at the mouth before departing from him in verse 39. Jesus having healed the boy in verse 42 having declared them all to be "a faithless and perverse generation" that he had to presently "bear" with them (in Matthew 17:19-20 Jesus telling the disciples that they had been unable to cure the boy because of their lack of faith) he subsequently went on to foretell again to his disciples that he would soon be delivered into the hands of men (i.e. at Jerusalem to be killed) but they understood not the saying in verse 45 it appearing to be almost supernaturally hidden from them (i.e. that the Scripture be fulfilled that they all lose faith in him at the moment of crisis) even Peter for all his possible insight upon the mountain now appearing to be no more knowing than the rest of them concerning what was soon to happen at Jerusalem.

Then the remainder of the chapter consists of various sayings of Jesus consisting of the need to receive a child as Jesus and Jesus as God in verse 48 which is associated with their being the least among them, the "humility" motif here then being associated with "becoming like little children" which Jesus speaks of in Matthew 18:3 in that it required that they depended upon God for all like a child its parents it being necessary for them to develop the faith of a child in this respect that God would provide and again in their humbling themselves they would be highly exalted in God's kingdom. After this in verses 49 and 50 Jesus forbids preventing other men from preaching in his name just because they did not belong to their own little discipleship for that man was still a follower of Jesus although he did not physically do it with them being from another town or place Jesus' words anticipating the coming great geographical distribution of Christianity in the first century it finally appearing in all parts of the Roman Empire and then in verses 51 to 56 Jesus rebukes his disciples for asking him to bring down fire upon the Samaritan villages like Elijah had done so in 1st Kings 1:9-15 to the apostate king's messengers who came to him declaring that he had come to save men's lives not destroy them although at that moment the Samaritans could not receive him as his face was set to go up to Jerusalem (i.e. to fulfill God's purpose for him there being the immediate priority). Finally on this chapter in verses 57 to 62 Jesus is approached by three men who wish to follow him but are still too concerned with worldly affairs to do so wholeheartedly none of them realizing the cost that his discipleship involved we thus reading from 57 to 62 "And it came to pass, that, as they went in the way, a certain man said unto him, Lord, I will follow thee whithersoever thou goest. And Jesus said unto him, Foxes have holes, and birds of the air have nests; but the Son of man hath not where to lay his head. And he said unto another, Follow me. But he said, Lord, suffer me first to go and bury my father. Jesus said unto him, Let the dead bury their dead: but go thou and preach the kingdom of God. And another also said, Lord, I will follow thee; but let me first go bid them farewell, which are at home at my house. And Jesus said unto him, No man, having put his hand to the plough, and looking back, is fit for the kingdom of God" one of the notable themes in this sequence which has been found already in the gospel is that people are so reluctant to leave their families and acquaintances behind to follow Jesus such as who did not share their new found faith Jesus being brutal upon this point in declaring "Leave the dead to bury their dead."

Luke Chapter 10

Luke chapter 10 for the larger part describes the apostolic mission in more detail with the lawyer's question in the second part of the chapter leading in to Christ's famous parable of the Good Samaritan upon the road from Jericho to Jerusalem after which by the end of the chapter Christ appears in the home of Martha and Mary at Bethany near Jerusalem presumably having followed that same transit route himself with his disciples as he had spoken the parable set upon that highway. Thus at the head of the chapter it is written of how the Lord (i.e. Jesus) appointed seventy others for his mission sending them out in pairs before him into every city or place where he himself would shortly arrive. However, in verse 2 there appear to be too few labourers in the envisaged harvest it being required therefore that they pray to the Lord of the harvest that he send forth more workers into it. Similar language is used in John chapter 4, verses 34 to 38 where Jesus describes finishing the one who had

34

sent him's work in terms of harvesting the imminent harvest with the ones who reaped and sowed rejoicing together in so much that fruit was gathered unto eternal life it being set forth as team work there in verse 8 as Paul had similarly written in 1st Corinthians 3:6 that he planted, Apollos watered but God gave the growth. It is of note that the harvesting allegory for the converting of converts is used within the immediate context of Christ's preaching to the Samaritans in John's gospel as indeed the Samaritan traveller is highlighted as having done what was right to the one fallen among thieves in Christ's parable in our present chapter in Luke it appearing that the harvesting motif reaches beyond a strictly Jewish vintage.

After this Jesus describes sending forth his disciples as "lambs in the midst of wolves" but nevertheless some perception of worldly thinking is not denied them in Matthew 10:16 when they must be as wise as serpents but as harmless as doves simultaneously as it were and indeed in verses 17 to 19 of this chapter they are empowered to exercise Jesus' authorities in casting out so called "demons" using the Greek word for the intermediary beings behind sickness, suffering and death they recognizing "the name" of Christ as expressing that authority over them in Hebrews chapters 1 and 2, in Hebrews 1:4 especially Christ having inherited a more excellent name than the angels to become the basis of their subordination to him and so in verse 18 Christ beheld the "adversary" (referring to the "angel of the Lord" in Numbers 22:22) fall "like lightning from heaven" referring to the lightning like movements of the Cherubim in Ezekiel's heavenly vision who would now fall down before Christ or man as their superior, hence "Let all God's angels worship him" in Hebrews 1:6 by coming down from heaven and so doing when God brought the first begotten into the world for there were now new "heavenly places" in Christ in Ephesians 1:3; 2:6 which were "in" him not exterior to him as positions of privilege for the Christians in relation to God through Christ relating to spiritual things but subsequently in the establishing of new Jewish "heavens and earth" referring to the government and common people below them in the so described political universe in Isaiah 34:4-5, Jeremiah 4:23, 28 (i.e. the sun eclipsed in the heaven in the king being taken into captivity), Ezekiel 32:7-8 they will exercise these positions of authority upon earth over the common people as their political "heaven" as it were and the angels that were adverse to humans in inflicting illness, suffering and death upon them relinquishing their God-given tasks to so do stepping down for the human government of Christ's redeemed to whom they will become subordinate as the new political "heaven" although literally exercising their dominion upon earth post-resurrectionally with Christ it being possible to interpret Revelation 5:10 "they shall reign upon earth" both literally and figuratively if we translate the Greek "epi ἐπί" "over" as in "over the earth" instead of "on" but the only certain thing being that they will not ascend to that "heaven of heavens" (1st Kings 8:27) where God apparently abides with his angels for although the latter set to be made subject to men dwell there as with Jesus now in the age to come God's kingdom is to be a terrestrial one without angelic activity over men but the power being invested within men themselves upon earth whose names nevertheless are "written in heaven" in verse 20 as they are "the congregation of firstborns written in heaven" in Hebrews 12:23 but not spatially located there at that time although in God's cognizance there at all times for which cause they may be elevated above his heavenly host who literally reside there. But it appears rather from Hebrews 12:22 that the "heavenly Jerusalem" is to be the new political heaven or seat of government in the age to come as it is so described in Isaiah 1:2, 10; 65:17-18 and it is to there that the remnant of humanity will resort to receive the word and will of God from the government there in the coming kingdom of God upon earth.

Returning from this digression to Luke chapter 10 from which we have digressed as in the last chapter Jesus instructs his missionaries whom he sends before him to carry neither purse, nor scrip, nor shoes, nor salute any man upon the way it appearing that the gospel is to be proclaimed only to those who welcome the apostles into their homes although not saluting men on the road may simply allude to not wasting time in frivolous greetings and conversation upon the highway when there was important work to be done. In verse 5 upon entering a house they were to invoke a blessing that their peace remain upon it but such "peace" (ultimately meaning "reconciliation with God" in Ephesians 2:15-17) was to return to them in the event of their rejection, verse 7 stating that the hospitality of food was acceptable for one who laboured in the gospel, for "the labourer was worthy of his hire," Paul having a long section upon the issue of those who preached the gospel living off the gospel in 1st Corinthians chapter 9 but he himself proudly claiming that he had used none of these privileges in having declared the word of God free of charge to them as it were in verses 15 and 18 there so it remains a contentious issue whether or not Christian preachers should be paid for their work as with the issue of marrying, Paul stating in 1st Corinthians 7:38 that marrying is good but refraining from marriage is "better" and so too he speaks in similar vein upon the issue of paid Christian preachers although admittedly in Jesus' picture only food is provided for his labourers rather than actual money for their time and effort which 1st Timothy 6:10 declares "is the root of all evil" in making a man do something not for itself but for the financial reward he might accrue from it. Then Jesus' command in verse 7 about not going from house to house may mean that one house in an area was sufficient for the gospel to spread for those they converted would tell their neighbours the gospel later so that it required every time that the Christian preachers go further afield to establish the gospel in new places. In verse 9 in the event of their being received they were to declare the nearness of the kingdom of God particularly after healing their sick in which miracles the powers of the kingdom were manifested in Hebrews 6:5, in verses 10 and 11 in the event of their rejection Jesus repeats from Luke 9:5 that they were to shake off the dust of that city scraping it from their shoes as pious Jews used to do upon entering Israel after leaving heathen territory. Since such cities had had the gospel of the kingdom directly preached to them by the apostles so that momentarily it was "at hand" for them they would receive the greater condemnation than even Sodom for all her immorality who had never had the gospel preached to them so precisely as they had had the privilege of so being visited by Christ's apostles. And similarly they were without excuse in the event of their having seen the miracles performed by Christ and his apostles for it was woe to Chorazin and Bethsaida for if the materialistic ancient cities of Tyre and Sidon had seen such works they would have long ago repented in sackcloth and ashes and in verse 15 Capernaum rather than being exalted to heaven is to be brought down to the grave (i.e. hades ᾅδης) showing the figurative use of heaven in this chapter to describe exaltation in status before God but not to do with the physical, spatial location of the subject, it referring more to exaltation of status before God. In verse 16 those who hear the apostles hear Christ and those who despise them in like manner despise Christ too in so much as they are all part of the same movement in salvation history that has its origin in God, hence in Matthew 10:40, John 13:20 the one receiving them receives Christ and the one who sent him and in verse 22 likewise that may be initiated into the revelation of secret knowledge of God in this threefold union so that "All things are delivered to me of my Father: and no man knoweth who the Son is, but the Father; and who the Father is, but the Son, and he to whom the Son will reveal him." Their power to then tread upon "serpents" and "scorpions" and "all the power of the enemy" in verse 19 so that "nothing could hurt them" was to be evidence enough of the presence of God with them for which cause the angels or "spirits" behind the afflictions they cure would indeed be subject to them as to God for they, Christ and God were all part and parcel of the same movement of human salvation that required the relinquishing of the angels of their God-given roles as the executors of suffering and death in this world as is clearly taught in the story of Job being a necessary "evil" so that man might learn obedience through the things that he suffered in Hebrews 5:8 by the testing of his faith to the limit even unto death in some cases that he might come forth as "purified gold" in his faith refining him in 1st Peter 1:7. Again the childlike demeanour of those to whom God chose to reveal himself is underlined in verse 21 in that hour Jesus rejoicing in spirit and saying "I thank thee, O Father, Lord of heaven and earth, that thou hast hid these things from the wise and prudent, and hast revealed them unto babes: even so, Father; for so it seemed good in thy sight" and in verses 23 to 24 Jesus turned to the humble Galilean fishermen who followed him, not to the educated teachers of the Law, declaring to them that their eyes were blessed for the things they saw and their ears likewise for what they heard for many prophets and kings of old had desired to hear and see such things and could not.

After this in verses 25 to 37 we have the parable of the Good Samaritan which as we have suggested was spoken upon the road from Jericho to Jerusalem let us suppose the lawyer approaching Christ in such a setting to ask him what he needed to do to inherit eternal life Jesus replying in terms of loving the Lord one's God with all one's heart, soul and strength and loving one's neighbour as oneself quoting from Deuteronomy 6:5 and Leviticus 19:18 but the lawyer seeks further clarification from Jesus concerning who precisely was his neighbour in verse 29 leading Jesus to tell his parable of the Good Samaritan upon that very highway which we envisage they were traversing and which accordingly features within the parable, the one left naked, wounded and half dead by the thieves upon that way being bypassed by a priest and Levite who preferred to cross the road and look the other way but finally a good Samaritan had compassion upon him, binding up his wounds having poured in oil and wine to alleviate his suffering and transporting him by his own beast to the inn where he leaves money with the innkeeper upon the morrow until his return to care for the man in his absence (i.e. the Christian principles until he returns) Jesus concluding the parable by telling the man to have mercy upon those less fortunate in life than he as the good Samaritan had so done within the story. After this Jesus with presumably his disciples still accompanying him although they drop out of the narrative here arrives at Bethany the home of Mary and Martha not far from

Jerusalem where according to his custom he entered their home and taught, Mary sitting at his feet paying attention to his words but Martha being distracted by her household chores for which cause Jesus rebukes her for criticizing Mary for not helping her declaring that Mary had indeed "chosen the good portion which would not be taken away from her" whereas Martha was too careful and troubled about many things that were not ultimately important.

Luke Chapter 11

Luke chapter 11 containing various sayings of Jesus as well as his confrontations with the Scribes and Pharisees and with the Lawyers towards the end of the chapter begins with his teaching his disciples the simple recitation of the Lord's prayer upon their asking him to so do so having observed how John the Baptist had taught his disciples how to pray and so Jesus began that they should address God as their Father who was in heaven, the idea of God as a Father being commonplace in all religious thought in the milieu of the influential Hellenistic culture that influenced them so that one of the Greek philosophers had written that "we are indeed his offspring" (i.e. Aratus Phaenomena 5), Paul quoting the words at the Areopagus or Mars Hill in Acts 17:28 to demonstrate that all nations were of a common paternity (i.e. God) ultimately it requiring them to return to God as their Father through Paul's adoptionist christology whereby their spiritual begettal in Christ would enable them to say "Abba, Father" in Romans 8:15, Galatians 4:6 it appearing that the bulk of mankind had hitherto gone astray from the one who had created their forefather Adam. Then in the words of the Lord's prayer now taught by Jesus in verse 2 God's name was holy and it required his kingdom come upon earth as his reign was already undeniably established in heaven, his angels "all ministering spirits" in Hebrews 1:14 and therefore completely conformed to his will although upon earth man was allowed a measure of free-will to follow his own sinful orientation and way contrary to God's heavenly rule Jesus anticipating a time therefore when sin would be eradicated from the earth (as in 1st Corinthians 15:24 28) in there being established a harmony therein resembling that which already exists in the heavenly host who speak with the plural name of God in Genesis 1:26 and 3:22 being "Elohimאֱלֹהִים" in token of the fact of it that they represent one singular God who is manifested in them in plurality, angels not being able to die in Luke 20:36 and therefore not being able to sin in so far as death is the punishment of sin in Romans 6:23, 1st Corinthians 15:56 (2nd Peter 2:4 and Jude 6's "the angels that sinned" obviously therefore referring to human messengers that did so). Moreover in verse 3 God was to provide for their every need in their asking him to give them their daily bread, in 4 their forgiveness of others is expected as a matter of course in order for God to forgive them their sins (as in Matthew 18:21-22 where one asks Jesus how many times one should forgive his brother he teaching not seven times but seventy seven times) but at the same time they were to pray to him not to lead them into temptation but deliver them from evil as indeed God led Christ into temptation by testing him in the wilderness Jesus teaching his disciples that they might be spared such testing of their faith. A lot of the teaching on forgiveness is related to sharing the love of God for one's brother for whom Christ died itself an expression of the greatest love that a man could give in giving his life for his friends in John 13:15;

38

15:13 for in 1st John 4:20-21 love of God and love of one's brother stand together for "If a man say, I love God, and hateth his brother, he is a liar: for he that loveth not his brother whom he hath seen, how can he love God whom he hath not seen? And this commandment have we from him, That he who loveth God love his brother also" for the truth was that man was made in the image of God and hating another man therefore was equivalent to hating God in whose image he had been made.

Then there follows a short parable from verses 5 to 8 of this chapter to show how even the stubbornness of human nature can be broken if one is persistent enough in one's plea for help subsequently explained in the following verses as showing that if even evil men know how to give good things to their children how much more will God to them that ask him Jesus envisaging a certain friend of a man who had a visitor come to him from a long journey and he having nothing to set before his visitor takes recourse to banging upon his friend's door, the hour being late having struck midnight imploring him to give him such things that he needed that he might provide the hospitality that his guest deserved after his travelling. But the answer from within the friend's house is not obliging to the man's request the so called friend declaring that late hour that he was already in bed with the door now locked and his children with him in bed and crying out from within the house to the man not to disturb him at this late hour but the man not being so easily deterred banged all the more upon his door and in his persistence the so called friend finally gives in to all the commotion outside and rising up finally gives the man the things that he needs but not without much grumbling doubtless at the lateness of the hour and couldn't he have come in the daytime etc. Now Jesus having drawn this portrait of the characteristic behaviour of selfish sin-oriented human nature then in verses 9 to 13 compares the so called friend in the parable to God who not being influenced by such selfish thinking will immediately provide for a man's need provided he prayed to him with an honest and unfeigned heart, hence there need be little doubt in the supplicant's mind that God will do this when even the worse of men will finally give in to constant nagging to deliver the goods as it were. Thus in verses 9 and 10 "And I say unto you, Ask, and it shall be given you; seek, and ye shall find; knock, and it shall be opened unto you. For every one that asketh receiveth; and he that seeketh findeth; and to him that knocketh it shall be opened." After this in verses 11 to 13 Jesus again compares God to our human fathers who despite being evil knew how to give good gifts to their children it being reasoned that if a son asked his father for bread none of them would give him a stone, or for a fish likewise would not give him a serpent or even a scorpion instead of an egg. So if their human fathers who were inevitably evil by their natural disposition unenlightened by moral law knew how to behave well towards their children in spite of their being by nature self-oriented then how would an entirely selfless and giving God do it so much more effectively as he did it upon the historical stage for all the world to see by giving his only begotten son as a human sacrifice for sin being the greatest gift any Father could give, to give his only Son.

Then in verses 14 to 20 of this chapter we have a further conflict between Christ and his anonymous accusers here not specifically identified although Matthew 9:34;

12:24 and Mark 3:22 have the Pharisees and Scribes as his interlocutors whereby they insinuate that Jesus was curing the people of their infirmities by the fictitious evil power of pagan deities even though Isaiah had laboured at length in chapters 41 to 46, especially in 45:7 (KJV), to show that God is the single omnipotent supernatural power in the spiritual realm and shared it with none other who might oppose his will and yet Jesus' accusers now accused him of casting out demons doubtless conjectured as being of the pagan variety according to the common usage of the word "daimonia δαιμόνια" (i.e. "demons") in colloquial speech by the late Philistine God of Ekron named "Baalzebub" (i.e. the Lord of the Flies" perhaps indicating a knowledge of disease spread by flies but if so Jesus does the opposite in restraining it not spreading it and could hardly have been enrolled in the power of such a God) but whatever the grounds of their accusation "Baalzebub" had long ago been declared by Elijah the prophet to be a fictitious lie in 2nd Kings 1:1-8 when king Ahaziah of Israel fell through the lattice of his upper chamber and sent messengers to Baalzebub the God of Ekron whom Elijah intercepts, upbraiding the king for not believing that there was a God in Israel in sending his messengers to fictitious pagan deities of inanimate wood or stone as they were invariably portrayed, for had any such deity really existed all God's claims to be the only true God and therefore all-powerful would accordingly be forfeit and he himself not exist. Nevertheless even in Jesus' time what the Bible declared to be pagan lies were still given credence to but Jesus argues against it when others also tempted (or "tested") him seeking a sign from heaven in verse 16 reasoning in verses 17 and 18 that a house or kingdom divided against itself cannot stand, the house falling or the kingdom being made desolate because of the conflict but in Jesus' miracles there was no conflict or contest of will between himself and those supernatural beings behind the conditions he cured (such as here the dumb man in verse 14 for both Jesus and the angels of God he commanded instituted by God to create human suffering, illness and death upon earth (i.e. Psalms 78:49 KJV) were working on the same team (i.e. for the one all-powerful God whose very existence forbade the existence of any other supernatural power that might be able to exert any influence in the world he only allowing man to disobey him upon the natural level so that man when he used his freedom of will to sin was the true enemy of God)). Thus far all is clear so that if the adversary in verse 18 (describing "the angel of the Lord" as a "Satan" or an adversary in Numbers 22:22) were divided against himself in Christ and the angel having different masters that angel would not obey Christ and no cure could be performed (as in the case of the Jewish exorcists in Acts chapter 19). But Jesus nevertheless went on to speak hypothetically entertaining the pagan fiction for the purpose of argument as he would later do with the consciousness of the dead that the Pharisees in their apostasy had come to believe in in Luke chapter 16, he declaring that if it were true that he cast out demons of the pagan kind by Baalzebub the Lord of the Flies so come to be believed in by the Pharisees in their apostasy, then whom did their sons call upon to cast them out for it must be an even more despicable pagan deity in that case because their cures did not work whereas Jesus' did, so that therefore they would be their judges in showing how ridiculous their accusations against Jesus were for he could only do what he was doing by the power of God (hence the blind man in John 9:33 now healed "if this man were not of God he could do nothing"). Thus Jesus concludes with the inevitable conclusion to his reasoning "But if I with the finger of God cast out devils, no doubt the kingdom of God is come upon you."

Then in verses 21 to 23 Jesus continues with another mini-parable to highlight the need for their being on God's side in that his miraculous cures were evidence enough of his superior power and therefore the Pharisees were wasting their time in opposing him, Jesus declaring "When a strong man armed keepeth his palace, his goods are in peace: But when a stronger than he shall come upon him, and overcome him, he taketh from him all his armour wherein he trusted, and divideth his spoils" (i.e. there is no protection for them in taking refuge in pagan religion or alternatively if "strong man" refer to the original name of God "El אֵל" meaning strength or power the allegory simply teaches Jesus' authority over God's angels as one made stronger than they by God or El Shaddai אֵל שַׁדַּי (i.e. "Strength" of the "Mighty Ones" plural) to take their "armour" or power away from them (literally "all their tools" πανοπλία coming from "pas πᾶς" (i.e. "all," "every") and hoplon ὅπλον (i.e. "tool")) in his miracles in which angels God trusts), Jesus finishing "He that is not with me is against me: and he that gathereth not with me scattereth." After this in verses 24 to 26 the miraculous curing of such and such a person is not sufficient as a means of salvation in so much as such a one may wax haughty and arrogant as the apparent subject of divine power his esteeming himself saved without true moral renewal accompanying the performance of some miracle upon him invariably making his last state seven times worse than when he was originally cured, Jesus explaining that this degeneration in him would subsequently then be angelically enhanced or "hardened" as in 2nd Thessalonians 2:9-12 where God sends "a strong delusion" (i.e. the returning seven angels or spirits) to prevent that person who had "pleasure in unrighteousness" in spite of the "lying wonder" performed upon him being saved, the "wonder" perhaps being attributed to the imaginary "Baalzebub" whereas God had been behind it in reality and with such a belief the man would soon degenerate into even worse depravity and sickness that he had been in originally as by God's own decree that they be "blinded" as to the import of the miracle wrought upon them to prevent them being saved. Thus the scenario is portrayed by Jesus with the simple allegory that "when the unclean spirit is gone out of a man, he walketh through dry places, seeking rest; and finding none, he saith, I will return unto my house whence I came out. And when he cometh, he findeth it swept and garnished. Then goeth he, and taketh to him seven other spirits more wicked than himself; and they enter in, and dwell there: and the last state of that man is worse than the first."

These seven spirits refer to the seven spirits before God's throne in Revelation 4:5 appearing as lamps of fire, the figure originally coming from Zechariah 4:2 where they are also described as seven "eyes" upon the unhewn altar stone symbolic of Christ who was not produced with "the tool of man" so to speak in John 1:13 also not "of bloods" (see Greek) meaning Joseph and Mary's together but as the word made flesh the engraving upon him was directly from God. Therefore the seven eyes stand for the Cherubic eyes that go throughout the earth in 2nd Chronicles 16:9, Zechariah 4:10, Proverbs 15:3 as corporate symbols of the angels and Christ's authority over them as the unhewn altar stone upon which they appear for it was these seven spirits that he brought against God's house in Israel in 70 AD having been given all authority in heaven and on earth in Matthew 28:18 including over the angels in Hebrews chapters 1 and 2 especially verse 5 so that they invisibly manipulated events to make Israel ripe for judgement when the preaching of John the Baptist had not had a permanent effect in making them a people prepared for the Lord (i.e. "the house swept and garnished" in the allegory for they subsequently rejected Christ both personally and in the preaching of the apostles to become seven times worse than they had been at the outset, seven being the number of completion that they had "filled up the measure of their fathers" in Matthew 23:32 (also as symbolized by "the ephah (i.e. measure) of wickedness" in Zechariah 5:6-8, cf. Genesis 15:16) and were therefore ripe for judgement Zechariah chapter 5 concluding that they would be taken by beings flying between heaven and earth to the land of Shinar (i.e. Babylon in Genesis 14:1, 9, Joshua 7:21, Isaiah 11:11 and Daniel 1:2) meaning the result of their judgement would be the Roman captivity or new"house" in the now symbolic land of Shinar.

After this returning to the record in Luke chapter 11 from which we have digressed in verses 27 to 28 a certain woman declares Jesus' mother blessed for having him whereas Jesus in his usual manner dismisses the natural family for the spiritual declaring rather that those who heard the word of God and kept it were truly blessed. In verses 29 to 32 no sign will be given to that evil generation except the sign of the prophet Jonah whose three days in the whale's belly before being ejected onto the dry land would correspond to Christ's period of interment in the grave in Matthew 12:40 and that generation would likewise be condemned by the Queen of Sheba and the Ninevites Jonah preached to, in that Christ was one greater then Solomon and Jonah who spoke to them. Then in verses 33 to 36 various imagery is pressed into service to express the importance of light, verse 33 about the candle being placed in the prominent place upon the candlestick to give light to all who entered about preaching Christ's word openly before men and not hiding it (as in the parable of the Pounds (or Talents)), in 34 "the light of the body," being the eye intended to teach that to receive God's word one had to have "a good and honest heart" (Luke 8:15) and not marred by evil interests so that the eye could no longer work effectively in receiving the truth, hence "the light of the body is the eye: therefore when thine eye is single, thy whole body also is full of light; but when thine eye is evil, thy body also is full of darkness. Take heed therefore that the light which is in thee be not darkness. If thy whole body therefore be full of light, having no part dark, the whole shall be full of light, as when the bright shining of a candle doth give thee light" it requiring a genuine, unfeigned faith to effectively receive God's word and shine it forth to others without any exterior motive (such as "Mammon" in Luke 16:13 for example).

Then the chapter concludes in verses 37 to 54 with Christ's tirade against the Pharisees and then Lawyers most of the material being found in Matthew chapter 15 about the Pharisees' accusation of Jesus' eating with unwashed hands and his reply concerning what was within that defiled them and in Matthew chapter 23 in his tirade against the hypocrisy of the religious leaders there, in verse 41 they believing they simply had to give alms to be clean from it all as though salvation could be bought in 42, tithing mint, rue and all kinds of herbs to make the Law "a heavy burden" without showing the love of God to judge those who were genuinely poor, and oppressed but whether consciously or not actively oppressing them with their numerous appendages to Moses' Law, in 43 loving the praise of men in public places, in 44 like open graves while they yet lived which men walk over unknowingly, the lawyers too in verse 46 burdening men with the Law, building the sepulchres of the righteous prophets their fathers killed as though to bear witness to the fact of it in 48, in verses 49 to 51 God's wisdom having foreordained it that they would slay and persecute all the prophets and apostles (possibly indicating later editing to the text here) sent by God for God to make a reckoning of the accumulated blood poured out with that generation "From the blood of Abel unto the blood of Zacharias which perished between the altar and the temple." Thus Jesus concludes his tirade in declaring they the Lawyers or Law-makers had taken away the key of knowledge neither "entering" themselves nor permitting others to "enter" (i.e. unto the eschatological kingdom). Finally on this chapter in verses 53 and 54 the Scribes and Pharisees begin to urge Jesus vehemently and to provoke him to speak of something whereby they having lain in wait might accuse him of something that they might catch from his mouth.

Luke Chapter 12

Luke chapter 12 then consists of various further sayings of Jesus some common themes running through it being the dangers of materialism and one's preparedness for Christ's coming, the scene being set for the many sayings the chapter contains in verse 1 with record of an innumerable number of people gathered unto Christ so much so that they trod upon one another Jesus beginning the discourse by warning them to beware of the leaven of the Pharisees which was "hypocrisy" "leaven" having been omitted from the Passover meals as signifying a negative element within the bread in Exodus 12:15-20 and in Christ's parable of its wholly permeating three measures of meal in Matthew 13:33, Luke 13:20-21 so as to make them completely leavened Christ may have had in mind the apostasy of the Scribes, Pharisees and Lawyers as three notable leaders of the people in religious matters who had mixed the pure religion of Yahweh with pagan superstition thus wholly leavening it as it were making the word of God "of none effect through their traditions" in Mark 7:13 as for example corrupting it directly with such practices as Corban in Mark 7:10-13 in declaring a thing "given to God" so that being thus consecrated they could not use it to help their mother and father thus effectively disannulling the fifth commandment. But judgement was certain in verse 2 Jesus continuing that "there is nothing covered, that shall not be revealed; neither hid, that shall not be known," in verse 3 emphasizing the need of confession to avoid a greater judgement from Christ later so that whatsoever they had spoken in darkness should be heard in the light and that spoken in the ear in closets proclaimed from the housetops for they had little to fear from men who could kill the body but could not prevent the life God could give them post-resurrectionally human victory always being short lived in God's justice inevitably triumphing in the end so that it required in verse 5 that they feared God who had the power to cast them into the grave (i.e. Greek "hades ᾅδης" covering the Hebrew "Sheolאֹול‎ שׁ " meaning "hidden place" as in the grave one's body is perpetually hidden from view) for this was "eternal destruction" in 2nd Thessalonians 1:9 whereas man's destructive acts were only of temporary duration in the certainty of the resurrection of the just this in itself being a test of faith. God's providential care for them is again reasserted in verses 6 and 7 that since God forgets not the sparrows five of whom may be sold for two farthings (i.e. the Greek "assarion ἀσσαρίων" in the genitive plural) certainly he would know such things that happened to men who were of infinitely more value to him he even being acquainted with the number of hairs upon their heads if that were possible.

In verse 8 then openness about the gospel in public is to be acknowledged by the "Son of man" confessing that man's name before God's angels in heaven in so much as they had confessed his name before men, verse 9 stating the inversion of this thus in the event that they denied his name before men so too would Christ deny them before God's angels in heaven. Verse 10 states however that an idle word (Matthew 12:36) spoken against the Son of man would be forgiven men but not blasphemy against the Holy Spirit such as belief in pagan fictitious deities for it limited the power of the all-powerful God to suggest that he was weak and did not have the power to control his own creation the charge being levelled against the Pharisees in Matthew and Mark's accounts of the Baalzebub acccusation. In verses 11 and 12 the disciples were therefore to have no fear when they were brought before synagogues, magistrates and powers in that "God would give them a mouth and wisdom which all their adversaries would not be able to gainsay nor resist" in Luke 21:15 not needing to think what to say for the Holy Spirit would teach them in that hour what they should say. In verses 14 to 21 Jesus then addresses the dangers of materialism as choking the spiritual life out of them with one asking him to command his brother to divide the family inheritance equally with him, Jesus saying that it was not his place to judge and divide their private inheritance but added more gravely that the people beware of covetousness and desire for material things in so much as a man's life did not consist in the abundance of his possessions Jesus telling a parable of a certain rich man whose ground brought forth plentifully and not having sufficient room to store them he purposes to tear down his current barns as no longer adequate and build greater new ones in which he might lay up his fruits and goods but Jesus declares the man a fool for thinking that he would have goods laid up for many years so that he might take his ease, eat, drink and be merry for that very night his life would be demanded of him and then whose would those goods be that he had provided for himself, for so it would be with him that laid up treasure for himself and was not rich towards God Christ recalling the words of Psalms 39:6 that "Surely every man walketh in a vain shew: surely they are disquieted in vain: he heapeth up riches, and knoweth not who shall gather them" and in Jeremiah 17:11 "he that getteth riches, and not by right, shall leave them in the midst of his days (i.e. in death), and at his end shall be a fool."

Then in verses 22 to 31 the theme of Christ's discourse returns again to the issue of God's providential care of the Christians they not to fret themselves unnecessarily about their lives, what they should eat or put on for life was more than food and the body more than clothing again it requiring that they look at how the birds were cared for by God in verse 24, the ravens neither sowing nor reaping nor indeed gathering into storehouses or barns but still God fed them and they were of infinitely greater value than the humble birds of the field. And so in verse 25 none of them by taking unnecessary thought and worry about the requirements of their daily living would be able to add a cubit to their lifespan for their lives were in the hand of God who "gave and took away" as he saw fit sending forth his spirit and men are created and renewing the face of the earth in Psalms 104:30, Elihu the Buzite declaring that the Spirit of God had made him and the breath of the Almighty had given him life in Job 33:4 and in 34:14-15 that if God gathered together his Spirit and breath all flesh would perish together into the dust from which it was created it being God alone who held the life-power ultimately and whose prerogative it was to continue it and knowing this the appropriate response from man was to fall upon God for the provision of all his daily needs as the one who had given him life in the first place not being able to preserve his own life any further than God permitted him. Thus in verse 26 since man could not do the least thing in keeping himself alive he should not worry about the rest of life's problems which God could likewise solve for him, as concerned their clothes and appearance in verse 27 they were to consider the beautiful lilies which neither toiled nor spun and yet Solomon in his most majestic robes and glory did not appear as beautiful as one of them so that if it were this way with the grass of the field which God clothed today and cast into the oven tomorrow being of such short duration how much more did God have the power to clothe man who was of infinitely more value than the grass of the field they needing therefore to have more faith not to seek after what they should eat or drink, neither be of a doubting mind in that these things were universally sought after by all the nations of the world and God knew that they needed them but for them it suffices to seek first God's kingdom and then all these things could be added unto them in God's providential care for those who cared about him. As such they were his little flock in verse 32 and it was God as their Father's good pleasure to give them the kingdom.

At this point the tenour of Jesus' words begins to move towards the theme of a coming day of judgement for which his followers should be prepared he advising them in verses 33 and 34 to sell their possessions giving alms to accumulate invisible heavenly treasure with God in their placing their trust in him to provide for them it requiring only that they provide themselves with bags that would not wax old suggesting a traveller's lifestyle with no fixed abode and in so doing they would show their heart was set upon the heavenly treasure God could give them which could not be stolen by a thief or corrupted by moths like earthly treasure could in that it was invisible but set to be manifested upon earth post-resurrectionally in 2nd Timothy 4:8, 1st Peter 5:4, Revelation 2:10; 22:12 etc. Therefore it was a matter of faith in seeking the invisible treasure that God could provide them more precious than anything conceivable in this life and with the objective of ultimately attaining to it they were to keep their loins girded about and their lights shining like the ten virgins had to keep their lamps in working order to be able to go out and meet the bridegroom in the parable in Matthew 25:1-13. Thus in verse 36 they were now to be like men waiting for their Lord when he returned from the wedding (presumably referring to Christ's inauguration as king in heaven as in Daniel 7:13-14, in Luke's parable the nobleman travelling to a far country to be appointed king and them to return in 19:12) so that being spiritually prepared they could open to him immediately when he came and knocked. The Lord's response to them would be in verse 37 that he himself would gird himself and make them sit down to eat and he himself would come to serve them as according to the manner of their salvation in Christ dying for them rather than they themselves earning it by their own works, they being recipients therefore of his service of "humbling himself unto death" in Philippians 2:5-8 as pictorially set forth in his humbling himself to wash his disciples' feet in John chapter 13 as a parallel to this verse in Luke. Then in verse 38 Christ's servants should be found continually prepared for Christ's coming whatever watch of the night he came and be like men protecting their households against the unexpected arrival of the thief at any moment of the night in 39 for in 40 the Son of man would come at such an hour that they thought not.

In verse 41 Peter then asks Jesus whether this parable was specifically addressed to them or to all Jesus replying in terms of "whoever" is that faithful and wise steward whom his Lord had made ruler over his household the words applying to all Christ's servants of all ages it requiring that they give their households (i.e. the church they were overseers over) their portion of food (i.e. spiritual food) in due season so as to be blessed to be found by their Lord so doing in verse 43, being exalted after the manner of Pharaoh with Joseph to be ruler over all that he had in 44. However, in the inversion of this the servant consumed with his own selfish interests seeing his Lord apparently delaying in his return who begins to beat both the men-servants and maid-servants, eating and drinking with the drunken will accordingly be caught and cut off by the unexpected return of his Lord being declared no better than an unbeliever although such a one had had the responsibility of knowledge and of the care of his Lord's household (i.e. the church). Then in verses 47 and 48 a distinction is made between the servant that knew his Lord's will (i.e. well) and failed to do it being beaten with many stripes and the one who did not know carrying not the same level of responsibility (as guilty of so called "sins of ignorance" in the Old Testament) and therefore receiving a much lighter punishment with fewer stripes from his master it appearing everyone being judged according to their respective knowledges and abilities with their being no constant, universal criteria of judgement applied to all men indiscriminately for it appearing every individual case is to be judged by the returned Christ upon its own merits. Thus "For unto whomsoever much is given, of him shall be much required: and to whom men have committed much, of him they will ask the more." In verses 49 and 50 Christ's judgement is associated with fire which will destroy the bodies of the rejected ones in Mark 9:43-48, Isaiah 66:24 but first he has a baptism of water to be baptized with that equates with his humility unto death at his first advent, not his return to kindle the judicial fire at his second that will consume the adversaries, baptism itself being an act of humility as expressed by Jesus' submitting to John's baptism of repentance even though he was sinless and did not therefore require it. In verses 51 to 53 men's reactions to Christ will cause the division of members of families between those who accept and reject him Jesus again returning to the theme of the natural family ultimately being displaced by the new spiritual family in Christ and in 54 to 56 the people's ability to discern the weather is contrasted with their inability to discern the signs of the times Jesus' words probably directed towards the Pharisees whom he characteristically addresses as "Ye hypocrites" throughout and in 57 to 59 Jesus concludes his discourse by warning about the importance of being reconciled with one's brother in a dispute that might arise before he deliver him to the magistrate and the magistrate to the judge and the judge to the officer and the officer cast one into the prison Jesus assuring them that they would not be let out until they had paid the last mite (i.e. a lepton one sixty fourth of a denarius the smallest Jewish coin used at the time).

Luke Chapter 13

Luke chapter 13 contains various other sayings of Jesus commencing with his words to them that their natural lives were not guaranteed in this world without hope of salvation for Christ gives two examples of sinners who met their deaths prematurely, the Galileans whose blood Pilate the Roman governor mixed with their sacrifices and the eighteen upon whom the tower of Siloam fell, the fact of their not meeting natural deaths not being because they were sinners above all others but simply because they happened to be in the wrong place at the wrong time, the so called laws of predestinarianism appearing to work blindly and mechanically upon those segments of humanity concerning whom God had no special concern in that he is acquainted only particularly with those who approach him in Christ but even in their cases martyrdom may have been required especially in the first century as the ultimate test of their faith until the end. Nevertheless in terms of final salvation they would all likewise perish as those poor unfortunates that Christ describes as meeting such a sanguinary end if they did not repent that day. In verses 6 to 9 Christ adopts the figure of the fig tree as an allegory already used for Israel in Jeremiah 8:13; 24:1-10 in the first of three short mini-parables in this chapter whereby the master of the vineyard comes to seek fruit upon his fig tree and having found none for the third successive year commands it to be cut down in so much as it encumbered the ground but the vinedresser asks his Lord's patience for one more year that it might yet bear fruit after which he might cut it down Jesus calling upon God to forgive his nation for rejecting and crucifying him in Luke 23:34 and there remained just short of forty years for the nation to bear spiritual fruit in accepting Christ in the early Christian preaching they being finally hewn down as the spiritually fruitless fig tree in the events of 70 AD coinciding with the call to the Gentiles in their stead. Nevertheless by the end of the chapter in Luke Jesus still entertains hope of their accepting him as their Saviour although conceding that it would not be at that present time declaring in verses 34 and 35 using the language from Isaiah 10:14 of the Assyrian king's conquering conquests as gathering the nations like eggs whereby none resisted to flap the wing or chirp so that here in similar language Jesus declared "O Jerusalem, Jerusalem, which killest the prophets, and stonest them that are sent unto thee; how often would I have gathered thy children together, as a hen doth gather her brood under her wings, and ye would not! Behold, your house is left unto you desolate: and verily I say unto you, Ye shall not see me, until the time come when ye shall say, Blessed is he that cometh in the in the name of the Lord." In the parallel Matthew 23:38-39 "until it may be that" (i.e. "that you say") in Greek "heos an ἕως ἄν" (the particle of uncertainty "an" not being retained in the Lukan variant of the verse) entertains the possibility of the tree bearing fruit thereafter in so far as it is reserved in the natural Jews' freedom of choice to do so but their time had grown short for saving the nation at that particular epoch before national calamity in

70 AD for John the Baptist had already warned them in Luke chapter 3 verses 8 and 9 that they should "Bring forth therefore fruits worthy of repentance, and begin not to say within yourselves, We have Abraham to our father: for I say unto you, That God is able of these stones to raise up children unto Abraham. And now also the axe is laid unto the root of the trees: every tree therefore which bringeth not forth good fruit is hewn down, and cast into the fire," the latter clause anticipating the 70 AD holocaust in the natural Jews' lack of response to Jesus and his gospel convinced of their own integrity without needing such a saviour as Jesus purely because they were Abraham's natural descendants to whom God had vouchsafed immutable promises that must surely be fulfilled in them but they had forgotten that their fulfillment depended upon righteousness.

Then in verses 10 to 17 of this chapter further Sabbath controversies ensue arising from Jesus' healing of a woman with a spirit of infirmity that caused her to have a stooping back, he curing her condition upon the Sabbath Day to the indignation of the ruler of the synagogue who retorted in verse 14 that there were six days upon which work could be done and upon which the people therefore need come and be healed but not upon the Sabbath Day he having beheld Jesus lay his hands upon the woman so that immediately she had been "loosed" from her infirmity and made straight glorifying God as for eighteen long weary years she had been bound down altogether and unable to lift herself up in any way. Since a great act of mercy had been performed upon the woman Jesus turns upon the synagogue ruler who had condemned him with indignation of his own declaring him to be a hypocrite in that he and his fellows equally zealous for keeping the Law routinely broke it upon the Sabbath Day in their loosing their ox and ass from the stall to lead them forth to watering and so why should he not help this true daughter of Abraham that believed in him (as "Abraham was justified by faith before works" in Romans 4:2-5, 9-10) to be loosed from her bond having been bound by Satan (or "the adversary" according to Numbers 22:22 referring to "the angel of the Lord") regardless of whether or not it was the Sabbath Day for Christ as "the end of the Law to all who believed" (Romans 10:4) was "the Lord of the Sabbath Day" (Matthew 12:8, Mark 2:28) just as much as he had authority over the angels and could therefore redirect their activities behind human suffering upon the Sabbath Day.

Then in verses 18 to 21 two parables follow from Christ prefaced by the question "Unto what is the kingdom of God like?" and "Whereunto shall I liken the kingdom of God?" the words coming from Isaiah 40:18 where the prophet asks "To whom then will ye liken God? Or what likeness will ye compare unto him?" and goes on to describe their making of idols that cannot compare to and be like the true God being constituted inevitably inferior as the imaginations and vanities of men's minds without any life or power to save of their own in contrast to the true God. Given then that a description of false religion follows what appears to be the same question in Luke there Christ's parables of the Mustard Seed that grows from the tiniest of seeds to become the greatest of trees in the branches of which all the birds of the aerial find a home and of the leaven in the three measures of meal that silently leavens them all are likely to describe the development of false religion, the three measures referring perhaps to the three principal branches of Christianity Roman

Catholicism, Greek Orthodoxy and Protestantism that are presented as being wholly leavened in Christ's word becoming adulterated by pagan philosophy in their institutions and organizations in 2nd Corinthians 11:2-4, James 4:4, in Acts 5:4 the "conception" of the evil thought leading to the germination of apostasy in Christ's church in the begettal of a man-child of sin in Revelation chapter 12 (i.e. 33 AD to 313 AD, the period of pregnancy 280 years (the official average exactly 280 days or 40 weeks) or approximately 9 months of years) elevated to the Roman political aerial as begotten by a woman whose true nature is as of a harlot in Revelation chapter 17 having committed adultery with all the kings of the earth in becoming wholly "leavened" or a "brazen woman" (Isaiah 48:4, Jeremiah 3:3 (RV)) in adopting their religious beliefs of immortal soulism and a weak God unable to control his own creation that are the hallmarks of these churches that have adulterated Christ's word by their paganization of it making his teaching of none-effect through their false religion for what is the purpose of Christ coming back to raise the dead if one goes to heaven upon the day of one's death and can exist non-corporeally as is affirmed by the erroneous teaching. Then in observing that the harlot of Revelation chapter 17 as a figure for the unfaithful church is code named "Babylon" and remembering in Daniel chapter 4 that king Nebuchadnezzar's pagan kingdom of Babylon is described as such a tree set to be hewn down by the watchers (i.e. angels in Daniel 7:13-14, 17, 23) in which all the birds of the air found their home in its branches as well as the beasts of the earth in its shadow beneath it in Daniel 4:10-12, 20-22 then we understand that this is the pseudo-kingdom of God or development of false Christianity from humble beginning though continually adulterating Christ's word with worldly philosophy that emerged as "Babylon the Great" in Revelation 17:5 in so much as it had inherited the religious and political ideologies of that ancient empire to appear the same as it in God's eyes in becoming indistinguishable in fact from it for the harlot rides Daniel's fourth beast or the Roman Empire in Daniel 7:23 in having traded the truth of Christ's word for political power and the so called "soul merchants" that inhabit its branches as "a cage of every unclean and hurtful bird" (Revelation 18:2) themselves doing business with "souls of men" in Revelation 18:13 by teaching the old worldly philosophy in a Christian guise that every life was already immortal and consequently entrapped or encaged those who followed them within this monstrous organization where no such liberty existed to be saved from it. If this interpretation is disputed then it has only to be remembered that when Christ did have occasion to talk about the coming of his real kingdom it was as a dramatic intervention of God suddenly in world history when men lest expected his coming and not at all a slowly growing, expanding and spreading out realm over time that the parable of the Mustard Seed would require its subject therefore being something other than the literal kingdom of God.

After having spoken these two short parables so pregnant with hidden meaning it is written in verse 22 that Jesus "went his way" through the cities and villages en route to Jerusalem with one saying to him obviously having understood something of the meaning of the preceding two parables whether it were true that there were few to be saved Jesus exhorting him in reply to "Strive to enter in at the strait (or narrow) gate for many would seek to enter in and not be able" the word translated "narrow" here "stene στενή" is used as synonymous with in the parallel of this verse in Matthew

7:14 "tethlimmene τεθλιμμένη" meaning literally "compressed" compared to the broad way that led to destruction and if this is indeed the correct sense it does not say much for "popular" religion that claims to be this narrow way for logic would dictate that it is invariably likely to be wrong if followed by the majority of people for whatever the true faith may be it is likely to be found by very few in Jesus' words in Matthew 7:14 and even fewer having found it may be found morally acceptable to pass through it or continue upon the narrow way that leads ultimately to life. Jesus was going "that way" in his route to Jerusalem to sacrifice himself there as an effective atonement for the sins of his fellow-travellers or indeed followers upon that route of every age having taken up their crosses and followed him thitherward denying themselves the pleasures of this life accordingly and even enduring the suffering of death like their master in some cases. But again men had only limited time to follow Christ before he came or indeed their natural deaths given that their Lord then "delayed" his coming but that moment of judgement would inevitably come for all such that called him "Lord" with the door having then been shut and they standing outside knocking upon it and imploring the Lord Jesus to open to them he would reply to them that he did not know them for they had not followed him faithfully although they believed themselves to have eaten and drunk in his presence (i.e. the Eucharist the taking of which whilst immoral leading to certain judgement in 1st Corinthians 11:27-31) and he to have taught in their streets but their religion will be revealed as counterfeit Jesus declaring to them in verse 27 that they should all depart from him as workers of iniquity and then in 28 presumably now in a post-resurrectional setting they would experience extreme mental anguish and pain described as "weeping and gnashing of teeth" in their seeing Abraham, Isaac and Jacob and all the prophets in the kingdom of God and they themselves cast out with the Gentiles coming from all compass directions to sit down in their stead for Christ declares concerning this coming inversion of how things were presumed to be by them that those who were despised as last would be first and they themselves who in their self-arrogance esteemed themselves to be first would inevitably find themselves the last when Jesus returned upon "that day" to "judge the secrets of men" in Romans 2:16.

After this the chapter draws to a close with Jesus being warned in verse 31 by certain of the Pharisees to get himself thence in the wake of a plot having been revealed to them that Herod sought to kill him Jesus replying to them that it was indeed his destiny to die at Jerusalem to where they were going but it was not according to Herod's or any other man's chronology but according to God's forepurpose that Jesus continue to wrought his miracles that day and the next he set to be "perfected" only upon the third day according to God's timing and not man's it being evident here that Jesus is not referring to literal days and his "perfection" upon the third day properly refers to his resurrection after a period of inactivity in the unconsciousness of death for at least something of the duration of a period of three days so it can only be that Jesus being "perfected" at Jerusalem after today and tomorrow upon the third day relates to his death and resurrection together the latter event arising from the former which halted Jesus' miracle-working for the interval of his repose in the tomb. "Go tell that fox!" as applied to Herod would appear to be a non-complimentary exclamation regarding the Tetrarch's character in seeking Jesus out to kill him like a fox after his prey and Jesus' having made his forecast that although he continued to work his miracles that day and the next it was incontestable that any prophet could perish away from Jerusalem then gives his bitter lamentation over the city's refusal to believe in and accept him declaring himself as a gentle hen trying to gather her unwilling brood to her in love and protection in contrast to the ravenous fox figure to describe the current king Herod and then mourning that they would not see him again until such time that they called him "blessed" as preeminently the one who "came in the name of the Lord" to them as in John 5:43 Jesus had declared that he had come in his Father's name and yet there too the stubbornness of human nature prevented them from accepting him preferring "Barabbas" (i.e. "the son of the Father" in Aramaic) who simply came to them in his own name without the divine begettal that Christ had truly begun his life with by which he was equipped to save them in truly bearing his Father's name or moral character in Exodus 33:18-19; 34:5-7 by his Father's hereditary influence in him as well as his being renewed and strengthened by that self-same Spirit or power of God by which he had been begotten continually in his ministry in John 3:34, Psalms 80:17.

Luke Chapter 14

Luke chapter 14 continues with various sundry sayings and parables of Christ dealing with the importance of humility, care for the poor, Israel's rejection of God's invitation to come to his banquet, counting the cost of discipleship and leaving all one's worldly concerns behind in following Christ only the first six verses really dealing with Jesus' interaction with others being another Sabbath Day healing narrated there. This time Jesus is invited into the house of one of the chief Pharisees to eat bread upon the Sabbath Day where there was predictably a certain man before him that had the dropsy (Greek "hudropikos ὑδρωπικός, " i.e. hydropsy, the body swollen due to excess water but nevertheless still thirsty) probably brought there quite deliberately so that they might have something to accuse Jesus of in his healing the man upon the Sabbath Day but Jesus accepted their challenge asking the Pharisees and Lawyers there assembled whether or not it was lawful to heal upon the Sabbath Day and they maintaining their silence Jesus took the man and healed him before them all and after having let the healed man go turned upon his accusers declaring to them that if they had had an ox or ass fallen into the pit they would have surely lost no time in pulling him out upon the Sabbath Day, Matthew 12:12 adding to this point "of how much greater value is a man" (i.e. than the restored animals) that Christ should exercise his compassion upon a human being upon the Sabbath day as Hosea 6:6 quoted by Christ in Matthew 9:13; 12:7 had taught "I desire mercy not sacrifice" with regard to the more important action that superseded even the keeping of God's Law (according to God's Law all humanity sentenced to death but God gave Christ as an act of mercy in John 3:16 showing he himself overriding the universal law of sin and death to save men) and Jesus' accusers knew how to be merciful to their own animals so could not Christ show that mercy to a human being that they showed to their ox or ass upon the Sabbath Day in rescuing them from the pit or was it because the animals helped them economically to be in possession of them in a fit and healthy state so that rather than having mercy upon animals which

51

is not a theme greatly stressed in the Bible their interests were purely self-centred in saving them from the pit or shaft into which they had fallen. That being the case they being purely money-minded in this respect they saw no intrinsic profit to themselves in men being healed by Christ upon the Sabbath Day and therefore opposed him being wholly rotten and self-centred to the core even in their saving of their own animals upon the Sabbath Day hardly an act of mercy but because they were useful to them. But the man with the dropsy (i.e. hydropsy) whom Christ healed served no practical use to them other than in Christ's performing the cure providing them with a pretext by which they might accuse him for they entirely lacked the compassion upon others that led Christ to do what he did not as a deliberate and blatant breaker of Moses' Law but the action of one who was led by a higher principle of love and compassion than that they were aware of.

In verse 6 then the Lawyers and Pharisees who contested the legitimacy of Christ healing upon the Sabbath Day having been put to silence in that he was uncovering their own hypocrisy in breaking the Sabbath Day themselves probably for a far less noble reason than the mission of love and compassion by which Christ was motivated Jesus observed that at the dinner table in that place that men who esteemed themselves to be something of high repute immediately chose out for themselves the chief places as though sitting at the head of the table was a matter of social prestige for them and a confirmation of their supposed high standing in society. Nevertheless rather than seeking "the praise of men" in this way Jesus as usual stressed the principle of humility in this social setting warning that if they deliberately chose the highest seats when a more honourable man than they arrived they would inevitably be asked to vacate their seat for such a one esteemed to be more honourable than they and begin again with shame to take the lowest seat Jesus in accordance with his maxim that "he who exalts himself shall be humbled and he who humbles himself shall be exalted" (here in verse 11) declares that it was required when one was invited to a feast that they took the lowest seat so that in the inversion of the before envisaged scenario he that had invited them might then subsequently invite him up higher upon the table so that he might gain respect and even worship from those there assembled in being directly called up to a higher position by his host in having hitherto exercised a spirit of humility in having selected the lowliest place as reckoning oneself to be of no great value that he "deserved" to occupy any high status as Christ practically illustrated this in taking on the role of a servant at the Last Supper with his disciples washing their feet as a humble servant in portraying his coming great act of service to them in "humbling himself unto death" upon the cross to thereafter be highly exalted by God in Philippians 2:11 to the universal applause of all who witness his exaltation being bowed to and confessed as "Lord" by all who witness God's exalting him by giving him a new name and status no longer "lowly" but "King of Kings" and "Lord of Lords" in Revelation 19:16 he thus "having worship in the presence of them that sit at meat with him" in Luke 14:10 Christ expressing the lesson of absolute humility leading to absolute exaltation most perfectly in his life and submission unto death to thereafter be highly exalted by God called to the most prestigious place upon the table and in Philippians 2:5 his followers are called upon to do the same it being required that "the same mind" be in them that was also in Christ who "made himself of no reputation, and took upon him the form of a servant, and was made in the likeness of men" (i.e. in Jesus' testing by God's angel he declining to seize God-like power over the kingdoms of the world given to the angel in Hebrews 2:5 at that precise moment humbling himself to play the role of a representative man in order to redeem those who associated with him as a man and not as a divine being such as would have had no ability to save man from sin and death in Hebrews 2:16 so that Jesus' "being found in fashion as a man, he humbled himself, and became obedient unto death, even the death of the cross. Wherefore God also hath highly exalted him, and given him a name which is above every name: That at the name of Jesus every knee should bow" (Philippians 2:7-10) in his dinner table parable Jesus calling upon his disciples to exercise the same spirit of mind that had been in him therefore. For this was the opposite to what those who followed the Law were doing for they boasted of themselves that they were something great and were therefore set to be put down from their high places by God himself whom they mistakenly believed themselves to represent.

After this in verses 12 to 14 and again in verses 15 to 24 there follow two parables based upon Jesus' present setting at a dinner-table Jesus having addressed himself to his host in verse 12 bade him not to invite his friends, brethren, kinsmen nor rich neighbours when he made a supper for it might so happen that they could repay his generosity in so having provided a supper for them by inviting him to a further supper that they would provide in return so that he would be "recompensed" by them for his trouble and work in his original banquet. But it required that the host be reconciled by God not by man for his generosity lest he be trying to impress men to get credit and respect from them but not necessarily with God Jesus advising therefore that to please God one should invite the poor, the maimed, the lame and the blind to one's banquet for in doing so they would truly be blessed precisely because these marginalized members of society could not repay them but there would ultimately be no loss to them but great gain in that God himself would repay them at the resurrection of the just it ultimately being firstly a matter of faith that God was there and knew about what one was doing and secondly a matter of conscience in that one who truly possessed the love and compassion of God as Christ had exhibited would automatically be "moved" by his inner voice as it were to perform some such good deed that Christ describes to the poor and unfortunate members of his society, he being indeed pricked with guilt in not taking action to help them.

Then after an interjection from one of Christ's fellow diners who heard his words in verse 15 that "Blessed was he that ate bread (i.e. supped) in the kingdom of God" Christ continues with a second supper-based parable in which he describes a certain man presumably intended to represent God who made a great supper and invited many sending forth at supper time his servants to invite his chosen guests (i.e. the Jews) relaying to them that all things were now ready for the banquet (i.e. corresponding to Christ's having been slain as "the lamb" in the historical parallel ready for them to "partake" of him in some way) but being bidden to now come to his banquet those invited according to God's original purpose begin to make excuses, in fact they "all" doing so with "one consent" standing for Israel's national rejection of Christ in the historical parallel, one having just bought a piece of land

and prayed be excused that he might go and see it (i.e. hoping to attain to the acquisition of the promised land through the accumulation of legalistic credit with God), another having bought five yoke of oxen and needing to go to prove them (i.e. the Law-enforcers making the Law "a heavy burden" upon their fellow men having been the Jewish leaders' principal fault), a further invitee had just married a wife and therefore asked to be excused ("marrying and giving in marriage" also appearing to be a higher priority than keeping awake for Christ's coming in Luke 17:27-30 people becoming too involved in worldly affairs as though there were nothing else the apostle Paul advising that because of the present trouble and that the time had grown short in 1st Corinthians 7:29 it were preferable to stay awake looking for the day of the Lord with singleness of purpose than marrying). After this in verse 21 in the parable the servant having returned word to his Lord of his invitees all having politely refused his invitation for various reasons the master of the house's reaction is one of great wrath he accordingly commanding her servant to go out quickly into the streets and lanes of that city to bring to his banquet the poor, maimed, halt and blind, these marginalized members of society of course standing for the Gentiles whom the Jews despised being invited or called to God's kingdom in their stead there still being room in verse 22 requiring the master of the house to send his servant further and further afield to find men in the highways and hedges (i.e. beyond the confines of the land of Israel) who are positively compelled to come to the Lord's great feast (i.e. the early Christian preaching to the Gentiles) so that his house might be filled with guests. The parable then concludes in verse 24 with the ominous words for Israel that none of those men who had originally been invited would ever taste of the Lord's banquet, they seeing Abraham, Isaac and Jacob and the prophets sitting and dining in the kingdom and they themselves locked out.

The remainder of Luke chapter 14 then largely concerns the cost of discipleship that it is no easy matter for a man to follow Jesus and requires considerable forethought lest one put one's hand to the plough and look back after the manner of Lot's wife incurring a greater judgement upon oneself. Thus in verse 26 Jesus again stresses the reoccurring theme in this gospel that one who seeks to follow him should not be held back by family ties when their family did not share their faith in Christ, in this sense Jesus having come not to bring "peace" but a "sword" in setting family members against one another as in Matthew 10:34-36 and here the inevitability of the family division is further stressed by one's being commanded to actually positively hate one's father, mother, wife, children, brethren, sisters and even one's own life to effectively follow Christ being prepared to go to martyrdom in verse 27 for Christ's name rather than deny him as their one true Lord and master thereafter, Paul in counting all things as "refuse" for the surpassing knowledge of "knowing" Christ and the "power of his resurrection" in Philippians 3:8-10 faith in which "resurrection" would enable Jesus' disciples to lay down their own lives in the certain conviction that it would not be the end. But the way to the cross was not a pleasant one they necessarily becoming alienated from their friends, families and former acquaintances it being required for them that they not fall away from their chosen vocation (i.e. especially through other people's influence) it being like a builder who began to build a tower without counting the cost and being unable to finish being mocked at in verses 28 to 30, or in 31 and 32 like a king going forth to war having not considered the greater numerical supremacy of the enemy king's forces and realizing his error being forced to send ambassadors to ask for conditions of peace. Thus in the case of following Jesus if they could not forsake all that they had they could not be his disciple the cost of following him being quite clear and if they were not up to the challenge it was better for them not to start lest they incur greater injury upon themselves and others than if they had never started along the road of Christian discipleship at all which involved leaving all the things of this world behind one to embrace in faith what they could not physically see but had to assume of its reality through the historical event of Christ's resurrection from the dead that showed a higher way beyond the ephemeral and transient pleasures of this life, anything that our physical possessions and unbelieving companions could give us being of no value in contrast to God's higher calling in Christ. Finally in verses 34 and 35 Jesus reminded his hearers that Christian discipleship was a continual walk along a way at variance with the way the rest of world was going (i.e. destruction) so that temptation would continue to come for as long as one walked that way and the possibility of one's losing one's way to fall from grace a very real one Jesus therefore expressing this truth allegorically that we must continually refresh ourselves with daily reading of God's word and Christian outreach to resemble Christ in denying our natural selfish desires, Jesus declaring "Salt is good: but if the salt have lost his savour, wherewith shall it be seasoned? It is neither fit for the land, nor yet for the dunghill; but men cast it out. He that hath ears to hear, let him hear" for our wandering aside from God's path would result in our being cast out of his kingdom forever in our hitherto not having counted the cost of what we were doing and finding ourselves suddenly unable to fulfill the high requirements of our Christian vocation when the subsequent crisis came upon us in our having been ill-prepared for what lay ahead.

Luke Chapter 15

Luke chapter 15 largely consists of three parables exploring the same theme, namely the parable of the Lost Sheep, the Lost Coin and the Prodigal Son the occasion for them being set in verses 1 to 3 with the Scribes and Pharisees murmuring against Jesus that he received tax-collectors and sinners and ate with them. This then is essentially the theme that the three parables spoken in response to this criticism of Jesus' behaviour seek to expound that Christ had not come to save those who believed themselves to be spiritually healthy but the lost. As regards the first two of these parables they are somewhat simpler and less detailed than the third parable of the Prodigal Son although it may be observed in each one the numerical value of the "lost" increases by percentage (i.e. in relation to the not "lost") so that firstly it is one of a hundred sheep, then one of ten coins and finally one of two sons it being brought to bear upon the Pharisees that the "lost" group is far greater than they imagined and even if it were not God would still desire the restoration to his love and concern of one sheep of a hundred as much as one son out of two no human being being forgotten by God for the sheer number of people in the world. There are similarities here of course with Abraham's plea to God's angel over Sodom in Genesis chapter 18 that firstly if fifty righteous are found in it would he spare the whole city for their sakes and so on with diminishing numerical values until it is assured that God would save the city for the sake of only ten found therein the basic point being that God cares about every individual that has the capacity to respond to him.

And so with regard to the parable of the Hundred Sheep bringing to mind Ezekiel's great shepherding discourse in his 34th chapter in which God will save his wandering sheep that have gone astray seeking them out upon "a cloudy and dark day" in Ezekiel 34:12 for want of sound leadership from their shepherds here too one of them would seek out the one lost sheep of ninety nine in the wilderness and having found it lay it upon his shoulders rejoicing, it appearing at first glance that the parable appears to exonerate the Pharisees as fulfilling their duties in seeking out the lost in contrast to Ezekiel where the shepherds are clearly condemned as abusing the sheep feeding upon them and letting them go astray but as in Jesus' critique of them for taking their ox or ass out of the pit into which it had fallen upon the Sabbath Day it appears they would certainly find the lost sheep not for the sheep's sake but for their own benefit in that they were covetous and every individual sheep increased their revenue in some way down to the last mite for it seems incongruous that Jesus would want to present them in a positive light in his parable whilst condemning them openly so that they might have indeed been happy for retrieving every last sheep but not for the right reason before God. Nevertheless in verses 6 and 7 Jesus interprets the parable another way identifying the shepherd who finds his lost sheep with God himself who is more joyful over the one assumed to be lost sinner who finally repents after a long period of having gone astray than over the ninety nine who not only did not need repentance at least in their own eyes and those of the people before whom they practised their religious piety but not necessarily in God's sight for God may have perceived them as overcome by their own self-arrogance and self-righteousness to have been unable to have evaluated their true spiritual status before him in not recognizing that they in fact needed repentance as much as the sinners whom they despised but of the latter they had nothing to hide never having previously "claimed" to be righteous so that in their public turning away from their former manner of life true repentance was indeed wrought such as the self-righteous Pharisees had no conception of in that they were not capable of repenting in being unable to recognize their sins were as deep as the tax-collectors and sinners they despised having taught themselves to believe that they were righteous but according to the wording of this parable God had no joy in them but rather in the other who could confess their sins openly without fear of loss of face or social prestige in so doing for this was a true and genuine repentance of which the Jewish elite had no idea having lulled themselves into a false sense of security that they needed none. Thus Jesus declared in verses 4 to 7 "What man of you, having an hundred sheep, if he lose one of them, doth not leave the ninety and nine in the wilderness, and go after that which is lost, until he find it? And when he hath found it, he layeth it on his shoulders, rejoicing. And when he cometh home, he calleth together his friends and neighbours, saying unto them, Rejoice with me; for I have found my sheep which was lost. I say unto you, that likewise joy shall be in heaven over one sinner that repenteth, more than over ninety and nine just persons, which need no repentance."

The parable of the Lost Coin then follows from verses 8 to 10 in similar vein although this time the numerical value is dropped from a hundred to only ten coins, the choice of money as the object of the woman's search for one of her ten pieces of silver suggesting the covetousness of the Pharisees or of the temple institution that controlled the treasury in Luke 21:1-4 in that every single coin of the poor ended up in their greedy hands to their own self-joy whereas the poor widow in chapter 21 who gave her entire life is rendered destitute whilst they rejoicing in growing rich from the people's offerings. Again we sense a double meaning to Christ's words implying the corruption of their religion by the love of Mammon if the woman stands for the religious teachers of the nation doing their job to "save the lost" with an exterior motive of rending such widows their prey and stripping them of their livelihood (in Matthew 23:14 they "devour widow's houses and for a pretence make long prayers" maintaining the outward appearance of being very virtuous servants of their God). Certainly the desire to find perishing money appears to be the theme here but once again according to the interpretation of the parable its primary surface meaning is not a critique upon Israel's corrupted religious leadership at all but a simple picture of God's angels in heaven rejoicing with one another (i.e. as represented by the women's friends and neighbours rejoicing with her) over the discovery of the lost coin or sinner that repents and returns into God's favourable "interest" as it were, it appearing that the main reason Jesus selects the image of a lost coin in the house for which the woman diligently sweeps is that it suits the domestic life of a woman as much as searching for the lost sheep the rural working life of the man and is simply a suitable image to adopt for a woman's gender while the parable makes the same basic point as the last one that one is joyful when one finds what is lost whether the sheep in the man's case or the coin in the woman's, both sharing their findings with great joy with their friends and neighbours as representing the angels rejoicing in heaven over the recovery by one of them particularly of the "lost" sinner. However in the parable of the Lost Coin the allegorical figure introduced of the woman using the lightstand to search which does not feature in the parable of the Lost Sheep clearly identifies her with the Christian preachers bearing witness to men (i.e. as "shining their light before them" in Matthew 5:16) in order to save the "lost" ones as indeed the seven churches in Revelation chapters 1 to 3 are depicted as seven lightstands surrounding the risen and ascended Christ at least symbolically with which "light" he can save the lost upon earth it appearing that in the parable of the Lost Sheep this image is replaced by the shepherd as presumably symbolic of Christ in this respect bearing the perishing sheep upon his shoulders (i.e. the cross of Christ as a means of saving men or the "lost" from their sins borne upon the shoulders of the model Christian or Simon of Cyrene where the sheep undergoes spiritual death upon it in being carried in the place where the cross would be when it did not have the power to survive of its own "strength" (i.e. the Law) by walking).

Finally then we come to the third and last parable in this sequence of three being the parable of the Prodigal or "Lost" Son from verse 11 to the end of the chapter being a vivid and shocking picture of Israel's resentment in the lost Gentiles having been "brought near" (Ephesians 2:13) back into divine favour through Christ when the elder son had served God so faithfully (i.e. by keeping the Law) all his life again deeming himself to have no need of repentance like his younger brother who had nothing to "lose" by making a public display by showing it whereas the elder brother could not do so not realizing that he needed to in his sins being hidden and not openly done and confessed as the younger son's but beneath the artificial facade of religious piety the older son is understood to have really been the failure by the end of the parable in not recognizing that he could not really have been perfect as he envisaged himself to be in his Father's service whereas he had no hesitation in condemning the younger brother. Thus the older brother is ultimately seen to be the judgemental one whereas his younger brother did not dare to undertake to judge him having the fear of God before his eyes by the end of the parable.

Thus at a certain time in verse 12 the younger son demanded his share of the family inheritance and having so gathered such things that were due him together travelled into a far land where he wasted his Father's money with riotous living particularly in verse 30 with prostitutes so that the money was soon exhausted and the younger foolish son left destitute and alone in that distant place without true friends or kin for the immoral women no longer wanted to know him now he had nothing to offer them in return. And so when that land was hit with a severe famine and he began to feel the unmistakable grip of real poverty enclosing upon him the young man endeavoured to enroll himself as a lowly farm labourer with a citizen of that country who sent him out into the fields to feed the swine where he would have gladly filled his belly with the husks that the swine fed on but no man would give him. The young man at last coming to his senses realized that it was now a choice between death (i.e. the plight of the Gentiles without Christ gone east to the land of Nod נוֹד or "Wandering" after the manner of Cain in Genesis 4:16, Jude 1:11) or returning to his Father's house ashamed for what he had done and openly confessing it before all, the young man recalling how his Father's servants had bread to the full and more besides while he wasted away in that "foreign" country he resolving that he would return and confess to his Father (i.e. God) that he had sinned both against himself and heaven and that he was no longer fit to be his son but if he could be treated as one of his lowly hired servants it would suffice him (i.e. "hired" or "bought" by Christ's blood when he could not pay the price himself it requiring therefore the confession of his sins in Acts 2:38, 1st John 1:9 before he could benefit from this sacrifice as doubtless represented by his Father's slaying of the fatted calf upon his return of which "thanksgiving" meal he partook). Thus when the son approached the house in a spirit of repentance the Father's attitude is not one of wrath and dismissal of him but quite the contrary for his heart yearned for his lost son seeing that he had repented so that having seen him coming while still a great way off the Father went out to him running in so much as he was moved with compassion for him falling upon his neck and kissing him and having almost brushed the young man's confession aside of how he had failed him treated him as a new person from that old sinful one commanding his servants to clothe him with the best robe and place a ring upon his finger and shoes upon his feet he being invested with "new garments" (Zechariah 3:3-5, Matthew 22:11, Galatians 3:27, Revelation 19:8 given her) as the fatted calf is slain and a great banquet instituted to celebrate the lost son's return who had hitherto been as good as dead but now miraculously lived.

The rest of the story follows as expected with the elder son out in the field being attracted by the sound of music and dancing from the house and inquiring of one of his Father's servants learnt that his younger brother had returned whom his Father had received safe and sound he thereafter becoming angry and complaining when his Father came out to meet him of how he had never transgressed his commandment and had so perfectly served him the Father assuring him that all that he had was his but it was fitting they slay the fatted calf for his younger brother had been dead but was now alive through his act of repentance, lost but now found whereas the older brother had needed no such recognition of his faithful service, not even the slaying of a kid, in so much as he esteemed himself already "righteous." But this again may have been the elder son's error although the parable does not clearly divulge it as in other places but we do get the impression that he was left in the field uninvited to that celebratory banquet at which the slain fatted lamb was partaken of by others who were able to "forgive" the young man as God had "forgiven" him (Matthew 6:14; 18:35, Ephesians 4:32).

Luke Chapter 16

Luke chapter 16 then mainly consists of two principal parables being the parable of the Unjust Steward and the parable of the Rich Man and Lazarus based upon the Pharisees' erroneous view of the death state entertained only for the purpose of argument and debate rather than for its essential truth. As regards the first parable it largely occupies the text from the start of the chapter until verse 13 and deals with a certain steward who deals dishonestly with money to provide himself with some when he is cast out of his stewardship either that he may pay for them to receive him into their houses in stealing his Lord's money after his rich master had given him a formal dismissal by reducing his creditor's bills firstly from a hundred to fifty and in the case of a second debtor from a hundred to forty measures of oil and wine respectively to get quick payment they presumably being unaware that he had been dismissed and he taking their money with him instead of returning it to his Lord to pay for his future lodging. Otherwise if this interpretation is not satisfactory we may understand his discount of his master's bills to his debtors as intended to arouse their sympathy with him in return for his helping them in order that they might receive him into their houses that way by way of returning the favour but whatever the case the steward acted very shrewdly with his Lord's financial dealings even after he had been dismissed from his post for wasting his Lord's goods although the debtors were unaware of it for in the case of the second understanding of the parable mentioned above it would not have mattered if he did not return the full amount to his Lord after he had been dismissed from his stewardship for he had already lost his position. Then the Lord commends the unjust steward upon finding out what he had done for he had done wisely in protecting himself after he had dismissed him even though it had lost him money for it showed the truth that the children of this world are wiser in their generation than the children of light meaning that in this life the unjust steward stood to survive but only in "their generation" or natural lives "the children of light" conversely "suffering themselves to be defrauded" in 1st Corinthians 6:7 in this life to attain to the heavenly riches.

Therefore in verse 9 Jesus takes the unjust steward's case as using money in this life fraudulently to assure himself an abiding place in this natural life as a figure for how his disciples should use the true riches to ensure themselves everlasting habitations it requiring them to be faithful in the least in this life and to be just in the least in this life in contrast to the unjust steward to show oneself to be trustworthy with the true invisible riches that appertained to God as their Lord finally and absolutely thus in verse 11 Jesus declared "If therefore ye have not been faithful in the unrighteous mammon, who will commit to your trust the true riches" and in 12 "And if ye have not been faithful in that which is another man's, who shall give you that which is your own" the latter verse meaning that immortality is not a commodity used like money that comes and goes from one's hand but one that appertains to one permanently to be "his own" in that no man can take it from them (John 10:28) whereas the unjust steward's desire for "everlasting habitations" or somewhere to live permanently after being cast out of his stewardship is really temporary and transient in so much that his efforts to "buy" the favour of other men through fraudulent activity with money will not see him any further than beyond his natural life although the Pharisees appeared through the accumulation of legal credit attained by defrauding men of their revenue through their exploitation of God's Law to this end (for they "devoured widow's houses" in Matthew 23:14) in the eyes of the people to be acting for God so that they might earn their salvation of the "everlasting habitations" spoken of in the parable but were in fact secretly putting aside the people's offerings for their own use for which cause the religious leaders of the nation would shortly be cast out of their stewardship by their divine master by those tragic events that transpired in 70 AD for they had been unfaithful in the unrighteous Mammon so that God would not entrust them with the true riches. Thus Jesus summarized the principal point of the parable in verse 13 that "No servant can serve two masters: for either he will hate the one, and love the other; or else he will hold to the one, and despise the other. Ye cannot serve God and mammon" the Pharisees also being very proud not wishing to lose face before the people for which cause they covered their faults rather than confessing them as in the parable the dismissed steward is too used to the comfortable life to do manual degrading work such as digging and to beg he is ashamed, the Pharisees facing not only lost of prestige and social standing but the comfort that an affluent lifestyle brought them as esteemed to be enrolled in God's service as it were. Thus in verse 14 it is written that the Pharisees also when they had heard this parable derided Christ for the narrator points out they were "covetous" seeking only to justify themselves before men not God in verse 15 so that they could be in good standing with men but not God when they fell for God knew their hearts and what was highly esteemed among men was abomination before God for the steward's human Lord had almost respected him for his duplicity in verse 8 in having shown cunning and guile in keeping a roof over his head but there was no such respect of double dealing with God in heaven who is ultimately all men's Lord and master.

Then in verses 16 and 18 fragments from Christ's "Sermon on the Mount" in Matthew's gospel appear preceding the parable of the Rich Man and Lazarus verse 16 declaring that the Law and the Prophets were until John since whom the kingdom of God was preached and every man pressed into it, this "friction" caused upon the spiritual plane by Christ's disciples using "the powers of the world to come" or kingdom age in Hebrews 6:5 prematurely or "before the time" (Matthew 8:29) in enforcing God's angels to relinquish their God-given roles to create illness and suffering upon earth (Psalms 78:49 KJV) is more clearly described in Matthew 11:12 that "from the days of John the Baptist until now the kingdom of heaven suffereth violence, and the violent take it by force" in so much that the powers of that epoch were prematurely manifested in the miracles the disciples were performing in Christ's name. In verse 17 it was easier for Israel as a nation to pass (described as "heavens and earth" particularly in Genesis 37:9-10, Deuteronomy 32:1, Isaiah 1:2, 10; 65:17-18, 2nd Peter 3:10-13) than for one "tittle" (i.e. small dot or stroke distinguishing the Hebrew letters) of the Law to fail in so much as Israel would be found transgressors of God's moral Law in particularly in the event of their crucifying and rejecting Christ and would accordingly pay the consequence (i.e. in 70 AD) for Christ "had come to fulfill the Law" in so much as it spoke of his sacrificial death the occasion for which was engineered by Israel's "necessary" rejection of him so that their "heavens and earth" or government and society was inevitably condemned to be removed by the fulfillment of their own Law whereby it spoke of the need for Christ's death "at the hands" of the nation (as their priests slew the animal sacrifices) throughout the symbology of its institutions or ordinances in John 5:46, Galatians 3:24-25 etc. Then verse 18 repeats Christ's teaching against remarriage after divorce found in Matthew 5:32 and 19:9 but without Matthew's exception clause "except for fornication" or pre-marital sex in one partner discovered before the marriage is consummated being divorce only or "breaking up" in the betrothal stage as it were, any separation following the consummation of the marriage due to adultery requiring the innocent party to remain celibate for the rest of their lives or else be regarded as an "adulterer" in like manner, Jesus declaring "Whosoever putteth away his wife, and marrieth another, committeth adultery: and whosoever marrieth her that is put away from her husband committeth adultery" in verse 18.

Finally upon this chapter then it requires that we offer up a brief explanation of the parable of the Rich Man and Lazarus that occupies it from verses 19 to 31 the parable being based upon the Pharisees' fictitious view of the death state in which they entertained the consciousness of the dead contrary to the Old Testament teaching that death is a state of thoughtlessness and utter unconsciousness forever if not interrupted by the event of the physical resurrection of the body as taught in Ecclesiastes 9:5, 10, Psalms 6:5; 39:13; 88:5, 10-12, 115:16-17, Psalms 146:4 (KJV), Isaiah 38:17-19, Daniel 12:2, John 5:28-29; 11:11-14, Ephesians 5:14 which belief the Pharisees were rejecting in believing in the consciousness of the dead elsewhere hence the parable ends with the words "Neither would they be persuaded if one rose from the dead" (as Lazarus the protagonist in the parable literally was in John chapter 11 leading the Jewish leaders to seek to murder Christ) for they were not really believing in the doctrine although here the physicality of Abraham who had a bosom, Lazarus who has a finger and the rich man who has a tongue at least comes closer to the Old Testament teaching than the modern teaching of the disembodied immortal soul for Lazarus is "carried to Abraham's bosom" as still physical by the angels but nevertheless it remains a fundamental teaching in the Bible that all organic life created by God cannot exist without a physical frame to support it, the Old Testament "living soul" constituting of that physical structure (i.e. the body or flesh) energized by blood (sometimes the Hebrew word "soul" referring to the blood element alone as in Isaiah 53:12 since both are necessary for the "living soul" to exist therefore it is the combination of flesh and blood that constitutes one) and animated by God's Spirit or power (as in Genesis 2:7, Job 33:4; 34:14-15 etc). Thus as the Pharisees had adopted a belief in Baalzebub the false Philistine God of Ekron in 2nd Kings 1:1-8 so too here in their apostasy they had come to believe in a fallacy in the dead being "conscious" before their physical resurrections from the grave and inheritance of the earth as Abraham, Isaac and Jacob had been promised post-resurrectionally in Acts 7:5, Hebrews 11:13, 39-40 etc for no other place had been promised and yet influenced by Greek and pagan philosophy an alternative afterlife was envisaged of which Josephus remarks of it in his "Dissertation V: Discourse to the Greeks concerning Hades" (although there is some evidence that it was actually written by Hippolytus of Rome) that in the Pharisaic belief there was an unbridgeable chasm separating the righteous and wicked with upon one side a fiery lake in "an unfinished part of the world" which separated the wicked from "Abraham's bosom" and the destination of the righteous upon that other side (although the Bible declares quite matter of factly that they "all died" (i.e. the faithful including Abraham of old meaning Biblically they are reposing unconscious in the grave) and therefore "had not yet received the promise" in remaining dead until the present day "that they might not be made perfect without us" (i.e. believers living now) in Hebrews 11:39-40 they all being "perfected" together upon that day of resurrection and judgement for all responsible upon one particular day of Christ's coming and not on many different days when they might have happened to have died.

Given then that the picture in this parable is contrary to the clear teaching of the Bible elsewhere we regard it as a parable based upon the fictitious beliefs of Jesus' opponents to show the illogicality of them for if the dead were conscious immediately after death and rewarded or not what purpose would there be in their future being resurrected for judgement or indeed what purpose in Christ's coming back to raise the dead and judge them when they had all already been dealt with upon the respective days of their deaths for this picture is as fictitious as Baalzebub being esteemed to be behind Christ's miracles but as in the case of Baalzebub Christ now forms his parable using the Pharisees' fictitious belief to show the illogicality of it for what need was there for resurrection and who indeed would "believe" in it being his crowning point in verse 31 if the dead were immediately conscious, judged and transported elsewhere after death as envisaged in the parable for there was none and yet the apostle Paul had declared that if there were no resurrection from the dead that their faith was in vain in 1st Corinthians 15:12-18 and those who had "fallen asleep in Christ had perished." Thus the purpose of the parable which does not teach itself but something else represented by the imagery as different varieties of trees abstaining to be anointed as king over the people in Jotham's parable in Judges 9:7-15 does not mean that we should understand that he is talking about literal trees (as in Ezekiel chapter 31, verse 9 where all the trees of Eden envied him (i.e. the king of Assyria) or Daniel talking about literal beasts in chapters 7 and 8 or a literal statue of gold in chapter 2 for these things were symbolic and a parable does not teach itself but something else, here that the rich were going to be brought down and the poor exalted ultimately, the former represented by the rich man who may possibly stand for Caiaphas the high priest who according to Josephus in Antiquities of the

Jews had five brothers-in-law Eleazar (high priest 16-17 AD), Jonathan (high priest spring 37 AD), Theophilus (37-41 AD), Matthias (43 AD), Annas (the Younger) (63 AD) who is enabled to speak "figuratively" but not literally in the parable to express his imagined remorse if he could have already been conscious after death of how he had abused the poor represented by Lazarus, for Jesus could not have introduced the dead high priest's testimony without allowing for the obviously fictitious possibility for those Biblically educated that the parable contains. So again like Baalzebub being entertained by Christ in Matthew 12:24-28 as the source of his power just for the sake of argument the parable is making a point just as if Baalzebub who does not really exist were divided against himself his kingdom could not stand making another point that Baalzebub could not really exist if Christ healed men for the powers he subdued must necessarily be on his side and co-operate with him for the cure to be successfully accomplished so that Christ pretends Baalzebub exists precisely to show the illogicality of it that he could not exist or Christ's miracles would result in conflict and desolation, not cures. Thus in the case of the parable of the Rich Man and Lazarus its mention of the resurrection of the dead at the end not only makes impossible the fictitious death state the parable describes but also underlines the fact that the Pharisees no longer believed in the true state of the dead as far as the Old Testament was concerned and the only means by which man might live again (i.e. by resurrection) which event itself in the case of Lazarus in John chapter 11 would not convince them of the error of their belief to make them "believe" because of their hard-heartedness.

Luke Chapter 17

Luke chapter 17 then deals with various themes, the importance of not causing offence to one's brother, forgiveness of one's brother, the power of faith, their humble Christian service, the healing of the ten lepers and the difference between Christ's two advents, whereas with regard to the first his enemies could not discern his presence among them for what it implied but with regard to his second it would be unmistakable like the lightning illuminating the night sky coming upon an unexpected world (unless this image is intended to be taken figuratively as suggested below) that would be in a similar state of immorality to that which had preceded Noah's flood. Thus as concerns the importance of not offending one's brother Jesus taught that it was woe unto the one whom offences came by so that for such a one it were better that a huge millstone be hung around his neck and he be thrown into the sea than that he should cause one of those little ones who believed in Christ to falter. We are reminded of Paul's picture in 1st Corinthians chapter 8 where one brother knowing that meat offered to idols is nothing and having no belief in it in partaking of the meat may cause the weaker brother to stumble in seeing them "at meat in the idol's temple" which might in the weaker one's eyes appear to be like an authorization of idol worship that such religious practice was acceptable. Therefore in verse 13 Paul concludes that it is better not to eat meat than cause his brother to offend. In verses 3 and 4 of Luke chapter 17 Christ then teaches them to rebuke their brother in the event that he trespasses against them but having done so afterwards forgive him, a procedure that could be repeated up to seven times a day in the event of one's brother expressing remorse and repenting of that bad thing that they had done for Paul taught in like manner that they should forgive one another as God forgave them in Christ in Ephesians 4:32.

After this in verses 5 and 6 in response to the disciples' request to increase their faith Jesus tells them that if they just had faith as small as a grain of mustard seed they would be able to declare to the sycamore tree that it be uprooted and transplanted into the sea and so it would obey them Jesus here not describing such miracles that were speeded up processes already occurring naturally in nature such as the grape turning water into wine, the grain of wheat germinating to produce a harvest, the progeniture of new life for such miracles that already appertained to the natural world were either done directly or dramatically speeded up in Jesus' miracles of the old creation but what Jesus is referring to here is a miracle of the "new creation" which will obey different physical laws such as in his walking upon water illustrating the power of his mind over matter rather than vice versa, the laws of nature controlling the physical organism to limit what it could do causing it to eventually "degrade" and die according to the second law of thermodynamics. Thus it is through faith that Jesus' disciples may eventually access the powers of this new age but Peter is not quite there in Matthew 14:27-31 his faith failing when Christ invites him to join him walking upon the sea so that matter took control of him causing him to sink he not having such a mind that could subdue the sinful tendency that caused him to obey the natural laws accordingly rather than vice versa in the possibility entertained of his suppressing and controlling them through not having the conscience of sin which ran according to natural law causing man to inevitably despite his best efforts run with it.

Then in verses 7 to 10 Jesus set out a brief parable to his disciples describing the principles of Christian service that they should not expect special thanks or treatment for what was their Christian duty as though they were doing it for reward like pursuing the works of the Law to gain legalistic credit with God for they were to expect nothing more than what their duty required for why did they do it in the first place, because they believed it was right or simply to get a reward? Thus Jesus envisages a servant plowing or feeding cattle in the field who having come in none of them would command him to sit down for supper without first preparing their own if they were their servant nor thank the servant for performing his duty with regard to preparing and bringing their suppers before eating his own for nothing more was expected than for the servant to fulfill his duties without any special commendation so that in verse 10 Jesus now asks his disciples to consider themselves in the servant's position he now teaching them to declare themselves as servants to be unprofitable ones who had simply done their humble service doing what was required of them for there was no place for the legalistic accumulation of credit before God through the keeping of the Law as though it might warrant the practitioner of the Law some special privilege or reward in return for having so "excelled" in his work.

Verses 11 to 19 then return to straightforward narrative with again it being recalled that Jesus was going up to Jerusalem to go his "way" to the cross ultimately, now passing through the regions of Samaria and Galilee where entering into a certain village Jesus is met by ten lepers standing afar off who addressing him as "Jesus, master" beg him to have mercy upon them Jesus doing so that all ten are healed of their leprosy having been dismissed by Jesus to show themselves to the priest to offer up those offerings prescribed in Leviticus chapter 14 for the cleansing of their leprosy it appearing that they are healed upon the way interestingly like Naaman the famous Old Testament leper cured by Elisha is healed away from the prophet's presence likewise in 2nd Kings chapter 5 in so much as leprosy was then regarded as a contagious condition which constituted physical contact a risk. Nevertheless the ten having been healed after it seems Jesus had already bid them depart in peace only one of them seeing that he had indeed been healed had the gratitude to return to Jesus, glorifying God and falling at his feet thanking him for the miracle that had been wrought upon him Jesus acknowledging that his faith had made him whole and commending the man who happened to be a Samaritan above the other nine who did not return to thank him glorifying God as this man did. Thus the extension of God's saving grace to non-Jews is anticipated here who would be grateful for the salvation wrought for them in Christ whereas the natural Jews would disdain and reject it, "the children of the kingdom" being "locked out" whilst "many would come from the east, west, north and south and sit down in the kingdom of God" (i.e. in Luke 13:29) because the Jews did not care upon the occasion of Christ's first advent to "acknowledge" him as their Saviour trying to go it alone through the works of the Law, hence the nine presumably Jewish lepers went straight to the priest to keep the Law of Moses rather then otherwise.

Then in verses 20 to 21 Jesus is approached by the Pharisees who demand of him when "the kingdom of God should come" he replying that upon that occasion it was not coming with signs to be observed with no man saying "Lo, here!" or "Lo, there!" for it was evident that as far as the kingdom of God existed at that time it existed in the person of Jesus who stood among them for it was through Jesus' sacrificial death that men might thereafter enter the kingdom and so Jesus told them that they should "behold that the kingdom of God was among them" (Greek "entos

ἐντὸς") Jesus' presence being synonymous of the kingdom in so much as its nucleus began from him in the subsequent crucifixion of "sin in the flesh" (Romans 8:3) in his flesh through which feat Jesus became the "doorway" through which man might enter into that sinless realm figuratively in John 10:9 and so it was because of this that the Synoptic phrase "kingdom of God" (or "heaven" in Matthew) is replaced with the person of Jesus in John's gospel and his famous "I Am" expressions concerning himself that he was "God manifest in the flesh" in 1st Timothy 3:16, John 1:14; 14:9 in the character of God being portrayed in his flesh (i.e. without sin) and therefore in his life, work and words as it will ultimately be everywhere in everyone through him in 1st Corinthians 15:28 in God being all in all ultimately but for now the kingdom of God began for them with the man Jesus Christ standing in their midst.

But after this in verses 22 to 37 Jesus apparently goes on to speak of the establishment of God's kingdom at his second coming which might have been in 70

AD had Israel accepted the first century Christian preaching for much of the language fits a first century Palestine context here, even the day of the Son of man being unmistakable like the lightning from one side of heaven to the other in verse 24 demonstrable as referring to the so called "lightning formation" or movements of the Roman Legions under Titus and Vespasian (particularly of the twelfth legion "Legio XII Fulminata" meaning "the lightning legion" or "lightning strike") who in the event of Israel's rejection of the Christian preaching came to destroy their temple in 70 AD with their "scorch-earth" strategy of burning and razing the city to the ground (i.e. as under Christ's direction from heaven "fulfilling the days of vengeance" in Luke 21:22) and certainly the last verse of this chapter in Luke fits into place as describing the Roman legions who portrayed the eagle upon the banners of their legions as a prominent symbol of the Roman Empire being wheresoever the carcase or spiritually dead nation of Israel was. Interpreting these verses as in a 70 AD context therefore the one man of two taken from the bed or field or woman from her companion at the mill is "caught away" to be with Christ in 1st Thessalonians 4:13-17, Matthew 24:31 declaring that the angels will be instrumental in gathering God's elect from the four winds of heaven leaving the one left behind in all cases as the rejected one who is left to face the coming holocaust but these verses surely require Christ's coming in 70 AD but that literal return of Christ having been postponed because of the Jewish people's rejection of him in Romans 11:25 we can only assume that the descriptions obviously suited to the land of Palestine in the first century present how things would have been if enough of the nation had accepted Christ. Thus in verse 22 they would soon desire to see one of the days of the Son of man and not see it presumably spoken to believers whilst Christ remained absent until their number grew as required in 1st Corinthians 11:25 in the interim Christ exhorting them to ignore the false prophets who said "See here!" or "See there!." In verse 25 Jesus reminds them that he as the Son of man need first be rejected by that generation before his enforced removal from Israel who nevertheless are still given opportunity until 70 AD for as long as that generation continued at least through the Christian preaching hence the language here explaining apparently more than one possibility of what might happen pending human response.

In verses 26 to 30 the times preceding the envisaged coming of the Son of man in 70 AD or other postponed time is to be marked by a significant decline of morality comparable to the world before Noah's flood or to Sodom and Gomorrah before they were destroyed, with eating and drinking, marrying and giving in marriage carrying on unabated as though nothing would happen to the world, it being like the day Lot went out of Sodom and Gomorrah and they were all suddenly destroyed by fire and brimstone, in verse 30 Jesus exhorting them to remember Lot's wife at this time and not look back to the old world, Paul also advising against "marrying" because "of the present distress" in 1st Corinthians 7:26 which chimes in for a first century context for Jesus' words about ongoing "marrying and giving in marriage" with impending destruction having then been imminent as of course the manner of Jerusalem's destruction being torched by the Roman legions also bears similarities with the destruction of Sodom and Gomorrah by fire manifestation thus strengthening the likelihood that these verses should properly be understood in a 70 AD context as does verse 30's warning not to go down from the rooftop to get one's possessions from the house or return from the field to get them although Luke does not include Matthew's reference to fleeing to the mountains here which is definitely suitable for describing a localized destruction within the land of Israel. Finally on this chapter Jesus' warning concerning whoever would seek to save his life would lose it and he who lost it would preserve it (i.e. post-resurrectionally) admirably suits the first century context where "separation from Israel" (possibly hinted at in Revelation 18:4 pending how Revelation is interpreted) was a matter of salvation seeing that the nation was doomed at that epoch for it may have been that in the siege that deserters were put to death by the Jewish forces protecting the city but they were fighting for a "loss" cause seeing that they had irrevocably rejected Christ by that time death only awaiting the people in the city who still clung to the national hope at least at that time if this context may be correct for Jesus' words here.

Luke Chapter 18

Luke chapter 18 then contains the parable of the Unjust Judge, the Self-righteous Pharisee and Humble Tax-collector, followed by Jesus' rebuking his disciples for not allowing the little children to come unto him "for unto such belonged the kingdom of God," followed by the story of the rich young ruler and the need to cut worldly ties and possessions to follow Christ, the chapter finally finishing after Jesus repeats his prophecy of his forthcoming death at Jerusalem to the disciples' bewilderment with the story of the healing of the blind man by the wayside at Jericho. Therefore to deal with each of these individual segments of the chapter in chronological order the first parable concerns a widow who pleaded repeatedly for the unjust judge who neither feared God nor man to avenge her upon her enemy who finally accedes to her request for sheer weariness at being repeatedly asked to do it the point being made in verse 7 that if even evil men will help rather than endure being constantly asked to, how much more will God avenge his own elect who cry day and night unto him Jesus declaring that he will avenge them speedily in verse 8 though "he bear long with them" in verse 7 it appearing that there are many such requests for help from the faithful that God must answer but nevertheless Jesus asks in verse 8 that when he himself comes as the Son of man again speaking of himself in the third person will he find "the faith" on earth in so much that people may cease asking God for anything even to the extent of denying his existence although God bore long with them as his salvific works in history bore testimony to his saving works with mankind so that men should know better by the time the day of judgement finally arrives for them for God had proved his saving concern with mankind repeatedly already in the past in having granted their petitions and delivered them although they continued to doubt and he to "bear with them" in spite of their lack of faith.

Then there follows in verses 9 to 14 the parable of the Self-righteous Pharisee and Humble Tax-collector the one respected as a religious guide of the people and the other despised as at the fringes of society and doing the Roman's dirty work in collecting their tax. The Pharisee indeed evidently held this stereotypical view of the tax-collectors as the dregs of society standing boldly and somewhat arrogantly in God's temple at the time of prayer declaring that he was not like him, not being like an extortioner, unjust person or adulterer which categories of people he associates with the tax-collector also as being of the same social rank as it were a sinner. Nevertheless the Pharisee boasts arrogantly of his fasting twice a week, of his tithes that he gave of all he possessed as though such "works" could truly justify himself before God when he had forgotten that beneath the artificial religious facade he was putting up as "a covering" (i.e. as Adam and Eve tried to make their own inadequate "covering for sin" in sewing fig leaves together in Genesis 3:7) he was still essentially a sinner as much as any man and needed atonement equally with the tax-collector who now stood afar off and refraining from even lifting up his eyes to heaven merely smote upon his chest beseeching God to be merciful to him for he was most certainly a sinner and did not claim to be anything else unlike the arrogant Pharisee who esteemed himself to be already "perfect" before God in all his good works that he did but did not know that he was "wretched and miserable and poor and blind and naked" (Revelation 3:17) as far as God's approximation of him was concerned for "man looked upon the outward appearance but God looked upon the heart" in 1st Samuel 16:7 so that the tax-collector went home justified set to be exalted by God for having appropriately humbled himself in being honest whereas the Pharisee went home condemned set to be toppled from his position of eminence by God within the process of time in his universal justice inevitably ultimately prevailing.

After this the people brought unto Christ the little children that he might lay his hands upon them but this displeased his disciples they rebuking the people upon his behalf without Christ having authorized it so that he in turn was forced to rebuke them commanding them to permit the little children to come unto him and not forbid them for unto such was the kingdom of God. It so transpired therefore that Christ was declaring in verses 16 to 17 that to enter the kingdom of God by coming unto him it required men cultivate a childlike mentality characterized by simplicity of thought such as a child might exhibit in not knowing yet how to manipulate circumstances to their own advantage especially for financial gain accepting things simply at face value for what they were without any other evil thinking of how they might benefit for themselves at the expense of their peers (such as adults are incessantly scheming and contriving to their own advantage). It required then that the disciples be as "innocent as doves" but not entirely ignorant with regard to the bad things of this world at least in so far as men could use them to their own profit they still nevertheless having to have some awareness of this evil in men in being paradoxically "as wise as serpents" in their dealings with them in Matthew 10:16 but without the corruption that other men allowed to dominate them to cheat and impoverish his fellows while they grew richer for in Christ's kingdom there is no place for such a covetous mind as this particularly when it involved hurting one's fellow man which was the cardinal crime of the Jewish religious leaders who exploited God's Law to their own advantage over those simple minded people whom Christ sought for his kingdom who had no such exterior motive for their simple religious confession.

Following this in verses 18 to 30 of Luke chapter 18 we have the story of the rich young ruler who initially approaches Christ with confidence albeit mistakenly addressing him as "good master" which Christ corrects in verse 19 declaring that God alone deserved the description of "good" Jesus probably playing down the Pharisaic mind-set here that one could be regarded as "good" for his many works before men which manner of thinking Jesus was actively attacking in his ministry that "good works" before men counted for nothing before God when accompanied by an exterior motive to impress men and Jesus doubtless did not want to be categorized alongside the Pharisees as performing such works before men for his own credit, "perfection" ultimately only appertaining to God alone as the way of Christ's "humility" would have dictated. Then in verses 20 to 22 we come to the crux of the matter that although the rich young ruler presumed he had done sufficiently to inherit eternal life through his keeping of the commandments among which are listed not committing adultery, killing, stealing, bearing false witness and honouring one's parents in verse 22 it appears that he was addicted to material things leading to Jesus' diagnosis of this addiction which hindered him living the selfless and altruistic life that God called upon his followers to follow Jesus telling him point blank that he must give up all his material possessions to which he was accustomed to having, distribute to the poor and after having done thus he might have the invisible treasure in heaven or credit with God which would result in a favourable outcome for him at Christ's coming to raise and judge the dead at which dispensation the reward of eternal life would be bestowed in Matthew 16:27, 2nd Timothy 4:8, 1st Peter 1:4, 13; 5:4, Revelation 22:12, pending a favourable judgement at that time.

This the rich young man had to accept as a matter of faith and to cling to the comforts of his material things was like an expression of doubt that something "better" was available and so Jesus found his materialism evidence for the inadequacy of his faith in spite of his protests to the contrary that he had never broken any of the commandments. Thus the young man was left downcast in verse 23 for it is remarked concerning him that he was very rich. In verse 24 Jesus comments upon this that it was well nigh impossible for those who had riches (and "trusted" in them in Mark 10:24, cf. 1st Timothy 6:17) to enter the kingdom of God in verse 25 contrasting it to trying to make a camel go through the eye of a needle to express the impossibility of it for "where one's heart was there would be where one's treasure was too" in Matthew 6:21, Luke 12:34 whether with God as invisible credit through faith or in the corruptible material things with which one might surround oneself upon earth, their trust in these objects to give them ultimate happiness and contentment finally causing them to "choke" him in Matthew 13:22, Mark 4:19, Luke 8:14 like eating food too fast to finally be unable to breathe from choking so too all the corruptible things one collected were in a state of decay leading to no lasting peace but guilt for not being generous to one's fellow-man in need, thus James declared the reality of all things "passing away" in this world (1st John 2:16-17) declaring "Your riches are corrupted, and your garments are motheaten. Your gold and silver is cankered; and the rust of them shall be a witness against you, and shall eat your flesh as it were fire. Ye have heaped treasure together for the last days" (James 5:2-3 he continuing to write of how the rich oppressed the poor by withholding his wages to feed his own materialistic craving for luxurious living but it seems that the rich young man Jesus spoke to was not as so far gone as that still having respect for the commandments as kept from his youth and yet covetousness was like a malignant cancer which could corrupt him even from this simplicity of following the commandments when it later might become a more powerful influence upon one than one's sense of religious obligation. Of course the disciples' reaction to Jesus' words is to be aghast they declaring "who then can be saved?" Jesus offering a ray of hope in answering that such things that were impossible with man might be possible with God pending his being disposed to be merciful to men. Nevertheless Peter speaking for the others protested to Christ that they had indeed left all to follow him Jesus replying in verse 29 that no man who had left house, parents, brethren, wife or children behind would not receive manifold more in the present time and in the world to come eternal life meaning that Christian discipleship for all its suffering at least gave one further hope which no amount of natural possessions could provide but conversely a feeling of guilt that one had pleased oneself at the expense of one's fellow-man who had nothing and therefore "a certain fearful expectation of judgement" in Hebrews 10:27.

In verses 31 to 34 Jesus then took the Twelve aside and forecast his coming sacrificial death at Jerusalem as ordained by God according to what had been written concerning him in the Prophets, that he would be delivered unto the Gentiles, mocked, spitefully entreated and spitted upon (as came to pass in the account of his passion narrative so treated by both the Jews and Romans before being crucified) he finally foretelling that they would scourge him and put him to death but that upon the third day he would rise again the meaning of Jesus' words being hidden from the disciples in verse 34 in so much as it was required that they play their part in forsaking him in Gethsemane to allow Jesus' arrest that subsequently led directly to his death for had they done anything differently from their natural reactions in not abandoning him in his moment of crisis as foretold by Zechariah 13:7 they would not only have falsified the Scripture but possibly prevented Jesus from going to his death in the way that God had appointed, hence God himself must have blocked their minds to prevent them from truly understanding the import of Jesus' words concerning what awaited him in Jerusalem in order that God might then fulfill his purpose with him the disciples evidently still regarding Jesus as a political Messiah who would lead an armed rebellion against the Roman governors of the land as it is clearly obvious that this was in their minds by Peter's action of drawing his sword in Gethsemane as well as the words of the two disciples upon the road to Emmaus in Luke 24:21 that they "had hoped" that he would have been the one to have "redeemed Israel" and had been left disappointed in that expectation by Christ's death.

The final nine verses of Luke chapter 18 tell the simple story of the blind beggar who sat by the wayside of the road in and out of Jericho who hearing Jesus' company passing by and having ascertained that it was the famous Jesus of Nazareth who passed by of whose miracles he had obviously been told the blind man waxing strong in faith cried out in spite of being rebuked by those around him to be quiet asking Jesus as "the son of David" (i.e. in other words the Messiah the blind man expressing his faith in whom he believed Jesus was) to "have mercy upon him" Jesus recognizing his faith healing him after they had brought him near declaring that his faith had saved him (i.e. Jesus' miracles being essentially salvific in so much as they depended upon the individual's faith as much as their overall salvation did). The chapter then concludes in verse 43 with the blind man having received his sight subsequently following Jesus glorifying God and all the people with him who had beheld the miracle collectively gave praise to God.

Luke Chapter 19

Luke chapter 19 then is roughly subdividable into four distinct sections being Jesus' encounter with Zacchaeus (from "Zakay יֹ ,כֹ_ֹיֹ" meaning "Pure or Righteous One"), the tax-collector, the parable of the Pounds, the story of Jesus' "Triumphal Entry" into Jerusalem leading finally to his cleansing of the temple as an immediately consecutive event to his crowd acclaimed entry in this account. With regard to Zacchaeus the account informs us that he was chief of all the tax-collectors in Jericho and was therefore a rich man who resorts to climbing a sycamore tree to catch sight of Jesus as he passed by for we are informed that he was small in stature and could not even so much as catch a glimpse of Jesus because of the crowd and the press resorting to desperate measures therefore to behold him. But Jesus in verse 5 with his uncanny supernatural insight appeared to already know the man and looking upward as he passed under that tree where he was invited him to come down declaring that he must abide at his house that day. Zacchaeus having descended received him with joy but the crowd being as judgmental as their Pharisaic leadership murmured against Jesus in saying that he had gone to be the guest of a man who was known to them as a sinner. Nevertheless Zacchaeus stood and vowed that he would give half his goods to the poor and in confessing his sins promised to restore anything four times such as he might have taken from any man by false accusation Jesus declaring concerning Zacchaeus' perhaps appearing to be almost miraculous change of heart from his former conduct that that day salvation had come to that house for here too was a "son of Abraham" referring back to God's promise to Abraham to give him the earth post-resurrectionally as in Acts 7:5, Hebrews 11:39-40 which Abraham and his spiritual offspring were to receive by faith in their belief in the promise through Christ his one literal offspring (the Hebrew and Greek words for "offspring" or "seed" being both denotive of a singular or plural one as dictated by context) constituting them spiritual offspring in him in Galatians 3:6-9, 16, 26-29 and so Jesus in naming the man a true son of Abraham accordingly inducts him into this new spiritual family of God whose belief is cemented together by their mutual faith in the promise to Abraham and in Christ as the primary one through which it was to be fulfilled for this was life from the dead according to Christ's reasoning in Luke 20:37-38 for God was not the God "of the dead" as done away with and forgotten but the "God of the living" in that he intended to raise Abraham, and all those that shared his faith so that they would inherit the earth in accordance with God's promise to Abraham. Thus with regard to Zacchaeus' case in being inducted into this hope through his faith in the promise to Abraham and Christ's fulfillment of it Christ declared that he as the Son of man had come to seek and save that which was lost as a representative man who would shortly undergo "the suffering of death" in order to accomplish this feat it showing "the righteousness of God" that sin-prone human nature deserved death whilst at the

71

same time being resurrected from it because of his sinless life rendered in that medium in Hebrews 4:15 as according to God's justice in Christ's case he literally being acquitted in not having been guilty of the crime (i.e. sin) but for other men their salvation was to come through Christ's atonement wrought in this medium of a morally perfect man incarcerated in sin-prone flesh which nature he bore had to be put to death to fulfill God's righteousness but he himself escaping eternal death by God's intervention in the physical laws of sin and death in resurrecting him by which his sacrifice was universally declared "accepted" by God for all men that chose to identify themselves with it by laying their hands upon "the lamb slain from the foundation of the world" "spotless and without blemish" (i.e. sinless in the antitype) in Revelation 13:8, 1st Peter 1:19-20, Colossians 2:19 to identify themselves with Christ's atonement as a matter of public declaration before men.

Then returning to Luke chapter 19 we next have the very important parable of the Pounds spoken by Jesus apparently upon the highway as they approached Jerusalem (although Matthew's very similar parable of the Talents was spoken it appears upon the Mount of Olives slightly later) Jesus telling the parable because there were some who thought the kingdom of God would be established immediately whereas he was going to Jerusalem to die there, be raised and ascend into heaven God's dwelling place for a long period Jesus explaining this in the parable in terms of a nobleman going into a far country to receive himself a kingdom and then to return (i.e. the inauguration of the Son of man as king of the world before God's angels in heaven having been foreseen in Daniel's apocalyptic vision in 7:13-14) Jesus distributing before he left ten pounds to his servants that they might trade profitably so that he might receive the interest of their trading upon his return referring to the preaching obligation to convert others upon his followers (possibly in the first century context also to the Spirit gifts and miracles that testified to the truth of their message until he might have come in 70 AD had Israel accepted the early Christian preaching in Matthew 23:39, Luke 13:35, Romans 11:15 history sadly for them postponing this event because of their disbelief), one preacher turning his pound into ten more, another into five more receiving authority over ten and five cities respectively when Christ finally did return to take up his kingdom upon earth (i.e. the restored kingdom of Israel in Luke 1:32-33, Acts 1:6 etc) but another Christian preacher being negligent as regards the responsibility of using his knowledge that he had been given to convert others (described as his doing nothing with his pound but simply laying it up in a napkin) for which cause he is condemned by his Lord in so much that he knew Jesus expected harvest in his absence when he was no longer upon earth from his followers converting others to the true faith in his absence, the slothful servant even declaring it himself for which Jesus condemns him from his own lips the man declaring that he feared Christ because he was "an austere (i.e. "hard") man" in so much as he "took up what he had not laid down and reaped what he had not sown" the returned Christ then commanding that "his pound be given to the servant with ten pounds" in spite of the surprise of those who stood by that that one already had ten pounds and was he to be given more? Jesus then concludes the parable by declaring that to everyone who had would more be given and he that had not even what he had would be taken away from him (i.e. in the man's subsequent condemnation and lost hope of life in Christ's kingdom).

Then a parallel theme that runs throughout this parable that is not so prominent in the Matthean equivalent in Jesus' parable of the Talents is Israel as a people's rejection of him we reading in verse 14 that upon the nobleman's departure to go into a far country (i.e. heaven) to have himself appointed king that his citizens (i.e. the Jews) hated him and sent a message after him declaring that they did not wish him to rule over them (i.e. in real history they rejected and even killed his witnesses) so that we have at the climax of the parable in verse 27 that Christ's enemies who did not want him to reign over them were brought forth (i.e. post-resurrectionally) and publicly slain before him after the manner of the kings of old such as Nebuchadnezzar of Babylon who had all the nobility of the conquered Judah slain before him in Jeremiah 39:6; 52:10.

And so after having spoken this parable Jesus ascended up to Jerusalem and upon the occasion of their having arrived at Bethphage (i.e. the house of Unripe Figs) and Bethany (the house of Figs, also possibly "affliction," "humility" or "poverty" if from "ani י נ ע " to described the socially marginalized without sustenance or property) which were situated within the vicinity of the Mount of Olives Jesus sent two of his disciples before him into the village over against them where upon entering they would find a colt tied which no man had ever used and having loosed it they were to bring it to Jesus that he might sit upon it in his ascent up to the temple mount, if any man stopping them he told them to simply explain that "the Lord had need of it" as though Christ's use of the animal had already been arranged but it seems more likely that men had heard far and wide of Jesus' miracles and it had become local knowledge that he was approaching the great city Jerusalem or how else can we explain the crowds that cheered and lauded him as he went up to the temple mount upon the humble animal as appropriately chosen as the purpose of Jesus' coming to Jerusalem was to "humble himself unto death" (Philippians 2:8) upon the cross not to take the kingdom there and then upon a mighty war stallion with an army of Galilean and Judaean farmers and fishermen behind him and it had been in prophecy of this that Zechariah had foretold "Rejoice greatly, O daughter of Zion; shout, O daughter of Jerusalem: behold, thy King cometh unto thee: he is just, and having salvation; lowly, and riding upon an ass, and upon a colt the foal of an ass" in 9:9 in foretelling the humble character of Christ's mission of his first advent as envisaged by the lowly animal by which he entered the city for his ultimate mission there was the suffering of the submission unto death that was required of him there. Nevertheless as Jesus ascended the mountain the people laid their clothes in the way and coming nigh unto the city at the descent of the Mount of Olives in the midst of the Kidron valley "the whole multitude of the disciples began to rejoice and praise God with a loud voice for all the mighty works that they had seen; Saying, "Blessed be the King that cometh in the name of the Lord: peace in heaven, and glory in the highest"" in verses 37 and 38. This led to some of the Pharisees in that crowd that was accompanying Jesus up the slope to ask him, respectfully addressing him as "master," to rebuke his disciples Jesus replying that the very stones would cry out if they were indeed forced to hold their peace.

Nevertheless in spite of the popular support Jesus appeared to be receiving at that particular moment he knew things would soon turn sour in the people losing their enthusiasm in him seeing him arrested and delivered to the Romans by their leaders so that it would have subsequently appeared to them at that moment that he must have surely been a deceiver and a false Messiah far from leading a popular uprising being taken into custody and condemned to death. Thus when Jesus came near the city he wept over it in that its leaders knew not at that time "the things that made for peace" that Christ could give them they being intent upon destroying him so that "those things" were "hidden from their eyes" perhaps intentionally so as far as God's purpose was concerned that they inadvertently fulfill it by delivering up Christ to be crucified. Then in verses 43 and 44 Jesus moved with sorrow envisages the day of judgement that would come upon the city for rejecting him he describing how their enemies (i.e. the Romans) would cast a trench around the city and encompass them around hemming them in upon every side in the straightness of the siege (Deuteronomy 28:53) that was set to befall upon them in 70 AD and even worse in verse 44 they would level the city to the ground and leave their children slain lying upon the ground likewise (Deuteronomy 28:53, 57 says the besieged people themselves will eat them!) with not one stone being left upon another because they had not known the day of their visitation, the expression for Christ's coming hearkening back to Luke 1:78 where Zacharias foretold how "the dayspring from on high had visited them" in so much that Christ was not just a political Messiah such as the people were expecting but "God manifest in the flesh" in 1st Timothy 3:16 in so much as the deity dwelt in him by his Spirit strengthening him to offer his life "spotless and unblemished" as a perfect sacrifice upon the moral place for the accumulated sins of mankind but personal "forgiveness through his blood" (Romans 3:24-25, Ephesians 1:7) pended upon one's deliberate and willful association with this sacrifice through "the obedience of faith" in Romans 1:5; 16:26 involving "baptism into Christ's death" (Romans 6:3-6) as a public declaration of one's faith that one wished to die to sin with Christ to subsequently "walk" with him "in newness of life" by becoming united with him not only in his death but also in his resurrection in being "buried" under the water and subsequently "raised up" with Christ in the act of baptism by which one became "conformed to his death" (Philippians 3:10) and in such a deliberately chosen association having the hope of being conformed to him in his resurrection unlike the dead physically perfect animals that the offerers laid their hands upon in becoming joined to them in their deaths for these never came alive again to offer permanent forgiveness of sins dealing with the defilement of sin upon the physical level but not upon the moral plane to make a man live forever for this awaited the man strengthened by God to be as perfect morally as those animals had been physically, in other words "the visitation of the day spring from on high" for "God was in Christ reconciling the world unto himself" in 2nd Corinthians 5:19.

Then Jesus having expressed his grief at his people's rejection of him our chapter then concludes with Jesus' subsequent entry into the temple precincts (in so much as the temple could be Jesus' only destination in that his mission at that time was not political but related to the moral status of the nation) and in anger Jesus began to cast out those who bought and sold there quoting the words of Jeremiah 7:11 in verse 46 that God had said his house would be "a house of prayer for all nations" but they had made it into "a den of thieves." Nevertheless in spite of having so disturbed the commercial activity of the temple as a foretaste of what was to come for it in 70 AD because of the corruption of the nation's religious leaders and their seat of power in his temple (2nd Thessalonians 2:4 appears to even envisage Mammon enthroned therein as a new deity masquerading as the true one) Jesus is still permitted thereafter to teach daily in the temple in what little time he had left whilst the chief priests, scribes and chiefs of the people secretly plotted to destroy him as teaching and taking action that undermined their power-base in the temple for it appeared they thrived from its commercialism. Moreover in verse 48 Jesus was not immediately to be given into their hands for he was protected by the crowds of people that surrounded him and who were giving heed to his words so that his enemies could for the moment not find what they might do to get at him for Jesus was still very popular among the common people preceding his arrest and imprisonment they doubtless hoping that "he would be the one to redeem Israel" and saw no evidence as yet to dampen their enthusiasm with regard to this.

Luke Chapter 20

Luke chapter 20 largely concerns Jesus' conflicts with the chief priests and scribes within the environs of the temple concourses where he taught the people they endeavouring to trap him in his words and he successfully evading the traps that they set for him. The first of these was the question of authority they asking him by what authority he did the things he did possibly referring back to his so called "cleansing of the temple" in the previous chapter Jesus evading the trap of declaring that he had a higher authority than God's "official" representatives in the temple by asking them first about from where John's baptism proceeded whether it were indeed of God from heaven or of men they reasoning among themselves that if they answered "from heaven" then Jesus could show their folly for not believing in him but if they said "from men" then they feared the people in whose eyes John was highly esteemed as a prophet sent from God so perceiving that Jesus had put them in a corner as far as answering this question was concerned answered him that they did not know from where John's baptism originated Jesus retorting in return that neither would he tell them by whose authority he did the things he did if they could not answer his question first.

Following this in verses 9 to 18 Jesus told his parable of the Tenants in the Vineyard which was intended to portray the religious leaders of the nation as disrespecting and maltreating God's prophets who he sent to them until finally killing his beloved son whom he at last sends to them in desperation (whom he believes they might "reverence") that he might receive the fruits of his vineyard from them. The vineyard was a familiar figure for the nation of Israel as pressed into service by Isaiah in his song of the Beloved and his Vineyard in his fifth chapter which instead of producing the satisfactory vintage that God required brought forth "wild grapes" in the nation's failure for God looked for "justice" and there was only "a cry" of oppression in verse 7 there and similarly in Jeremiah 2:21-22 Israel (or Judah) as originally planted as a noble vine had clearly degenerated into a degenerate plant of a strange vine to God her incessant washing with nitre and soap failing to erase the mark of their iniquity having been a simple allegory of the nation's failure to justify itself before God through pursuing the works of the Law for although they took unto themselves much soap their iniquity could not be removed by much scrubbing and toil. In Luke chapter 20 then it is the land of Israel that is itself a "vineyard" let out to tenants or the Jews who did not literally possess it showing conclusively that the nation's occupation of the land was never a fulfillment of the promises to Abraham, Isaac and Jacob which required them to personally receive the land not for a generation but forever post-resurrectionally with their chosen "offspring" immortalized with them post-resurrectionally and Israel's possession of God's "vineyard" like "Eden" as "the garden of the Lord" in Ezekiel 28:13, 31:8-9; 36:35 using a similar figure was never intended to fulfill God's promises to the Jewish Patriarchs being merely a typification of it but not the very substance which involved the resurrection and immortalization of the persons involved.

Thus as with Jesus' parable of the Pounds a certain man who had planted a vineyard having let it out to tenants (or "husbandmen" in the KJV) went into a far country for a long time but here the owner of the vineyard cannot be Christ but God for Christ is subsequently introduced into the parable as the Lord of the Vineyard's Son whom the tenants murder in understanding that he was the heir of it and by murdering him they might seize the vineyard for themselves, but not before they had already treated God's servants whom he sent to collect the fruits of the vineyard in its seasons shamefully, sending them back empty handed, beating one and wounding another and casting him out of the vineyard as though indeed it were their permanent property and they themselves forgotten that they were but tenants "sojourners in the land" (Hebrews 11:9, 13) themselves with no lasting claim to it. Their whole attitude therefore was humanistic and egotistical doubting the power of the invisible landlord to take them to hand or even perhaps that he existed to so carry on as they did so mistreating his servants until finally things came to a head between them and the absent landlord by their murdering of his beloved son whom he had thought surely they would respect they treating him more abominably than all that had come before him casting him forth from the vineyard and killing him. Thus the rhetorical question is then asked concerning what the Lord of the Vineyard would then do unto them it naturally following that he would destroy them and give the vineyard out to others (i.e. the Gentiles) who would render to him the fruits of it in their seasons the people answering Christ "God forbid!"

Jesus then went on to be more explicit concerning the fate of those who rejected the Son and that the Son's death would not be "the end" but the beginning of something altogether new for in Psalms Psalms 118:22-24 it had been written that the stone the builders rejected would become the head of the corner being "the Lord's doing and marvellous in their eyes" the Psalm goes on to say for here recollection is made of king Ahaz of Judah's Assyrian altar which he installed in the temple of the Lord in 2nd Kings 16:10-16, Isaiah 8:13-15 in the place of the brazen altar of burnt offerings but the underlying altar foundation stone he could not move although he rejected it stuck hard in the earth it subsequently becoming associated with false religion as Christ's name likewise would do so but the point is that Christ as the rejected "altar-stone" in Zechariah 3:9 written by God alone (John 1:14) would become a new building stone in a new temple "the head of the corner" in fact by which it would be made complete whereas without him it was incomplete he being the cohesive force therefore by which the other stones in the new temple framed themselves into a temple now constituent of Christ and God spiritually abiding with the believers in John 14:2-3, 23 in God's having forsaken the house of bricks and mortar at Jerusalem due to the nation's apostasy to become immanent in a "spiritual temple" instead composed of men who "accepted" his Son and were conformed to him in his death to sin and death at least upon the spiritual plane in Philippians 3:10 to form a fit abode for the deity to thereafter inhabit, Christ himself being "the chief cornerstone" in Ephesians 2:20 and the others "living stones" in 1st Peter 2:4-8 whereas "a stone of stumbling and rock of offence" for the disobedient (i.e. the Jews in the parable) so that in Ephesians 2:21-22 "in whom (i.e. the chief cornerstone Christ by which the temple is made complete in John 1:3, Colossians 1:16) all the building fitly framed together groweth unto an holy temple in the Lord: In whom ye also are builded together for an habitation of God through the the Spirit." Then the certainty of Israel's coming judgement is expressed in verse 18 in the parable so that whosoever would fall upon that stone would be broken (i.e. in its association with false religion thereafter but more likely the fate of those who tried to entrap Jesus in his words here as he said in John 15:22 that "If I had not spoken to them they would have had no sin" and moreover his word is a touch-stone by which men would be judged in John 12:48 (the meaning of "basanizo βασανίζω" in Matthew 8:29, Revelation 20:10 meaning "to rub with a touch-stone" in that they would hurt themselves upon the Christ-stone in touching it as in Zechariah 12:3 "I will make Jerusalem a burdensome stone for all people: all that burden themselves with it shall be cut in pieces"). However the second part of verse 18 in Luke chapter 20 undoubtedly refers to the day of judgement as in Christ as "the unhewn altar stone" (Zechariah 3:9 (not hewn by man), Deuteronomy 27:5-6) not having "the imprint" of man upon him in God having been his Father in John 1:13 (see Greek "born not of bloods" signifying Mary and Joseph's together) must at his second coming smash the image of human dominion in Daniel chapter 2 as "the stone made (i.e. cut out) without hands" in verses 34 and 45 there (i.e. no human imprint of Joseph) to smithereens as the chaff of the summer threshing floor ultimately for Christ's coming would grind the disobedient who trusted in themselves for salvation (like a mighty statue standing erect of its own strength) to pieces (i.e. the inversion of Isaiah 3:15).

Then following this in verse 19 the chief priests and Scribes sought to lay hands upon Jesus in so much as that they perceived he had spoken his parable against them but they were unable to accomplish their objective fearing the people who at that moment were still believing in Jesus before his arrest must have necessarily put them off and finding no other way to accomplish their objective they sent forth spies feigning themselves to be honest men who sought to entrap Jesus in his words that he might be given over to the authority and power of the governor. Thus in verse 21 feigning respect for Jesus as one who taught rightly without partiality the way of God they asked him if it were lawful for them to pay taxes to Caesar or not but Jesus perceiving their craftiness asked them why they tempted (i.e. "tested") him for if he said it was not lawful then they could accuse him before the Romans but if he said it were then he would appear as a traitor to their national hope and certainly no

Messiah at all of any description. Thus Jesus replied in terms of returning that which was Caesar's to Caesar and that which was God's to God so that there was no "criss-crossing" of the use of one's for the other or vice versa for if the coin portrayed Caesar's image and inscription then it should be returned to him for it was only money and not of any such great value to God as to where one's heart was, for this was the true treasure by which men were valued in his eyes in Matthew 6:21, Luke 12:34. Thus they could not take hold of Jesus' words to accuse him in his separating God and Caesar into two entirely autonomous areas of requirement upon men which did not at all impact upon each other's fulfillment in being kept entirely separate from one another.

After this Jesus is approached by the Sadducees who denied the resurrection of the dead who propound to him the paradox of seven brothers who all consecutively took the same wife as they consecutively died in accordance with the commandment of Deuteronomy 25:5-10 that one should raise up seed or offspring for one's deceased brother they asking Christ whose wife she would be after the resurrection in so far as they all had her. Jesus therefore in verses 34 to 36 corrects their mistaken notion in explaining that being like the angels post-resurrectionally (who appearing as "men" are sexless beings as far as sexual progeniture is concerned for they are immortal) they neither marry nor give in marriage because they cannot die anymore being the reason why the production of offspring is no longer necessary. Then in verses 37 and 38 Jesus reminded the Sadducees that God is not called "the Lord God of Abraham, Isaac and Jacob" at the burning bush to Moses in Exodus 3:15 for nothing as though these men were dead and gone and done away with for God was the God "of the living" in that he intended to raise these men to personally fulfill his promises to them that they inherit the land forever lest he be found a liar by not doing so, both Stephen in Acts 7:5 and possibly Paul writing in Hebrews 11:13, 39-40 stressed that God's promises to them remained unfulfilled in that they had never personally possessed God's land as their possession forever but had rather been nomads in it during their natural lives thus necessitating their resurrection to life to not be "made perfect without us" who also believed in God's promise and had lived in later ages all being resurrected back to life upon the day of Christ's coming to receive the promises made to the Patriarchs with them in which all had believed that God had promised them the earth. Thus in this respect Jesus concluded "all (finally) live unto God" he not forgetting anyone who had manifested faith in his word and particularly in what he had promised concerning life after death here. Then in verses 39 and 40 one of the Scribes commended Christ for his wise answer and they (i.e. his adversaries) dared not ask him any further questions after that.

But Jesus himself asked them a question in verses 41 to 44 of Luke chapter 20 quoting from Psalms 110:1 asking how David could address his offspring or descendant as "Lord" when he was his son, the Psalm reading "the Lord said unto my Lord, Sit thou at my right hand, until I make thine enemies thy footstool." The point was that Christ as the promised son and legitimate heir to the Davidic throne was also "Son of God" begotten by God's Spirit which was poured out upon him throughout his ministry inspiring him to speak God's words in John 3:34 and "strengthening" him (Psalms 80:17) to reveal God's character within the medium of his sin-prone flesh from his mother Mary so that Christ was "God manifest in the flesh" (1st Timothy 3:16) in so much that God figuratively and spiritually (but not physically) dwelt in him through his Spirit and spoke through him David recognizing his descendant who must rule over his kingdom forever would "become" (John 1:14) "one" (John 10:30) with God in his life of obedience empowered by his begettal and strengthening by God's Spirit to thus be David's superior in so much as God would "dwell" in him like in the new Spirit-temple through Christ likewise which other men through him would become constituent of, Christ building God's temple in 2nd Samuel 7:1-17 when David had proposed to do so thus making Christ his descendant the greater one and superior to him. Luke chapter 20 then concludes with three verses which appear to have become isolated here from chapter 11, verses 38- 52 (as they appear together with this material in Matthew chapter 23) in which Jesus warns his disciples publicly before the people to "beware of the scribes who desired to walk in long robes, and love greetings in the markets, and the highest seats in the synagogues, and the chief rooms at feasts" and "Who devoured widows' houses, and for a show made long prayers" for such would receive the greater condemnation in that their religion was a false facade hiding their true nature that they were in fact greedy and covetous making the weak and vulnerable in society their prey as it had similarly been in Isaiah's time in 1:17, 23; 10:2 and also in Jeremiah 7:6; 22:3, Ezekiel 22:7 widows are among those socially exploited by their evidently corrupted leadership of their society.

Luke Chapter 21

Luke chapter 21 then for the most part deals with the Lukan equivalent of Matthew's Mount Olivet Prophecy although it is not specifically stated in Luke's account that Jesus ascended the mountain to give the prophecy and some parts of it had already been incorporated into the latter half of Luke chapter 17. But preceding Jesus' discourse in this chapter we have the short story of the Poor Widow's Mites in the first four verses placed there to no doubt highlight the corruption of the temple system perhaps since the succeeding discourse largely deals with its destruction although it is unclear whether the woman was compelled to give her two mites as her entire livelihood by the temple establishment or gave them willingly of her own initiative, it appearing to be more likely to have been the latter given the way in which Jesus commends her in verse 4 compared with the other far richer offerers at the treasury who cast in not even a fragment of their wealth but whatever the case God's judgement upon the temple institution and all it represented quickly follows in this chapter Jesus' disciples drawing his attention to the expensive stones and gifts that adorned its buildings but Jesus answered them concerning these things that the days were coming when there would not be left one stone upon another that would not be thrown down his disciples asking him when these things would be of which he had spoken and what would be the sign that they were about to come to pass. Jesus' long answer then appears to deal chiefly with events leading up to the 70 AD holocaust to which he was referring in verses 8 to 24 whilst verses 24 to 36 appear more suited to the time of Christ's second coming requiring a "gap" in the prophecy between these two epochs of something like nearly two thousand years unless we take "the times of the Gentiles" mentioned in verse 24 which had to run their course as reflecting the later belief of the church and place the whole prophecy as originally referring to events culminating in Christ's literal physical coming in 70 AD which would then agree with the statement in verse 32 that that generation which was contemporary with Christ would not completely pass away before his return who had seen "all those things come to pass" that he had spoken of in the preceding verses. However we may observe from the use of the "an" particle in the expression "heos an ἕως ἂν" in Luke 9:27's "There are some standing here which shall not taste of death till (i.e. "heos an ἕως ἂν," i.e. "until it may be that") they see the kingdom of God" that it introduces an element of uncertainty to this timing that all would be fulfilled within that generation's lifetime and suggests that the fulfillment may depend upon human response to Christ and particularly Israel's here to the first century preaching that had indeed they accepted Christ then their kingdom would have been established in 70 AD rather than their temple destroyed which is precisely what did happen in their rejecting the first century preaching as Jesus appears to anticipate that they might do in this prophecy while other parts of it may reflect events that might have conversely transpired if Israel had accepted Christ, their acceptance of him being synonymous with the establishment of their kingdom both in Matthew 23:39 where the "an ἂν" particle is used and in Romans 11:15 where their acceptance as a nation is synonymous with "life from the dead."

Thus the ambiguity in the chronology of this prophecy may be attributable to its referring to two alternative outcomes simultaneously as it were, one in which Israel accepts Christ and their kingdom is established in 70 AD and the other obviously more likely eventuality that they reject him and their kingdom is postponed (although perhaps not indefinitely) with the destruction of their temple which appears to be the dominant line of thought with Jesus starting his discourse by announcing its destruction. (interestingly in Luke 21:7 Matthew 24:3's "What shall be the sign of your coming and of the close of the age" is changed to not refer specifically to the personal coming of Christ the disciples asking simply for the sign that related to the things coming to pass that Jesus describes rather than to his personal coming which chimes in with their expectation of the temple being destroyed and that personal coming of Christ postponed because of the expected rejection of Israel of their message indeed quite possibly having become a historical fact at the time of writing perhaps even leading them to amend the prophecy in the light of their current events to relate more exclusively to the events of 70 AD than to any personal coming of Christ that had been envisaged at that time, but with the apocalyptic descriptions of it still retained towards the end of the discourse in Luke their hope could not have been entirely lost sight of, verse 25 and Romans 11:15 explaining that time has to pass for "the fullness of the Gentiles to come in" before a personal coming of Christ might be envisaged but with Luke possibly having been written slightly later than Matthew's gospel we find the personal return of Jesus de-emphasized compared with the conjectured earlier gospel and the direct reference to "your coming" dropped from the disciple's question altogether.

And so to offer a brief summary of the essential content of the prophecy Jesus began by warning his disciples of the danger of false prophets who would come in his name pretending to be him especially so that such prophets are to be distinguished from other false Messianic pretenders of which two are mentioned by Gamaliel at the convening of the Sanhedrin in Acts chapter 5, verses 34 to 37 as having misled the people but having had no association with Christ's name which was just beginning to make inroads in the church's formative preaching at that time. Besides the increase in false "Christian" prophets there were to be rumours of wars and commotions but the disciples were not to be afraid of such things for they would come to pass in those days but the end was not yet with nation rising against nation and kingdom against kingdom, such political upheavals also being accompanied by natural ones with great earthquakes in diverse places, famines, pestilences and fearful sights with great signs from heaven if heaven-sent the famine and pestilence doubtless making special reference to those conditions inside the city during the siege of Jerusalem when the people perished for lack of bread and sanitation for three and a half years according to the Rabbinic record of Lam.R 1:31 (i.e. as according to the time period given in Revelation 13:5, Daniel 7:25). In verses 12 to 19 the Christians themselves were to be arrested and persecuted for Christ's name being delivered up unto synagogues and thrown into prison but in being brought before kings and rulers (as the long suffering prisoner Paul eventually before Caesar) it would allow them to give their testimonies concerning Jesus before the powers that were Jesus telling them not to worry about what they would speak beforehand for he himself would give them a mouth and wisdom which their enemies would not be able to gainsay or resist but nevertheless their Christian conviction would result in their being rejected by their natural families who might even betray them leading directly to their own martyrdoms for Christ, in verse 17 Jesus concluding that they would be hated by all men for his name's sake. Nevertheless in 18 and 19 divine protection is assured them in so long as martyrdom was not required of them by God to test their faith to the upmost, Jesus declaring that not a hair of their heads would perish (as in Matthew 10:30 God knew all the hairs of their head by number) and that in their patience (i.e. in realizing that Christ's coming was a long way off- the later understanding of this prophecy) they would possess their souls (i.e. "lives," Greek "psuchai ψυχαί").

After this in verses 20 to 24 the prophecy moves unmistakably to the 70 AD context with the sight of Jerusalem encompassed by the Roman armies being a sure sign for them that its desolation was near so that those in Judaea were to flee to the mountains, those in the midst of Judaea to depart hastily from therein and others already outside of the land of Judaea were upon no occasion to enter it for they were "the days of vengeance" that all things written concerning God's people in the Law if they disobeyed him might come upon them it being woe to those pregnant and with newly-born at that time to escape from the upheaval in the land, for there would be great distress there and wrath upon God's people for all their disobedience culminating in their murder of his only beloved Son Jesus Christ. Thus in verse 24 the nation having been taken into captivity among all nations of the Roman world Jerusalem was to be trodden down by the Gentiles until that time of non-Jewish occupation of the temple mount terminated in "the sanctuary" being "restored" or "cleansed" in Daniel 8:14 referring to 2300 day-years from the time the Medo-

Persian ram met with the Grecian he-goat (i.e. Alexander the Great) at the battle of Issus (or Issos) in 333 BC and of Granicus in 334 BC through to 1967 when Israel got control of the temple mount in the Six Days War but this does not fulfill the precise requirements of the prophecy for that victory was purely political and the Dome of the Rock remains upon the temple mount until this day.

Following this the prophecy descends into the apocalyptic symbols of a political universe used extensively in the Old Testament but particularly of Israel whose "heavens" was the national government or ruling authority "earth" under it its common people whom they ruled in Isaiah 1:2, 10; 65:17-18, its "sun" an outstanding political luminary such as the king being taken into captivity in its eclipse in Jeremiah 4:23, 28, the "moon" ecclesiasticism or the religious institutions of the nation that drew their light from the sun or state, the "stars" the prominent statesmen within that heaven, their "falling from heaven" in the parallel Matthew 24:29 representing great political turmoil in the demise of the prevailing powers, the "sea and waves roaring" representing the nations in Isaiah 8:7-8; 17:12-13; 57:20, Revelation 17:15; 21:1 signifying the world-shattering trends and tides of politics at that time with "distress of the nations with perplexity" and "Men's hearts failing them for fear, and for looking after those things which are coming on the earth: for the powers of heaven would be shaken" in verses 25 and 26. It was at this time that they would behold Christ as the Son of man "coming in a cloud with power and great glory" (referring back to his heavenly inauguration as king in Daniel 7:13-14) whether this is understood as a symbolic cloud of "raised" Saints in the political aerial (1st Thessalonians 4:13-17) evapoured by Christ from the "waters" which are "peoples, and multitudes, and nations, and tongues" in Revelation 17:15 in his rising in that aerial as "the sun of righteousness with healing in his beams" in Malachi 4:2 (see Hebrew and compare Psalms 110:3 with Isaiah 26:19 (i.e. Hebrew "Thy birth is as the dew of lights") or whether the clouds simply refer to God's Shekinah glory that appeared in this form in Exodus 40:34-35, 1st Kings 8:10-11 and in the Transfiguration accounts of course. Verse 28 appears to make it unlikely that the clouds represent an army of resurrected Saints in motion with Christ as they so represent an army in Ezekiel 38:9, 15-16 and the Saints are supposed to exercise God's judgements upon the nations post-resurrectionally in Deuteronomy 33:2 (KJV), Psalms 149:5- 9 because they appear before the living believers' redemption is accomplished (unless the thought is that they are constituent of the resurrected immortalized saints only leaving a sizable gap between "the dead in Christ will rise first" and "we that are alive at his coming will be caught away together with them in the air" in 1st Thessalonians 4:16-17), the still living believers being exhorted by Christ in verse 28 to lift up their heads at this time upon account of their redemption drawing near.

Then in verses 29 to 32 Jesus uses the figure of the fig tree as an Old Testament symbol of the nation of Israel (i.e. in Jeremiah 8:13; 24:1-10) putting forth its leaves to show the imminence of his kingdom for by it they knew that summer was near as would indeed have been the case in 70 AD if the natural Jews had accepted the first century preaching of Christ but in their rejecting this message this figure can only relate to modern times with Israel's political revival as a nation but it still does not allow their spiritual revival in actually bearing "fruit" not just leaves in that the Jews have returned to the land of Israel in the twentieth century in unbelief of the Messiahship of Jesus, the addition of "all the trees" (i.e. bearing leaves) in verse 29 suggesting the general revival of the Middle Eastern nations in modern times driven by the oil extraction in the area making them prosperous. Whatever the case the prophecy of the generation who witnesses these events not passing away before Christ comes is only tenable in a modern day context if "these things" that were "to come to pass" in verse 31 refer specifically to the revival of the Middle East and especially of Israel but nevertheless verse 33's reference to "heaven and earth passing away" then immediately takes us back to 70 AD when the Jewish government and 'society pictured as "heavens and earth" in Isaiah 1:2, 10; 65:17-18 was forcibly removed by the Romans as indeed the symbols are used in this way in 2nd Peter 3:10-13 in which we read that "the day of the Lord will come as a thief in the night; in the which the heavens shall pass away with a great noise, and the elements (i.e. weak and beggarly elements of the Law in Galatians 4:9) shall melt with fervent heat, the earth also and the works (i.e. of the Law) that are therein shall be burned up. Seeing then that all these things shall be dissolved, what manner of persons ought ye to be in all holy conversation and godliness, Looking for and hasting unto the coming of the day of God, wherein the heavens being on fire shall be dissolved, and the elements shall melt with fervent heat? Nevertheless we, according to his promise, look for new heavens and a new earth, wherein dwelleth righteousness" (i.e. the restoration of Israel's commonwealth under Jesus Christ). Nevertheless in Luke 21:33 in spite of the Jewish political heavens and earth politic being removed in 70 AD we clearly being back in 70 AD times now (unless reference is made to the northern Gog's possession of the temple mount immediately before Christ's coming in Ezekiel 38:8-9; 39:2, Daniel 11:45 wiping out Israel once again (as possibly also referred to in Revelation 17:16 according to the Preterist school of interpretation) who will then turn to Christ for deliverance (i.e. now sent by God for "he who touched them touched the apple of his eye" in Zechariah 2:8)) in the interim before Christ came understanding the passing away of Israel from the political heaven and earth (or "land" if referring to the land of Israel from the same Greek and Hebrew words) his words would continue with them, there almost being a sense of pathos in this that they had lost sight of the assurance of Jesus' personal presence and coming by the time this was written.

After this the prophecy concludes with a general warning from Christ not to be overcome with surfeiting and drunkenness and the cares of this life so that that day of his coming come upon them unawares, it coming as a snare upon all the inhabitants upon the face of the whole earth who may largely have been too busy enjoying the sinful pleasures of life to want it; the disciples being admonished to watch so that that day would not catch them unawares and that they would be accounted worthy to escape and stand before the Son of man when all those things that he had foretold had come to pass. The chapter then concludes in verses 37 and 38 with the historical recollection that "in the day time he (i.e. Christ) was teaching in the temple; and at night he went out, and abode in the mount that is called the Mount of Olives. And all the people came early in the morning to him in the temple to hear him."

Luke Chapter 22

Luke chapter 22 is very much a long narrative chapter in which sayings of Jesus are interspaced with the account of those events leading up to his arrest in Gethsemane and accusation of blasphemy before the chief priests, elders and scribes. Since a lot of it is narrative it should not require too much writing to summarize the main events without analyzing the inner meanings of Jesus' words greatly although it does include his institution of the Eucharist as the official commemoration of the early church of Christ's sacrificial death as often as they partook of the bread and wine they "declaring the Lord's death until he came" in 1st Corinthians 11:26. Thus verse 1 informs us that the feast of Unleavened Bread called the Passover was drawing nigh when it behoved Jesus to die in his sacrifice being the antitype of that of the Passover Lamb in the Old Testament history that had delivered God's people from his angel of death (Psalms 78:49 (KJV)) that slew the Egyptian firstborn who had no such required offering to save them from it. And so with the feast approaching in verse 2 the chief priests and scribes are recorded as eager to find any way by which they might dispose of Jesus but they feared the people who gave credence to him still at that time before his finally being taken into their custody later in this chapter. And so in verse 3 one of Jesus' disciples, Judas, who was "covetous" in John 12:4-6 saw an opportune way to get money by betraying Jesus he being encouraged to do so by the angel of the Lord (called "Satan" in Numbers 22:22 or "an adversary" literally) entering into him to inflame his greed and covetous streak to resolve upon this fatal decision for the supernatural influence upon Judas and evidently from God as God's purpose required Jesus to die at Passover time precisely and now through Judas' actions he now engineered a way by which it might be done albeit Judas was an unknown tool in the hands of deity here God's angel being "adverse" to Judas or blocking the way for him to pursue any other course of action as it had done so long ago blocking Balaam's way to prevent him from going to curse Israel, no other course of action being permitted by divine intervention within the sequence of events for it had not been God's "will" either that Balaam curse Israel. Thus here in verses 4 to 6 Judas agreed with the chief priests and captains for a sum of money for betraying Jesus and awaited his chance to do so at such a moment when Jesus would not be surrounded by the multitudes that attended to his words within the temple precincts feigning loyalty to Jesus right up to the very end by betraying him with a kiss in the secluded garden of Gethsemane in the dark night time where the kiss ironically given identified him as the man they sought.

Then in verse 7 of the current chapter the day of Unleavened Bread arrived when the Passover should be killed and Jesus dispatched Peter and John ahead of him to prepare the Passover meal they being shown by a man already identified by Jesus as carrying a pitcher of water a large furnished upper room, he leading them to the house and its owner literally showing them the room in verse 12 where they might prepare the Passover meal. Verses 14 to 20 then record the details of Jesus' words over the bread and cup of wine during the meal that same night he identifying the bread with his body given for them and the wine with his spilt blood, these emblems of his sacrificial death as an effective atonement for their sins being learnt by rote and passed on to the apostle Paul in 1st Corinthians 11:23 who delivered unto them what he had also received from the Lord that they should take the bread and wine weekly ("upon the first day of the week" in Acts 20:7) as a memorial for what Christ had done for them but the Eucharist or "Giving Thanks" was also forward looking in anticipating that day when Christ would drink the fruit of the vine anew with them in his Father's kingdom in verse 18 in Luke. After Christ's institution of the Eucharistic emblems of his body and blood by which through partaking of them they would share in his sacrificial death weekly as the ancient Israelites were joined to their sacrificial offering by placing their hands upon its head whether lamb, calf or ram in its death and the spilling of its blood whereby their particular sins associated with that offering could be forgiven Christ having done this "once and for all" in Hebrews 10:10, 14 as a morally perfect man in contrast to the physically unblemished animals that typified him in this respect then after this in verses 21 to 23 Judas' defection to the side of Christ's enemies is foretold although he is not identified to the others by name here leaving them in doubt as to which one of them would do this thing but lest there was any doubt Jesus declared that God was behind this man's action "as it was determined" meaning "that the Scripture be fulfilled" in Matthew 26:24 "The Son of man goeth as it is written of him" and it being "woe" to Judas that he had been born to fulfill the necessary role of Jesus' betrayer as one of God's (pictured by Paul as the divine potter) "vessels fitted to destruction" in Romans 9:22 whose heart God hardened (as with Pharaoh in the Old Testament history that God might fulfill his purpose in multiplying his miracles in the land of Egypt) Judas therefore having been created for "menial use" and not as a "vessel prepared beforehand for glory" in Romans 9:23.

Then in Luke after this in verses 24 to 27 a quarrel among Jesus' disciples concerning who among them should be considered the greatest leads Christ to rebuke them telling them that they should not be like the Gentiles whose kings exercised lordship over them and those who exercised authority over them were called benefactors receiving the tribute and homage of their subjects but for Christ's disciples the younger would be the greatest and he that served (as he would serve them in cleansing them from their sins in his "humility unto death" in Philippians 2:8) as their chief, Jesus setting everything in the inversion to what their natural thinking supposed pointing out that he was as one who served them there whilst they sat at meat (although Luke does not record the footwashing episode at the Last Supper that John records in his thirteenth chapter). Then in verses 28 to 30 like the second part of the sequence in Philippians 2:5-11 Jesus foretells the coming exaltation of his disciples who had continued with him in his temptations or "suffering unto death" that in due course they would be appointed by Christ his kingdom as God had appointed it to him, the coming exaltation both here for the disciples and for Christ in Philippians 2:5-11 always being by appointment and never of one's own self-will to exalt oneself as though one could be in God's place who alone has the prerogative to do this ultimately. Thus Christ envisages in the future that his disciples would once again eat and drink at his table in his kingdom whilst they were similarly exalted (i.e. not of their own will but God's ultimately) to sit upon twelve thrones judging the twelve tribes of Israel.

After this in verses 31 to 34 comes Christ's foretelling of Peter's denial whom Satan or the adversary had desired to have him to sift him as wheat meaning either that there was a profound conflict between Peter's natural instincts for self-preservation and following Jesus to martyrdom ultimately so that it is the wayward tendency of his own human nature that is personified as his adversary just as sin-prone human nature and its innate power of death (Romans 6:23, 1st Corinthians 15:56) is personified as the Devil or "false accuser" of God in making men act contrary to his declared moral word in falsely accusing God of being a liar was crucified to death or destroyed in Christ's death within his own human nature in that it had no power to keep him dead in his not having yielded to it in Hebrews 4:15. Thus we suspect it is the adverse propensities of human nature with which Peter is fighting but if Satan or "the adversary" as the word should be translated refers to the personal influence of the angel of the Lord upon him here then it can only be in the sense of removing the impurities from Peter's thinking by causing him to disown Christ to show himself how fickle his own nature was despite all his attestations that he could remain faithful to Christ, for only by undergoing loss of faith could his faith be subsequently strengthened in recognizing the "evil" within him that had got the mastery over him at that moment when he had not perceived it previously. According to this second line of interpretation in Jesus' words about his faith failing (i.e. his threefold denial before the cock crew in verse 34) and his then being "converted" in his not losing his faith altogether thereafter but its being restored prior to the evidence of Christ's resurrection in his strengthening others in this moment of greatest hopelessness was a sequence of events ordained by God to put human nature in its true perspective as hopelessly weak but illustrating however that in the realization of this one could recover successfully from its effect. Otherwise Peter's "conversion" refers to the moment he "believed" in seeing the empty tomb in John 20:8 it being declared of the beloved disciple whom Jesus loved but assuming that Peter was similarly at that moment convinced by the incontestable evidence of the empty tomb and discarded grave clothes in which case his subsequent "strengthening" of the other Christians could be equated with Christ's command to him to feed his lambs and sheep in John 20:15-17 but certainly being suddenly "weak" in faith and then "strong" in faith to teach Peter the lesson of his own fallibility as a lesson of humility that he was not infallible as he had supposed would fulfill the "sifting" process that he is subjected to as wheat in the granary in verse 31 with remedial effect to leave him finally with a far greater faith (i.e. the purification process) than he had ever possessed when he had not been aware of how fallible he truly was and of how he "genuinely" needed Christ's help to overcome it the whole process in fact putting Peter in his place lest he had hitherto thought too highly of himself taking the kingdom by force of arms without any need for an atonement by which it was necessary to teach him that he was really "weak" before God before Christ's atonement could be of benefit to him in his having been brought to realize this and his inherent need for it.

Then as concerns the rest of this chapter verses 35 to 53 narrate the sequence of events in Gethsemane in 35 Christ now telling is disciples to take those things necessary for self-survival that he had told them not to take upon their preaching endeavour in Luke 9:3 when it had been required that they depended upon God to provide for them but now Jesus wanted them to have the opposite mind with purse, scrip (i.e. shepherd's leather bag) and even sword making them think of self-preservation and survival to make them react precisely in the way required in Gethsemane in seeing the superior force of Judas' arrest party (in verse 52 the chief priests, elders and captains of the temple being armed with swords and staves) so that they would flee abandoning Jesus to his fate according to God's purpose although Peter alone drew his sword severing the high priest's servant's right ear in verse 50 which Jesus touches and heals in 51 declaring "suffer ye thus far" in so much that these things had been ordained to happen and could not be averted by Peter's show of putting up a fight for it Jesus having been strengthened in verse 43 by an angel from heaven for what lay ahead whilst the disciples had dozed off and slept as Jesus prayed there again showing the weakness of their own human natures that they were not able to stay awake with Christ to keep watch with him for one hour as a lesson to them as it were. Then Jesus as the submissive "lamb led to the slaughter" in Isaiah 53:7 in not resisting his arresters as according to God's purpose decreed for him remonstrated with them in verses 52 and 53 concerning their present show of force when he had taught daily in their temple and none had laid hands upon him but this he conceded was their hour, and the power of darkness it literally requiring them to operate in the darkness to affect the arrest of an "innocent" man which they could not arguably do in the broad daylight in front of the people who still up unto that point respected Jesus before being alienated from him by his subsequent arrest and condemnation. But the meaning of "their hour and the power of darkness" strikes deeper than this for it was the moment universal human ignorance sought to "overcome" the light that Jesus was shining for them in the darkness but as John 1:5 (Revised Version) puts it "the darkness could not overcome it."

The last part of the chapter then follows as a matter of course Jesus being escorted under armed guard to the high priest's house with Peter following afar off in verse 55 we finding him in the hall with the high priest's servants having kindled a fire there around which Peter endeavoured to warm himself a maid immediately declaring she recognized him as having been with Jesus leading Peter to deny it, then a little while later a man-servant likewise with Peter similarly being compelled to deny his association with Jesus and finally in verse 59 after an hour had passed another confidently affirmed it of him that he had undoubtedly been with him for he was a Galilean leading Peter to deny it most vehemently the last time after which immediately the cock crew in verse 60. It is at this juncture in 61 that the Lord turned and looked at Peter having been in plain sight of him whichever part of the house he was being held in and Peter remembered his words that before the cock crew he would deny him three times and subsequently went out and wept bitterly in the realization of how the weakness of his own human nature had caused him to fail which he now recognized most clearly as his internal "adversary" or "enemy" as it were as far as doing the right thing was concerned. Jesus meanwhile was mocked, and smitten and blindfolded and asked to prophesy which one of the high priest's men had struck him and so spoke many blasphemous things against him as the night progressed towards the daybreak and at the break of day the elders, chief priests and scribes convened their counsel asking Jesus if he were the Christ and he replying indirectly in speaking the truth of them that if he told them they would not believe him nor answer his own question or let him go but still he said they would see "the

Son of man sitting upon the right hand of power" (i.e. God, the original Hebrew word for God "El אֵל " meaning "power") and then in verse 70 to their question as to whether or not he were the Son of God he answered in the affirmative after which in 71 they declared themselves to have no further need of witnesses in so much that they had heard his presumed "blasphemy" from his own mouth declaring Jesus to be self-condemned by his own words.

Luke Chapter 23

Luke Chapter 23 then narrates Jesus' audiences before Pilate and Herod, Pilate's conviction of Jesus' innocence and his resolving to release him, the Jewish people led on by their chief priests rejecting Jesus in favour of the criminal Barabbas to be released and the account of Jesus' crucifixion, death and burial predominantly towards the end of the chapter. Jesus being led to Pilate in verse 1 the whole multitude of the Jews who accused him fabricated a false charge before him that Jesus forbade the forgiving of tribute or tax to Caesar seeking to nail him to the cross upon a political charge before the Roman governor the reader knowing from Luke chapter 20, verses 21 to 26 that Jesus had taught no such thing that taxes should not be paid to Caesar he having declared that they should render to Caesar the things that were Caesar's and to God the things that were God's when asked concerning the question and it seems that within the narrative of Luke chapter 23 Pilate is unconvinced of Jesus' guilt he declaring that he "found no fault in him" in verse 4 when Jesus' accusers accused him of perverting their nation and forbidding the paying of tax to Caesar in declaring that he himself was Christ the king in Caesar's stead there. Jesus himself in verse 3 ascribes such words to Pilate's own mouth implying that he had taught no such thing that the Jews were insinuating for in John 18:36 Jesus had answered Pilate that his kingdom had not been of that world or of that particular system of things that prevailed in first century Palestine it requiring Christ's crucifixion of "sin in the flesh" (Romans 8:3) within his own body to destroy its inherent power in all men that inevitably brought sin and death to them before the pure kingdom in which God would ultimately be king could be established upon earth not by force of arms but through divine intervention.

Moreover in verse 5 the Jewish accusation against Jesus further incriminated him in accusing him of stirring up the people throughout Judaea and Galilee, Pilate having ascertained that Jesus was a Galilean and belonged to Herod's jurisdiction summoned Herod who happened to be at Jerusalem at that time who was most glad to become acquainted with Jesus at last for he had heard much concerning him and was desirous to see a miracle performed by him that he might ascertain the truth of the stories concerning Jesus that he had heard. However he was sorely disappointed upon this point for not only did Jesus do no miracle but answered Herod not a word when the latter sought to examine him, thus fulfilling the words of Isaiah 53:7 that he was "as a sheep before his shearers is dumb." Nevertheless the chief priests and scribes standing by began to more vehemently accuse Jesus during the proceedings Herod and his men setting Jesus at nought and clothing him in a "gorgeous robe" before sending him back to Pilate (the parallel in John 19:1-5 has Pilate's soldiers dressing Jesus in a scarlet robe (as the colour of blood symbolically) with "a crown of thorns" platted upon his head (as in Genesis 3:17-19 the land would bring forth thorns and thistles unto the man in his being condemned to work it a fitting symbol of man's mortal lot which "labour and toil" Jesus would ultimately redeem them from (hence the crown representing conquest over) so that for now he is associated with mortality in it requiring he die the death of all men in going to the earth (albeit very briefly) as a representative man as it were). Verse 12 in Luke chapter 23 then recollects that Pilate and Herod made friends that day whereas prior to that day they had been at enmity as Paul later observes in Acts 4:25-28 that their leaders and the Gentiles had been united in putting Jesus to death although Pilate as the Gentile representative repeatedly stresses Christ's innocence having found "no fault in him" in verse 14 and Herod's investigation too having found no evidence against Christ of such things that he was accused of.

Thus with the amnesty now coming up coinciding with the feast time Pilate offered Christ's release after having chastised him but the people spurred on by their rulers were adamant in demanding that Barabbas be released who had been thrown into prison for sedition in Jerusalem and for murder demanding that Christ conversely be crucified (this "Barabbas" figure whose name means "the Son of the Father" in Aramaic being set forth as the opposite to Christ in every way being not "the Son of God" the Father but the son of his Father the False Accuser (i.e. the genetic false-accusing principle leading all men to sin and die by hereditary by nature as it were which Christ destroyed in his own sin-prone body upon the cross by rendering a sinless life within its medium in Hebrews 4:15) who in John 8:44 personified was "a murderer from the beginning" in bringing sin and death upon the human race from Adam and Eve onwards the false accusing principle originally getting installed into the first human pair by the carnal reasoning of the serpent not having been made in God's image to be capable of reflecting his moral character whose "carnal animal-like reasoning" came to the conclusion that God had lied about the man dying if he did not obey God for it saw no empirical evidence to the contrary and having installed the "earthy mind" (John 3:31; 8:23, James 3:15) into Adam and Eve in their acting upon the serpent's lie they too falsely accused God by their action (i.e. the first sin) that he was a liar and his moral word bad for them after which the tendency became part and parcel of human nature thereafter mankind bringing death upon himself by being infected by it and Barabbas set forth as a prime example of the tendency at work in that like the original Edenic serpent long since dead his actions resulted in murder or death in the serpent's case God having permitted it the vocal apparatus to express its carnal reasoning (Romans 7:14-15; 8:6-7) in order to bring about the present probation of man learning to serve God willingly rather than as an automaton). Then returning to Luke Pilate having contested Jesus' innocence three times finally concedes to the voices of that crowd and their chief priests prevailing over his impressing upon him that keeping Jesus alive would be tantamount to starting a stampede and riot in the city but as Jesus was led away to be crucified in verse 26 it may have been that the Roman governor may have enacted one last act of mercy upon Jesus in commanding his men to lay hold of one Simon of Cyrene coming in from the country to carry Jesus' cross after him Simon of Cyrene therefore standing in the text as the role model disciple taking up his cross and following Christ in Luke 9:23 but also anticipating the many Christian martyrs who would go to their deaths under Roman instrumentality in later years.

Then in verse 27 a great company of people and of women bewailing and lamenting Christ followed him Jesus turning to them behind him and declaring in anticipation of the coming 70 AD holocaust that they should weep not for him but for themselves and their children he declaring to them that days were coming when they would call the barren and unbearing wombs blessed and likewise the breasts that never gave their milk, it being a day in which they would call upon the mountains to fall upon them and the hills to cover them in there being nowhere to flee from the Roman incursion of their land under the Emperor Vespasian and his son Titus who succeeded him to the purple's ruthless "scorched-earth" policy where the legions destroyed every living thing which they encountered finally with the use of fire. Then Jesus' words in verse 31 "For if they do these things in a green tree, what shall be done in the dry" imply the Jewish tree (now not specifically "a fig tree" which in Matthew's and Mark's gospels Jesus withers in finding no fruit upon it as presently then green as having some measure of autonomy under the Roman rule at least to be leafy if not spiritually fruitful but soon it would be shrivelled, withered or dried up in the coming Roman holocaust sucking it clean of all moisture and life and that, said Jesus, was the time when they need truly weep for it was the death of their nation. Verses 32 and 33 then describe Jesus' arrival at Calvary with the other two presumed malefactors with whom he was crucified one on the left and one on the right Jesus forgiving to the end in verse 34 asking his Father to forgive them for they knew not what they did whilst the Roman soldiers at the foot of the cross cast lots to divide his garments between them thus fulfilling the words of Psalms 22:18 though not quoted by Luke in his record. After this the rulers who stood by there derided Christ inviting him to save himself if he were truly the Christ, God's chosen one, for hadn't he supposed to have saved others? The soldiers likewise in verses 36 and 37 presumably of Pilate's detachment mocked him offering him vinegar and inviting him to save himself if he were the king of the Jews they similarly having mocked Jesus in John 19:1-3 in clothing him with the scarlet robe and crown of thorns being more conscious of the political charge against Jesus than the religious one. Indeed the superscription was written above Christ's cross in verse 38 in Luke in Greek, Latin and Hebrew for all men to read that this was the king of the Jews that they were crucifying lest anyone doubt as to the precise manner of the charge and suppose that the Romans had any interest in the "Law" and religious disputes of the Jews (Acts 18:14-16) such as their accusation far more important to them that Jesus claimed to be "the Son of God."

After this in verses 39 to 43 of Luke chapter 23 we have the famous story of the repentant thief one of the two deriding Christ as the other bystanders but the other rebuking him for having no fear of God since they were all under the same condemnation (i.e. death because of inheriting "sin in the flesh" (Romans 8:3) they condemned to death from birth by their inevitable following of their natural propensities) but in their cases the two thieves were "guilty" of the crime whereas Christ was "innocent" (dying unjustly in that he had committed no sin throughout his life although his nature which he had inherited from his human mother was sentenced to death by God's decree and could not therefore continue indefinitely like any man's without God's subsequent intervention in bringing him back to life because of his "innocence" in that nature condemned to death). The repentant thief then calls upon Jesus to remember him when he "comes into his kingdom" being a future event when Jesus' second "coming" back to the earth would result in that repentant man being remembered in the physical resurrection of the dead upon that day and being given a name and a place in that kingdom at that time, hence Jesus replied that he was promising him that very day that he would be with him in paradise at that time, Ezekiel 31:8-9 describing the earth and particularly the environs of the land of Israel being like the garden of Eden or paradise using the same Persian word in the Septuagint "paradeisos παράδεισος" for "a walled garden or park" applied likewise to the renewal of the earth's fertility and beauty during the kingdom age therefore.

Then after the story of the repentant thief the Egyptian Passover symbolism is recalled in a supernatural darkness supervening across the earth from the sixth to the ninth hour after which Jesus expired declaring that he would give his life into God's safekeeping finally who alone had the power to restore it. In verse 47 the Roman centurion seeing how Christ had died declares he was surely "a righteous man" as representing the believing Gentiles subsequently in the record here for he too understood that Jesus was non-deservant of death being the fundamental truth in the Christian gospel upon which all salvation for every man depended. Similarly all the onlookers gathered together and having smote their breasts returned to the city although Luke does not describe the supernatural phenomena accompanying Christ's death that Matthew does in his account that might have accounted for the people's reverence at this time for they saw "how" or "the way" Jesus died in verses 47 and 48 particularly although Luke tones it down to speak of their seeing "what had been done." Moreover in verse 49 all Jesus' acquaintances and the women who had followed him from Galilee stood afar off beholding what was done and in verse 50 a good and just man, an honourable counsellor, named Joseph of Arimathaea, a city of the Jews, who was also waiting for the kingdom of God begged the body of Jesus from Pilate that he might wrap it in a linen shroud and lay it in his new tomb in which no man had yet been laid (in that Jesus until the end was associated with the living not the dead) hewn of stone and that day being the day of Preparation (i.e. of the Sabbath not the Passover specifically here) and the Sabbath drawing on Joseph hastily sealed the tomb the women who had accompanied Jesus from Galilee beholding the place where he was laid and returning to the city prepared spices and ointments and rested upon the Sabbath Day in accordance with Moses' Law intending to return to Jesus' tomb early upon the first day of the week that they might anoint his body properly for burial as according to the custom.

Luke Chapter 24

Luke chapter 24 then contains the account of the appearance of God's angels to the women at the empty tomb early upon the first day of the week as they came to anoint Jesus' body, Peter's consequent inspection of the empty tomb, the appearance of Christ to the two disciples upon the road to Emmaus one of whom is named

"Cleopas" meaning "Vision of all (i.e. glory)" from "κλεω kleo," to tell of or make famous combined with the adjective "πας pas," meaning "all"), the Lord Jesus being made known to them at the inn in the breaking of bread with him and finally Jesus' subsequent appearance to the eleven gathered together, his eating before them and expounding of the Scriptures until at last leading them out of the city as far as Bethany from which locality he was carried up to heaven in their sight they returning to Jerusalem to continually praise and bless God in his temple. Such then is the general outline of the chapter and as regards its minute details we are told that the women who had followed Christ from Galilee came to the tomb very early upon the Sunday morning immediately after the Sabbath had passed as soon as light allowed them to inspect Jesus' body that they might anoint it according to the burial custom of the Jews they bringing the spices which they had prepared and certain others with them ("others" is not clear in the Greek but would appear to refer to other people accompanying them in Matthew 27:56 compared with 28:1 only two women are clearly identified Mary Magdalene and Mary the mother of James and Joses, in Mark presumably the same Mary Magdalene and Mary the mother of James and Salome the name Joses disappearing to be replaced by the daughter Salome's, in John's gospel Mary appears coming to the tomb and then returning to it after Peter and John's inspection of it (assuming John to have been the beloved disciple) entirely alone with no mention of the other Mary accompanying her although the absence of references to other women in John does not necessarily imply that they may not have been with her of course but that John did not deem them important enough to mention them in his narrative focusing exclusively upon Mary's own encounter with the Lord (compared with Matthew's account where the two Marys fall at Christ's feet to worship him when he does appear to them in 28:9 but again Matthew may have passed over the earlier appearing to be singular revelation of Christ to Mary appearing to be entirely alone in John's account to have possibly appeared a second time just as Matthew and Mark's record of only one angel in or within the vicinity of the empty tomb announcing Christ's resurrection to the women compared with Luke's two does not necessarily prove inaccuracy in the record for the second angel might have come or gone during the process of the interview just as the first may have been alternatively in and outside of the tomb so that none of these superficial differences upon the surface of the accounts really prove anything regarding their respective accuracies but rather different moments and aspects of the women's encounters with the angels and risen Christ are stressed and de-emphasized or even omitted as according to the writer's purpose in recording them quite possibly to create his own dramatic effect in retelling the story in the way that he thought best.

Thus as regards Luke's narrative the women in whatever number they may have come upon approaching the tomb found the boulder rolled away from its entrance it being suggested by comparison with Matthew that Mary Magdalene and Mary the mother of James and Joses may have actually seen this happen for the angel appears to address the women from outside the tomb in Matthew 28:5 but again upon entering the tomb in Mark and Luke's accounts Jesus is not there and given the physicality of Christ's resurrection body as stressed in Luke 24:39-40 it seems incongruous that Christ could have left the tomb without the women seeing him whilst they conversed with the angel sitting upon the boulder outside the tomb in

Matthew's account in Matthew 28:6 they being invited by the angel to see the place where Christ had lain so that we may conclude that although the two Marys saw the angel outside the tomb they could not have witnessed its descent and unsealing of the tomb although witnesses to the earthquake caused by the event for otherwise they would have seen the risen Christ emerging from the tomb at the same time as they set eyes upon his angel. But in Luke's account they see two angels in the interior of the tomb upon entering the sepulchre and that accompanied by possibly "other women" from which detail we might deduce that either there were three angels one positioned outside and two within or that the first angel had departed and the other women joined the two Marys to behold a further two angels actually inside the tomb (Mark 16:5 has only one seated upon the right side inside but this difference may be explained away from the women's vantage point if one were out of sight around the curve of the wall for example for the interior of the tomb would not have been spacious neither of necessarily straight dimensions, John 20:12 stating that Mary saw two angels positioned at the space of the head and feet of where Jesus had lain which would have therefore been separated by the length of Jesus' body and if the entrance to the tomb entered into it at any other angle than straight on into its interior and the women stood in the entrance afraid to enter in further then of course one of these angelic beings may have been at least partly hidden from view to some of them which might then account for the appearing to be contradictory eye-witness accounts concerning the number of angels present in the tomb, one or two). However in Luke's account they are described as two men standing by them in shining garments which might suggest that they were relatively close enough to the angels to have been able to both see them both plainly but again if they were accompanied by other women some of them may have turned back in fear before having penetrated deeply enough into the tomb to have been able to see both of the angels such as Luke's account allows the possibility of and then the "one angel" only tradition in the tomb may have arisen from their subsequent testimony when in fact there were two and numerous other ingenious theories may doubtless be proposed to explain away these ambiguities within the respective gospel accounts of the discovery of the empty tomb.

Then as concerns the angels' message in verses 5 to 7 the angels ask the women why they sought the living among the dead declaring to them that Jesus whom they sought was not there because he had risen as he had indeed foretold them whilst they still abode in Galilee with him that "the Son of man would be delivered into the hands of sinful men, be crucified and upon the third day rise again" the women now remembering Christ's words with sudden new understanding to their import in verse 8 returning from the sepulchre and telling the eleven disciples what had happened it being recounted that it was Mary Magdalene and Mary the mother of James and now from the unnamed women alluded to earlier in verse 10 of Luke chapter 24 Joanna is identified as having been among them being mentioned as the wife of Chuza Herod's steward in Luke 8:3 introduced into the narrative after Mary Magdalene there along with Susanna and many other women, that ministered to Jesus and his disciples presumably, from their substance in Luke 8:2-4 they presumably all being again the same women that accompanied Mary to the tomb at the head of their party. In verse 11 the women's testimony is rather disregarded by the disciples as idle words it perhaps being ingrained in the contemporary thinking and certainly in the teaching of Paul that a woman's testimony was inferior to a man's Paul not permitting women to speak in church (1st Corinthians 14:34) nor to teach men (1st Timothy 2:12) in so much as "Eve was caught in the transgression not Adam" in 1st Timothy 2:14 the first woman teaching the first man to sin so that in the business of salvation the man was ordained to teach the woman and not vice versa as the inversion of what happened in the Fall in which the woman played the conspicuous part in bringing about the man's downfall. Whether the disrespect for the women's testimony was due to the religious view of her role being subject to man not exercising any superiority over him in salvific matters or whether it was simply the secular thinking of the time that the woman's word did not carry the same weight or authority as man's who was the stronger, braver and dominant one in Greek and Roman culture whereas the woman may have been considered to be subject to untoward emotional excess and weakness compared with the hardened male stereotype of the time is not a question we can be sure of but in spite of the general reluctance of the disciples to believe the women's testimony we do find Peter attentive enough to them to personally investigate the tomb himself in verse 12 he bending down and beholding the linen clothes laid by themselves and departed wondering what had come to pass.

After this attention shifts in Luke's narrative to the two disciples upon the road to Emmaus about sixty furlongs (i.e. each furlong equalling 660 feet or 1/8 of a mile) from Jerusalem in verse 13 Jesus drawing near and joining onto their company as they walked discussing what had transpired among them one of them having been Cleopas possibly identified as the husband of Mary who witnessed Christ's crucifixion in John 20:25 identified as Jesus' mother's sister. Jesus then having joined the two travellers it is noted in verse 16 in Luke that their eyes were held to prevent them from recognizing him supernaturally as it were as the disciples had previously been supernaturally prevented from understanding the import of Christ's words concerning the necessity of his death at Jerusalem they believing him such a Messiah who would finally lead them in armed rebellion against their Roman Overlords and it seems that the two men still believed that Christ would "have been the one to redeem Israel" in verse 21 now hypothetically only in the past as it was now the third day since his crucifixion they told their interlocutor not knowing that he was Jesus although confessing that he had been a prophet, mighty in word and deed before the people. In verses 22 to 25 they recount to Jesus how the women had told them of their vision of angels claiming Christ had risen but upon their own inspection of the tomb (at least of "some of them who were with them" in verse 24 if Cleophas as Jesus' mother's sister's husband is not to be identified with Peter whom we are told in verse 12 went there) no such appearance of Jesus followed although the tomb appeared empty as according to the women's report now verified by their superior and more trustworthy "male" eyes as it were according to the mentality of the time but Jesus having heard their lack of faith in verses 25 to 27 upbraids them for it as "fools" and "slow of heart" to believe all that the prophets had written that Christ should suffer these things and enter into his glory and beginning at Moses and then all the prophets Jesus expounded to them the things concerning himself as they walked. And as they drew near to the village and inn where it required they spend the night he (Jesus) looked as though he would go further but they invited him to sup with them it being evening and the day far spent and as they sat at meat Jesus took the bread, blessed it, broke it and gave it to them after had been his manner at the Last Supper which distinctive characteristic action of Jesus broke their "hypnosis" so that they recognized him and as they did so he disappeared from their sight there being some precedent here for at least one of the two disciples having been present at the Last Supper but more likely both of them although Jesus had of course performed the same procedure in his multiplication miracles but still it seems that the husband of Jesus' mother's sister was not present at the supper as not one of the elect twelve disciples unless he be identified as Simon Peter due to verse 34's "The Lord has risen indeed and appeared to Simon" being their first words to the eleven disciples upon returning to Jerusalem but this seems impossible for if Simon Peter were one of the two then there could not have been "eleven" disciples left to return to at Jerusalem.

Nevertheless the two having self-criticized themselves for their hearts burning within them as they were upon the way and Jesus had opened up to them the Scriptures with doubt and uncertainty when they should have believed then Jesus himself appears to the assembled disciples in that place where they were in Jerusalem lest any of them still doubt he eating broiled fish and honeycomb before them in proof that he was no Spirit or trick but truly physically raised from the dead inviting them to behold his hands and feet where the nails had been Jesus again opening the Scriptures to his overjoyed disciples from the Law of Moses, Prophets and Psalms concerning how it had so been foretold of him that all such things that had happened had been forepurposed by God concerning him, that it behoved him to suffer, be risen from the dead and that repentance and remission of sins be subsequently taught unto all nations in his name commencing from Jerusalem they themselves having been witnesses of these things. Having spoken thus Jesus instructed them to remain in the city Jerusalem until they would be clothed upon with power from on high for their ministry as it so came to pass upon the day of Pentecost in Acts chapter 2 and Jesus having led them out as far as Bethany lifted up his hands, blessed them and was parted from them carried up into heaven (Acts 1:9 stating that "he was taken up and a cloud received him out of their sight") and the disciples having worshipped him and returned to Jerusalem with great joy were continually in the temple praising and blessing God thereafter upon which joyful note Luke closes his account with a solemn "Amen" meaning "in truth" or "Let it truly be" from the original Hebrew.

Gospel of Luke, King James Version

Luke

Luke.1

[1] Forasmuch as many have taken in hand to set forth in order a declaration of those things which are most surely believed among us,

[2] Even as they delivered them unto us, which from the beginning were eyewitnesses, and ministers of the word;

[3] It seemed good to me also, having had perfect understanding of all things from the very first, to write unto thee in order, most excellent Theophilus,

[4] That thou mightest know the certainty of those things, wherein thou hast been instructed.

[5] There was in the days of Herod, the king of Judaea, a certain priest named Zacharias, of the course of Abia: and his wife was of the daughters of Aaron, and her name was Elisabeth.

[6] And they were both righteous before God, walking in all the commandments and ordinances of the Lord blameless.

[7] And they had no child, because that Elisabeth was barren, and they both were now well stricken in years.

[8] And it came to pass, that while he executed the priest's office before God in the order of his course,

[9] According to the custom of the priest's office, his lot was to burn incense when he went into the temple of the Lord.

[10] And the whole multitude of the people were praying without at the time of incense.

[11] And there appeared unto him an angel of the Lord standing on the right side of the altar of incense.

[12] And when Zacharias saw him, he was troubled, and fear fell upon him.

[13] But the angel said unto him, Fear not, Zacharias: for thy prayer is heard; and thy wife Elisabeth shall bear thee a son, and thou shalt call his name John.

[14] And thou shalt have joy and gladness; and many shall rejoice at his birth.

[15] For he shall be great in the sight of the Lord, and shall drink neither wine nor strong drink; and he shall be filled with the Holy Ghost, even from his mother's womb.

[16] And many of the children of Israel shall he turn to the Lord their God.

[17] And he shall go before him in the spirit and power of Elias, to turn the hearts of the fathers to the children, and the disobedient to the wisdom of the just; to make ready a people prepared for the Lord.

[18] And Zacharias said unto the angel, Whereby shall I know this? for I am an old man, and my wife well stricken in years.

[19] And the angel answering said unto him, I am Gabriel, that stand in the presence of God; and am sent to speak unto thee, and to shew thee these glad tidings.

[20] And, behold, thou shalt be dumb, and not able to speak, until the day that these things shall be performed, because thou believest not my words, which shall be fulfilled in their season.

[21] And the people waited for Zacharias, and marvelled that he tarried so long in the temple.

[22] And when he came out, he could not speak unto them: and they perceived that he had seen a vision in the temple: for he beckoned unto them, and remained speechless.

[23] And it came to pass, that, as soon as the days of his ministration were

accomplished, he departed to his own house.

[24] And after those days his wife Elisabeth conceived, and hid herself five months, saying,

[25] Thus hath the Lord dealt with me in the days wherein he looked on me, to take away my reproach among men.

[26] And in the sixth month the angel Gabriel was sent from God unto a city of Galilee, named Nazareth,

[27] To a virgin espoused to a man whose name was Joseph, of the house of David; and the virgin's name was Mary.

[28] And the angel came in unto her, and said, Hail, thou that art highly favoured, the Lord is with thee: blessed art thou among women.

[29] And when she saw him, she was troubled at his saying, and cast in her mind what manner of salutation this should be.

[30] And the angel said unto her, Fear not, Mary: for thou hast found favour with God.

[31] And, behold, thou shalt conceive in thy womb, and bring forth a son, and shalt call his name JESUS.

[32] He shall be great, and shall be called the Son of the Highest: and the Lord God shall give unto him the throne of his father David:

[33] And he shall reign over the house of Jacob for ever; and of his kingdom there shall be no end.

[34] Then said Mary unto the angel, How shall this be, seeing I know not a man?

[35] And the angel answered and said unto her, The Holy Ghost shall come upon thee, and the power of the Highest shall overshadow thee: therefore also that holy thing which shall be born of thee shall be called the Son of God.

[36] And, behold, thy cousin Elisabeth, she hath also conceived a son in her old age: and this is the sixth month with her, who was called barren.

[37] For with God nothing shall be impossible.

[38] And Mary said, Behold the handmaid of the Lord; be it unto me according to thy word. And the angel departed from her.

[39] And Mary arose in those days, and went into the hill country with haste, into a city of Juda;

[40] And entered into the house of Zacharias, and saluted Elisabeth.

[41] And it came to pass, that, when Elisabeth heard the salutation of Mary, the babe leaped in her womb; and Elisabeth was filled with the Holy Ghost:

[42] And she spake out with a loud voice, and said, Blessed art thou among women, and blessed is the fruit of thy womb.

[43] And whence is this to me, that the mother of my Lord should come to me?

[44] For, lo, as soon as the voice of thy salutation sounded in mine ears, the babe leaped in my womb for joy.

[45] And blessed is she that believed: for there shall be a performance of those things which were told her from the Lord.

[46] And Mary said, My soul doth magnify the Lord,

[47] And my spirit hath rejoiced in God my Saviour.

[48] For he hath regarded the low estate of his handmaiden: for, behold, from henceforth all generations shall call me blessed.

[49] For he that is mighty hath done to me great things; and holy is his name.

[50] And his mercy is on them that fear him from generation to generation.

[51] He hath shewed strength with his arm; he hath scattered the proud in the

imagination of their hearts.

[52] He hath put down the mighty from their seats, and exalted them of low degree.

[53] He hath filled the hungry with good things; and the rich he hath sent empty away.

[54] He hath holpen his servant Israel, in remembrance of his mercy;

[55] As he spake to our fathers, to Abraham, and to his seed for ever.

[56] And Mary abode with her about three months, and returned to her own house.

[57] Now Elisabeth's full time came that she should be delivered; and she brought forth a son.

[58] And her neighbours and her cousins heard how the Lord had shewed great mercy upon her; and they rejoiced with her.

[59] And it came to pass, that on the eighth day they came to circumcise the child; and they called him Zacharias, after the name of his father.

[60] And his mother answered and said, Not so; but he shall be called John.

[61] And they said unto her, There is none of thy kindred that is called by this name.

[62] And they made signs to his father, how he would have him called.

[63] And he asked for a writing table, and wrote, saying, His name is John. And they marvelled all.

[64] And his mouth was opened immediately, and his tongue loosed, and he spake, and praised God.

[65] And fear came on all that dwelt round about them: and all these sayings were noised abroad throughout all the hill country of Judaea.

[66] And all they that heard them laid them up in their hearts, saying, What manner of child shall this be! And the hand of the Lord was with him.

[67] And his father Zacharias was filled with the Holy Ghost, and prophesied, saying,

[68] Blessed be the Lord God of Israel; for he hath visited and redeemed his people,

[69] And hath raised up an horn of salvation for us in the house of his servant David;

[70] As he spake by the mouth of his holy prophets, which have been since the world began:

[71] That we should be saved from our enemies, and from the hand of all that hate us;

[72] To perform the mercy promised to our fathers, and to remember his holy covenant;

[73] The oath which he sware to our father Abraham,

[74] That he would grant unto us, that we being delivered out of the hand of our enemies might serve him without fear,

[75] In holiness and righteousness before him, all the days of our life.

[76] And thou, child, shalt be called the prophet of the Highest: for thou shalt go before the face of the Lord to prepare his ways;

[77] To give knowledge of salvation unto his people by the remission of their sins,

[78] Through the tender mercy of our God; whereby the dayspring from on high hath visited us,

[79] To give light to them that sit in darkness and in the shadow of death, to guide our feet into the way of peace.

[80] And the child grew, and waxed strong in spirit, and was in the deserts till the day of his shewing unto Israel.

[1] And it came to pass in those days, that there went out a decree from Caesar Augustus, that all the world should be taxed.

[2] (And this taxing was first made when Cyrenius was governor of Syria.)

[3] And all went to be taxed, every one into his own city.

[4] And Joseph also went up from Galilee, out of the city of Nazareth, into Judaea, unto the city of David, which is called Bethlehem; (because he was of the house and lineage of David:)

[5] To be taxed with Mary his espoused wife, being great with child.

[6] And so it was, that, while they were there, the days were accomplished that she should be delivered.

[7] And she brought forth her firstborn son, and wrapped him in swaddling clothes, and laid him in a manger; because there was no room for them in the inn.

[8] And there were in the same country shepherds abiding in the field, keeping watch over their flock by night.

[9] And, lo, the angel of the Lord came upon them, and the glory of the Lord shone round about them: and they were sore afraid.

[10] And the angel said unto them, Fear not: for, behold, I bring you good tidings of great joy, which shall be to all people.

[11] For unto you is born this day in the city of David a Saviour, which is Christ the Lord.

[12] And this shall be a sign unto you; Ye shall find the babe wrapped in swaddling clothes, lying in a manger.

[13] And suddenly there was with the angel a multitude of the heavenly host praising God, and saying,

[14] Glory to God in the highest, and on earth peace, good will toward men.

[15] And it came to pass, as the angels were gone away from them into heaven, the shepherds said one to another, Let us now go even unto Bethlehem, and see this thing which is come to pass, which the Lord hath made known unto us.

[16] And they came with haste, and found Mary, and Joseph, and the babe lying in a manger.

[17] And when they had seen it, they made known abroad the saying which was told them concerning this child.

[18] And all they that heard it wondered at those things which were told them by the shepherds.

[19] But Mary kept all these things, and pondered them in her heart.

[20] And the shepherds returned, glorifying and praising God for all the things that they had heard and seen, as it was told unto them.

[21] And when eight days were accomplished for the circumcising of the child, his name was called JESUS, which was so named of the angel before he was conceived in the womb.

[22] And when the days of her purification according to the law of Moses were accomplished, they brought him to Jerusalem, to present him to the Lord;

[23] (As it is written in the law of the Lord, Every male that openeth the womb shall be called holy to the Lord;)

[24] And to offer a sacrifice according to that which is said in the law of the Lord, A pair of turtledoves, or two young pigeons.

[25] And, behold, there was a man in Jerusalem, whose name was Simeon; and the

same man was just and devout, waiting for the consolation of Israel: and the Holy Ghost was upon him.

[26] And it was revealed unto him by the Holy Ghost, that he should not see death, before he had seen the Lord's Christ.

[27] And he came by the Spirit into the temple: and when the parents brought in the child Jesus, to do for him after the custom of the law,

[28] Then took he him up in his arms, and blessed God, and said,

[29] Lord, now lettest thou thy servant depart in peace, according to thy word:

[30] For mine eyes have seen thy salvation,

[31] Which thou hast prepared before the face of all people;

[32] A light to lighten the Gentiles, and the glory of thy people Israel.

[33] And Joseph and his mother marvelled at those things which were spoken of him.

[34] And Simeon blessed them, and said unto Mary his mother, Behold, this child is set for the fall and rising again of many in Israel; and for a sign which shall be spoken against;

[35] (Yea, a sword shall pierce through thy own soul also,) that the thoughts of many hearts may be revealed.

[36] And there was one Anna, a prophetess, the daughter of Phanuel, of the tribe of Aser: she was of a great age, and had lived with an husband seven years from her virginity;

[37] And she was a widow of about fourscore and four years, which departed not from the temple, but served God with fastings and prayers night and day.

[38] And she coming in that instant gave thanks likewise unto the Lord, and spake of him to all them that looked for redemption in Jerusalem.

[39] And when they had performed all things according to the law of the Lord, they returned into Galilee, to their own city Nazareth.

[40] And the child grew, and waxed strong in spirit, filled with wisdom: and the grace of God was upon him.

[41] Now his parents went to Jerusalem every year at the feast of the passover.

[42] And when he was twelve years old, they went up to Jerusalem after the custom of the feast.

[43] And when they had fulfilled the days, as they returned, the child Jesus tarried behind in Jerusalem; and Joseph and his mother knew not of it.

[44] But they, supposing him to have been in the company, went a day's journey; and they sought him among their kinsfolk and acquaintance.

[45] And when they found him not, they turned back again to Jerusalem, seeking him.

[46] And it came to pass, that after three days they found him in the temple, sitting in the midst of the doctors, both hearing them, and asking them questions.

[47] And all that heard him were astonished at his understanding and answers.

[48] And when they saw him, they were amazed: and his mother said unto him, Son, why hast thou thus dealt with us? behold, thy father and I have sought thee sorrowing.

[49] And he said unto them, How is it that ye sought me? wist ye not that I must be about my Father's business?

[50] And they understood not the saying which he spake unto them.

[51] And he went down with them, and came to Nazareth, and was subject unto

them: but his mother kept all these sayings in her heart.

[52] And Jesus increased in wisdom and stature, and in favour with God and man.

Luke.3

[1] Now in the fifteenth year of the reign of Tiberius Caesar, Pontius Pilate being governor of Judaea, and Herod being tetrarch of Galilee, and his brother Philip tetrarch of Ituraea and of the region of Trachonitis, and Lysanias the tetrarch of Abilene,

[2] Annas and Caiaphas being the high priests, the word of God came unto John the son of Zacharias in the wilderness.

[3] And he came into all the country about Jordan, preaching the baptism of repentance for the remission of sins;

[4] As it is written in the book of the words of Esaias the prophet, saying, The voice of one crying in the wilderness, Prepare ye the way of the Lord, make his paths straight.

[5] Every valley shall be filled, and every mountain and hill shall be brought low; and the crooked shall be made straight, and the rough ways shall be made smooth;

[6] And all flesh shall see the salvation of God.

[7] Then said he to the multitude that came forth to be baptized of him, O generation of vipers, who hath warned you to flee from the wrath to come?

[8] Bring forth therefore fruits worthy of repentance, and begin not to say within yourselves, We have Abraham to our father: for I say unto you, That God is able of these stones to raise up children unto Abraham.

[9] And now also the axe is laid unto the root of the trees: every tree therefore which bringeth not forth good fruit is hewn down, and cast into the fire.

[10] And the people asked him, saying, What shall we do then?

[11] He answereth and saith unto them, He that hath two coats, let him impart to him that hath none; and he that hath meat, let him do likewise.

[12] Then came also publicans to be baptized, and said unto him, Master, what shall we do?

[13] And he said unto them, Exact no more than that which is appointed you.

[14] And the soldiers likewise demanded of him, saying, And what shall we do? And he said unto them, Do violence to no man, neither accuse any falsely; and be content with your wages.

[15] And as the people were in expectation, and all men mused in their hearts of John, whether he were the Christ, or not;

[16] John answered, saying unto them all, I indeed baptize you with water; but one mightier than I cometh, the latchet of whose shoes I am not worthy to unloose: he shall baptize you with the Holy Ghost and with fire:

[17] Whose fan is in his hand, and he will throughly purge his floor, and will gather the wheat into his garner; but the chaff he will burn with fire unquenchable.

[18] And many other things in his exhortation preached he unto the people.

[19] But Herod the tetrarch, being reproved by him for Herodias his brother Philip's wife, and for all the evils which Herod had done,

[20] Added yet this above all, that he shut up John in prison.

[21] Now when all the people were baptized, it came to pass, that Jesus also being

baptized, and praying, the heaven was opened,

[22] And the Holy Ghost descended in a bodily shape like a dove upon him, and a voice came from heaven, which said, Thou art my beloved Son; in thee I am well pleased.

[23] And Jesus himself began to be about thirty years of age, being (as was supposed) the son of Joseph, which was the son of Heli,

[24] Which was the son of Matthat, which was the son of Levi, which was the son of Melchi, which was the son of Janna, which was the son of Joseph,

[25] Which was the son of Mattathias, which was the son of Amos, which was the son of Naum, which was the son of Esli, which was the son of Nagge,

[26] Which was the son of Maath, which was the son of Mattathias, which was the son of Semei, which was the son of Joseph, which was the son of Juda,

[27] Which was the son of Joanna, which was the son of Rhesa, which was the son of Zorobabel, which was the son of Salathiel, which was the son of Neri,

[28] Which was the son of Melchi, which was the son of Addi, which was the son of Cosam, which was the son of Elmodam, which was the son of Er,

[29] Which was the son of Jose, which was the son of Eliezer, which was the son of Jorim, which was the son of Matthat, which was the son of Levi,

[30] Which was the son of Simeon, which was the son of Juda, which was the son of Joseph, which was the son of Jonan, which was the son of Eliakim,

[31] Which was the son of Melea, which was the son of Menan, which was the son of Mattatha, which was the son of Nathan, which was the son of David,

[32] Which was the son of Jesse, which was the son of Obed, which was the son of Booz, which was the son of Salmon, which was the son of Naasson,

[33] Which was the son of Aminadab, which was the son of Aram, which was the son of Esrom, which was the son of Phares, which was the son of Juda,

[34] Which was the son of Jacob, which was the son of Isaac, which was the son of Abraham, which was the son of Thara, which was the son of Nachor,

[35] Which was the son of Saruch, which was the son of Ragau, which was the son of Phalec, which was the son of Heber, which was the son of Sala,

[36] Which was the son of Cainan, which was the son of Arphaxad, which was the son of Sem, which was the son of Noe, which was the son of Lamech,

[37] Which was the son of Mathusala, which was the son of Enoch, which was the son of Jared, which was the son of Maleleel, which was the son of Cainan,

[38] Which was the son of Enos, which was the son of Seth, which was the son of Adam, which was the son of God.

Luke.4

[1] And Jesus being full of the Holy Ghost returned from Jordan, and was led by the Spirit into the wilderness,

[2] Being forty days tempted of the devil. And in those days he did eat nothing: and when they were ended, he afterward hungered.

[3] And the devil said unto him, If thou be the Son of God, command this stone that it be made bread.

[4] And Jesus answered him, saying, It is written, That man shall not live by bread alone, but by every word of God.

[5] And the devil, taking him up into an high mountain, shewed unto him all the kingdoms of the world in a moment of time.

[6] And the devil said unto him, All this power will I give thee, and the glory of them: for that is delivered unto me; and to whomsoever I will I give it.

[7] If thou therefore wilt worship me, all shall be thine.

[8] And Jesus answered and said unto him, Get thee behind me, Satan: for it is written, Thou shalt worship the Lord thy God, and him only shalt thou serve.

[9] And he brought him to Jerusalem, and set him on a pinnacle of the temple, and said unto him, If thou be the Son of God, cast thyself down from hence:

[10] For it is written, He shall give his angels charge over thee, to keep thee:

[11] And in their hands they shall bear thee up, lest at any time thou dash thy foot against a stone.

[12] And Jesus answering said unto him, It is said, Thou shalt not tempt the Lord thy God.

[13] And when the devil had ended all the temptation, he departed from him for a season.

[14] And Jesus returned in the power of the Spirit into Galilee: and there went out a fame of him through all the region round about.

[15] And he taught in their synagogues, being glorified of all.

[16] And he came to Nazareth, where he had been brought up: and, as his custom was, he went into the synagogue on the sabbath day, and stood up for to read.

[17] And there was delivered unto him the book of the prophet Esaias. And when he had opened the book, he found the place where it was written,

[18] The Spirit of the Lord is upon me, because he hath anointed me to preach the gospel to the poor; he hath sent me to heal the brokenhearted, to preach deliverance to the captives, and recovering of sight to the blind, to set at liberty them that are bruised,

[19] To preach the acceptable year of the Lord.

[20] And he closed the book, and he gave it again to the minister, and sat down. And the eyes of all them that were in the synagogue were fastened on him.

[21] And he began to say unto them, This day is this scripture fulfilled in your ears.

[22] And all bare him witness, and wondered at the gracious words which proceeded out of his mouth. And they said, Is not this Joseph's son?

[23] And he said unto them, Ye will surely say unto me this proverb, Physician, heal thyself: whatsoever we have heard done in Capernaum, do also here in thy country.

[24] And he said, Verily I say unto you, No prophet is accepted in his own country.

[25] But I tell you of a truth, many widows were in Israel in the days of Elias, when the heaven was shut up three years and six months, when great famine was throughout all the land;

[26] But unto none of them was Elias sent, save unto Sarepta, a city of Sidon, unto a woman that was a widow.

[27] And many lepers were in Israel in the time of Eliseus the prophet; and none of them was cleansed, saving Naaman the Syrian.

[28] And all they in the synagogue, when they heard these things, were filled with wrath,

[29] And rose up, and thrust him out of the city, and led him unto the brow of the hill whereon their city was built, that they might cast him down headlong.

[30] But he passing through the midst of them went his way,

[31] And came down to Capernaum, a city of Galilee, and taught them on the

sabbath days.

[32] And they were astonished at his doctrine: for his word was with power.

[33] And in the synagogue there was a man, which had a spirit of an unclean devil, and cried out with a loud voice,

[34] Saying, Let us alone; what have we to do with thee, thou Jesus of Nazareth? art thou come to destroy us? I know thee who thou art; the Holy One of God.

[35] And Jesus rebuked him, saying, Hold thy peace, and come out of him. And when the devil had thrown him in the midst, he came out of him, and hurt him not.

[36] And they were all amazed, and spake among themselves, saying, What a word is this! for with authority and power he commandeth the unclean spirits, and they come out.

[37] And the fame of him went out into every place of the country round about.

[38] And he arose out of the synagogue, and entered into Simon's house. And Simon's wife's mother was taken with a great fever; and they besought him for her.

[39] And he stood over her, and rebuked the fever; and it left her: and immediately she arose and ministered unto them.

[40] Now when the sun was setting, all they that had any sick with divers diseases brought them unto him; and he laid his hands on every one of them, and healed them.

[41] And devils also came out of many, crying out, and saying, Thou art Christ the Son of God. And he rebuking them suffered them not to speak: for they knew that he was Christ.

[42] And when it was day, he departed and went into a desert place: and the people sought him, and came unto him, and stayed him, that he should not depart from them.

[43] And he said unto them, I must preach the kingdom of God to other cities also: for therefore am I sent.

[44] And he preached in the synagogues of Galilee.

Luke.5

[1] And it came to pass, that, as the people pressed upon him to hear the word of God, he stood by the lake of Gennesaret,

[2] And saw two ships standing by the lake: but the fishermen were gone out of them, and were washing their nets.

[3] And he entered into one of the ships, which was Simon's, and prayed him that he would thrust out a little from the land. And he sat down, and taught the people out of the ship.

[4] Now when he had left speaking, he said unto Simon, Launch out into the deep, and let down your nets for a draught.

[5] And Simon answering said unto him, Master, we have toiled all the night, and have taken nothing: nevertheless at thy word I will let down the net.

[6] And when they had this done, they inclosed a great multitude of fishes: and their net brake.

[7] And they beckoned unto their partners, which were in the other ship, that they should come and help them. And they came, and filled both the ships, so that they began to sink.

[8] When Simon Peter saw it, he fell down at Jesus' knees, saying, Depart from me; for I am a sinful man, O Lord.

[9] For he was astonished, and all that were with him, at the draught of the fishes which they had taken:

[10] And so was also James, and John, the sons of Zebedee, which were partners with Simon. And Jesus said unto Simon, Fear not; from henceforth thou shalt catch men.

[11] And when they had brought their ships to land, they forsook all, and followed him.

[12] And it came to pass, when he was in a certain city, behold a man full of leprosy: who seeing Jesus fell on his face, and besought him, saying, Lord, if thou wilt, thou canst make me clean.

[13] And he put forth his hand, and touched him, saying, I will: be thou clean. And immediately the leprosy departed from him.

[14] And he charged him to tell no man: but go, and shew thyself to the priest, and offer for thy cleansing, according as Moses commanded, for a testimony unto them.

[15] But so much the more went there a fame abroad of him: and great multitudes came together to hear, and to be healed by him of their infirmities.

[16] And he withdrew himself into the wilderness, and prayed.

[17] And it came to pass on a certain day, as he was teaching, that there were Pharisees and doctors of the law sitting by, which were come out of every town of Galilee, and Judaea, and Jerusalem: and the power of the Lord was present to heal them.

[18] And, behold, men brought in a bed a man which was taken with a palsy: and they sought means to bring him in, and to lay him before him.

[19] And when they could not find by what way they might bring him in because of the multitude, they went upon the housetop, and let him down through the tiling with his couch into the midst before Jesus.

[20] And when he saw their faith, he said unto him, Man, thy sins are forgiven thee.

[21] And the scribes and the Pharisees began to reason, saying, Who is this which speaketh blasphemies? Who can forgive sins, but God alone?

[22] But when Jesus perceived their thoughts, he answering said unto them, What reason ye in your hearts?

[23] Whether is easier, to say, Thy sins be forgiven thee; or to say, Rise up and walk?

[24] But that ye may know that the Son of man hath power upon earth to forgive sins, (he said unto the sick of the palsy,) I say unto thee, Arise, and take up thy couch, and go into thine house.

[25] And immediately he rose up before them, and took up that whereon he lay, and departed to his own house, glorifying God.

[26] And they were all amazed, and they glorified God, and were filled with fear, saying, We have seen strange things to day.

[27] And after these things he went forth, and saw a publican, named Levi, sitting at the receipt of custom: and he said unto him, Follow me.

[28] And he left all, rose up, and followed him.

[29] And Levi made him a great feast in his own house: and there was a great company of publicans and of others that sat down with them.

[30] But their scribes and Pharisees murmured against his disciples, saying, Why do ye eat and drink with publicans and sinners?

[31] And Jesus answering said unto them, They that are whole need not a physician; but they that are sick.

[32] I came not to call the righteous, but sinners to repentance.

[33] And they said unto him, Why do the disciples of John fast often, and make prayers, and likewise the disciples of the Pharisees; but thine eat and drink?

[34] And he said unto them, Can ye make the children of the bridechamber fast, while the bridegroom is with them?

[35] But the days will come, when the bridegroom shall be taken away from them, and then shall they fast in those days.

[36] And he spake also a parable unto them; No man putteth a piece of a new garment upon an old; if otherwise, then both the new maketh a rent, and the piece that was taken out of the new agreeth not with the old.

[37] And no man putteth new wine into old bottles; else the new wine will burst the bottles, and be spilled, and the bottles shall perish.

[38] But new wine must be put into new bottles; and both are preserved.

[39] No man also having drunk old wine straightway desireth new: for he saith, The old is better.

Luke.6

[1] And it came to pass on the second sabbath after the first, that he went through the corn fields; and his disciples plucked the ears of corn, and did eat, rubbing them in their hands.

[2] And certain of the Pharisees said unto them, Why do ye that which is not lawful to do on the sabbath days?

[3] And Jesus answering them said, Have ye not read so much as this, what David did, when himself was an hungred, and they which were with him;

[4] How he went into the house of God, and did take and eat the shewbread, and gave also to them that were with him; which it is not lawful to eat but for the priests alone?

[5] And he said unto them, That the Son of man is Lord also of the sabbath.

[6] And it came to pass also on another sabbath, that he entered into the synagogue and taught: and there was a man whose right hand was withered.

[7] And the scribes and Pharisees watched him, whether he would heal on the sabbath day; that they might find an accusation against him.

[8] But he knew their thoughts, and said to the man which had the withered hand, Rise up, and stand forth in the midst. And he arose and stood forth.

[9] Then said Jesus unto them, I will ask you one thing; Is it lawful on the sabbath days to do good, or to do evil? to save life, or to destroy it?

[10] And looking round about upon them all, he said unto the man, Stretch forth thy hand. And he did so: and his hand was restored whole as the other.

[11] And they were filled with madness; and communed one with another what they might do to Jesus.

[12] And it came to pass in those days, that he went out into a mountain to pray, and continued all night in prayer to God.

[13] And when it was day, he called unto him his disciples: and of them he chose twelve, whom also he named apostles;

[14] Simon, (whom he also named Peter,) and Andrew his brother, James and John, Philip and Bartholomew,

[15] Matthew and Thomas, James the son of Alphaeus, and Simon called Zelotes,

[16] And Judas the brother of James, and Judas Iscariot, which also was the traitor.

[17] And he came down with them, and stood in the plain, and the company of his disciples, and a great multitude of people out of all Judaea and Jerusalem, and from the sea coast of Tyre and Sidon, which came to hear him, and to be healed of their diseases;

[18] And they that were vexed with unclean spirits: and they were healed.

[19] And the whole multitude sought to touch him: for there went virtue out of him, and healed them all.

[20] And he lifted up his eyes on his disciples, and said, Blessed be ye poor: for yours is the kingdom of God.

[21] Blessed are ye that hunger now: for ye shall be filled. Blessed are ye that weep now: for ye shall laugh.

[22] Blessed are ye, when men shall hate you, and when they shall separate you from their company, and shall reproach you, and cast out your name as evil, for the Son of man's sake.

[23] Rejoice ye in that day, and leap for joy: for, behold, your reward is great in heaven: for in the like manner did their fathers unto the prophets.

[24] But woe unto you that are rich! for ye have received your consolation.

[25] Woe unto you that are full! for ye shall hunger. Woe unto you that laugh now! for ye shall mourn and weep.

[26] Woe unto you, when all men shall speak well of you! for so did their fathers to the false prophets.

[27] But I say unto you which hear, Love your enemies, do good to them which hate you,

[28] Bless them that curse you, and pray for them which despitefully use you.

[29] And unto him that smiteth thee on the one cheek offer also the other; and him that taketh away thy cloke forbid not to take thy coat also.

[30] Give to every man that asketh of thee; and of him that taketh away thy goods ask them not again.

[31] And as ye would that men should do to you, do ye also to them likewise.

[32] For if ye love them which love you, what thank have ye? for sinners also love those that love them.

[33] And if ye do good to them which do good to you, what thank have ye? for sinners also do even the same.

[34] And if ye lend to them of whom ye hope to receive, what thank have ye? for sinners also lend to sinners, to receive as much again.

[35] But love ye your enemies, and do good, and lend, hoping for nothing again; and your reward shall be great, and ye shall be the children of the Highest: for he is kind unto the unthankful and to the evil.

[36] Be ye therefore merciful, as your Father also is merciful.

[37] Judge not, and ye shall not be judged: condemn not, and ye shall not be condemned: forgive, and ye shall be forgiven:

[38] Give, and it shall be given unto you; good measure, pressed down, and shaken together, and running over, shall men give into your bosom. For with the same measure that ye mete withal it shall be measured to you again.

[39] And he spake a parable unto them, Can the blind lead the blind? shall they not

both fall into the ditch?

[40] The disciple is not above his master: but every one that is perfect shall be as his master.

[41] And why beholdest thou the mote that is in thy brother's eye, but perceivest not the beam that is in thine own eye?

[42] Either how canst thou say to thy brother, Brother, let me pull out the mote that is in thine eye, when thou thyself beholdest not the beam that is in thine own eye? Thou hypocrite, cast out first the beam out of thine own eye, and then shalt thou see clearly to pull out the mote that is in thy brother's eye.

[43] For a good tree bringeth not forth corrupt fruit; neither doth a corrupt tree bring forth good fruit.

[44] For every tree is known by his own fruit. For of thorns men do not gather figs, nor of a bramble bush gather they grapes.

[45] A good man out of the good treasure of his heart bringeth forth that which is good; and an evil man out of the evil treasure of his heart bringeth forth that which is evil: for of the abundance of the heart his mouth speaketh.

[46] And why call ye me, Lord, Lord, and do not the things which I say?

[47] Whosoever cometh to me, and heareth my sayings, and doeth them, I will shew you to whom he is like:

[48] He is like a man which built an house, and digged deep, and laid the foundation on a rock: and when the flood arose, the stream beat vehemently upon that house, and could not shake it: for it was founded upon a rock.

[49] But he that heareth, and doeth not, is like a man that without a foundation built an house upon the earth; against which the stream did beat vehemently, and immediately it fell; and the ruin of that house was great.

Luke.7

[1] Now when he had ended all his sayings in the audience of the people, he entered into Capernaum.

[2] And a certain centurion's servant, who was dear unto him, was sick, and ready to die.

[3] And when he heard of Jesus, he sent unto him the elders of the Jews, beseeching him that he would come and heal his servant.

[4] And when they came to Jesus, they besought him instantly, saying, That he was worthy for whom he should do this:

[5] For he loveth our nation, and he hath built us a synagogue.

[6] Then Jesus went with them. And when he was now not far from the house, the centurion sent friends to him, saying unto him, Lord, trouble not thyself: for I am not worthy that thou shouldest enter under my roof:

[7] Wherefore neither thought I myself worthy to come unto thee: but say in a word, and my servant shall be healed.

[8] For I also am a man set under authority, having under me soldiers, and I say unto one, Go, and he goeth; and to another, Come, and he cometh; and to my servant, Do this, and he doeth it.

[9] When Jesus heard these things, he marvelled at him, and turned him about, and said unto the people that followed him, I say unto you, I have not found so great

faith, no, not in Israel.

[10] And they that were sent, returning to the house, found the servant whole that had been sick.

[11] And it came to pass the day after, that he went into a city called Nain; and many of his disciples went with him, and much people.

[12] Now when he came nigh to the gate of the city, behold, there was a dead man carried out, the only son of his mother, and she was a widow: and much people of the city was with her.

[13] And when the Lord saw her, he had compassion on her, and said unto her, Weep not.

[14] And he came and touched the bier: and they that bare him stood still. And he said, Young man, I say unto thee, Arise.

[15] And he that was dead sat up, and began to speak. And he delivered him to his mother.

[16] And there came a fear on all: and they glorified God, saying, That a great prophet is risen up among us; and, That God hath visited his people.

[17] And this rumour of him went forth throughout all Judaea, and throughout all the region round about.

[18] And the disciples of John shewed him of all these things.

[19] And John calling unto him two of his disciples sent them to Jesus, saying, Art thou he that should come? or look we for another?

[20] When the men were come unto him, they said, John Baptist hath sent us unto thee, saying, Art thou he that should come? or look we for another?

[21] And in that same hour he cured many of their infirmities and plagues, and of evil spirits; and unto many that were blind he gave sight.

[22] Then Jesus answering said unto them, Go your way, and tell John what things ye have seen and heard; how that the blind see, the lame walk, the lepers are cleansed, the deaf hear, the dead are raised, to the poor the gospel is preached.

[23] And blessed is he, whosoever shall not be offended in me.

[24] And when the messengers of John were departed, he began to speak unto the people concerning John, What went ye out into the wilderness for to see? A reed shaken with the wind?

[25] But what went ye out for to see? A man clothed in soft raiment? Behold, they which are gorgeously apparelled, and live delicately, are in kings' courts.

[26] But what went ye out for to see? A prophet? Yea, I say unto you, and much more than a prophet.

[27] This is he, of whom it is written, Behold, I send my messenger before thy face, which shall prepare thy way before thee.

[28] For I say unto you, Among those that are born of women there is not a greater prophet than John the Baptist: but he that is least in the kingdom of God is greater than he.

[29] And all the people that heard him, and the publicans, justified God, being baptized with the baptism of John.

[30] But the Pharisees and lawyers rejected the counsel of God against themselves, being not baptized of him.

[31] And the Lord said, Whereunto then shall I liken the men of this generation? and to what are they like?

[32] They are like unto children sitting in the marketplace, and calling one to another, and saying, We have piped unto you, and ye have not danced; we have

mourned to you, and ye have not wept.

[33] For John the Baptist came neither eating bread nor drinking wine; and ye say, He hath a devil.

[34] The Son of man is come eating and drinking; and ye say, Behold a gluttonous man, and a winebibber, a friend of publicans and sinners!

[35] But wisdom is justified of all her children.

[36] And one of the Pharisees desired him that he would eat with him. And he went into the Pharisee's house, and sat down to meat.

[37] And, behold, a woman in the city, which was a sinner, when she knew that Jesus sat at meat in the Pharisee's house, brought an alabaster box of ointment,

[38] And stood at his feet behind him weeping, and began to wash his feet with tears, and did wipe them with the hairs of her head, and kissed his feet, and anointed them with the ointment.

[39] Now when the Pharisee which had bidden him saw it, he spake within himself, saying, This man, if he were a prophet, would have known who and what manner of woman this is that toucheth him: for she is a sinner.

[40] And Jesus answering said unto him, Simon, I have somewhat to say unto thee. And he saith, Master, say on.

[41] There was a certain creditor which had two debtors: the one owed five hundred pence, and the other fifty.

[42] And when they had nothing to pay, he frankly forgave them both. Tell me therefore, which of them will love him most?

[43] Simon answered and said, I suppose that he, to whom he forgave most. And he said unto him, Thou hast rightly judged.

[44] And he turned to the woman, and said unto Simon, Seest thou this woman? I entered into thine house, thou gavest me no water for my feet: but she hath washed my feet with tears, and wiped them with the hairs of her head.

[45] Thou gavest me no kiss: but this woman since the time I came in hath not ceased to kiss my feet.

[46] My head with oil thou didst not anoint: but this woman hath anointed my feet with ointment.

[47] Wherefore I say unto thee, Her sins, which are many, are forgiven; for she loved much: but to whom little is forgiven, the same loveth little.

[48] And he said unto her, Thy sins are forgiven.

[49] And they that sat at meat with him began to say within themselves, Who is this that forgiveth sins also?

[50] And he said to the woman, Thy faith hath saved thee; go in peace.

Luke.8

[1] And it came to pass afterward, that he went throughout every city and village, preaching and shewing the glad tidings of the kingdom of God: and the twelve were with him,

[2] And certain women, which had been healed of evil spirits and infirmities, Mary called Magdalene, out of whom went seven devils,

[3] And Joanna the wife of Chuza Herod's steward, and Susanna, and many others, which ministered unto him of their substance.

[4] And when much people were gathered together, and were come to him out of every city, he spake by a parable:

[5] A sower went out to sow his seed: and as he sowed, some fell by the way side; and it was trodden down, and the fowls of the air devoured it.

[6] And some fell upon a rock; and as soon as it was sprung up, it withered away, because it lacked moisture.

[7] And some fell among thorns; and the thorns sprang up with it, and choked it.

[8] And other fell on good ground, and sprang up, and bare fruit an hundredfold. And when he had said these things, he cried, He that hath ears to hear, let him hear.

[9] And his disciples asked him, saying, What might this parable be?

[10] And he said, Unto you it is given to know the mysteries of the kingdom of God: but to others in parables; that seeing they might not see, and hearing they might not understand.

[11] Now the parable is this: The seed is the word of God.

[12] Those by the way side are they that hear; then cometh the devil, and taketh away the word out of their hearts, lest they should believe and be saved.

[13] They on the rock are they, which, when they hear, receive the word with joy; and these have no root, which for a while believe, and in time of temptation fall away.

[14] And that which fell among thorns are they, which, when they have heard, go forth, and are choked with cares and riches and pleasures of this life, and bring no fruit to perfection.

[15] But that on the good ground are they, which in an honest and good heart, having heard the word, keep it, and bring forth fruit with patience.

[16] No man, when he hath lighted a candle, covereth it with a vessel, or putteth it under a bed; but setteth it on a candlestick, that they which enter in may see the light.

[17] For nothing is secret, that shall not be made manifest; neither any thing hid, that shall not be known and come abroad.

[18] Take heed therefore how ye hear: for whosoever hath, to him shall be given; and whosoever hath not, from him shall be taken even that which he seemeth to have.

[19] Then came to him his mother and his brethren, and could not come at him for the press.

[20] And it was told him by certain which said, Thy mother and thy brethren stand without, desiring to see thee.

[21] And he answered and said unto them, My mother and my brethren are these which hear the word of God, and do it.

[22] Now it came to pass on a certain day, that he went into a ship with his disciples: and he said unto them, Let us go over unto the other side of the lake. And they launched forth.

[23] But as they sailed he fell asleep: and there came down a storm of wind on the lake; and they were filled with water, and were in jeopardy.

[24] And they came to him, and awoke him, saying, Master, master, we perish. Then he arose, and rebuked the wind and the raging of the water: and they ceased, and there was a calm.

[25] And he said unto them, Where is your faith? And they being afraid wondered, saying one to another, What manner of man is this! for he commandeth even the winds and water, and they obey him.

[26] And they arrived at the country of the Gadarenes, which is over against Galilee.

[27] And when he went forth to land, there met him out of the city a certain man, which had devils long time, and ware no clothes, neither abode in any house, but in the tombs.

[28] When he saw Jesus, he cried out, and fell down before him, and with a loud voice said, What have I to do with thee, Jesus, thou Son of God most high? I beseech thee, torment me not.

[29] (For he had commanded the unclean spirit to come out of the man. For oftentimes it had caught him: and he was kept bound with chains and in fetters; and he brake the bands, and was driven of the devil into the wilderness.)

[30] And Jesus asked him, saying, What is thy name? And he said, Legion: because many devils were entered into him.

[31] And they besought him that he would not command them to go out into the deep.

[32] And there was there an herd of many swine feeding on the mountain: and they besought him that he would suffer them to enter into them. And he suffered them.

[33] Then went the devils out of the man, and entered into the swine: and the herd ran violently down a steep place into the lake, and were choked.

[34] When they that fed them saw what was done, they fled, and went and told it in the city and in the country.

[35] Then they went out to see what was done; and came to Jesus, and found the man, out of whom the devils were departed, sitting at the feet of Jesus, clothed, and in his right mind: and they were afraid.

[36] They also which saw it told them by what means he that was possessed of the devils was healed.

[37] Then the whole multitude of the country of the Gadarenes round about besought him to depart from them; for they were taken with great fear: and he went up into the ship, and returned back again.

[38] Now the man out of whom the devils were departed besought him that he might be with him: but Jesus sent him away, saying,

[39] Return to thine own house, and shew how great things God hath done unto thee. And he went his way, and published throughout the whole city how great things Jesus had done unto him.

[40] And it came to pass, that, when Jesus was returned, the people gladly received him: for they were all waiting for him.

[41] And, behold, there came a man named Jairus, and he was a ruler of the synagogue: and he fell down at Jesus' feet, and besought him that he would come into his house:

[42] For he had one only daughter, about twelve years of age, and she lay a dying. But as he went the people thronged him.

[43] And a woman having an issue of blood twelve years, which had spent all her living upon physicians, neither could be healed of any,

[44] Came behind him, and touched the border of his garment: and immediately her issue of blood stanched.

[45] And Jesus said, Who touched me? When all denied, Peter and they that were with him said, Master, the multitude throng thee and press thee, and sayest thou, Who touched me?

[46] And Jesus said, Somebody hath touched me: for I perceive that virtue is gone out of me.

[47] And when the woman saw that she was not hid, she came trembling, and falling down before him, she declared unto him before all the people for what cause she had touched him and how she was healed immediately.

[48] And he said unto her, Daughter, be of good comfort: thy faith hath made thee whole; go in peace.

[49] While he yet spake, there cometh one from the ruler of the synagogue's house, saying to him, Thy daughter is dead; trouble not the Master.

[50] But when Jesus heard it, he answered him, saying, Fear not: believe only, and she shall be made whole.

[51] And when he came into the house, he suffered no man to go in, save Peter, and James, and John, and the father and the mother of the maiden.

[52] And all wept, and bewailed her: but he said, Weep not; she is not dead, but sleepeth.

[53] And they laughed him to scorn, knowing that she was dead.

[54] And he put them all out, and took her by the hand, and called, saying, Maid, arise.

[55] And her spirit came again, and she arose straightway: and he commanded to give her meat.

[56] And her parents were astonished: but he charged them that they should tell no man what was done.

Luke.9

[1] Then he called his twelve disciples together, and gave them power and authority over all devils, and to cure diseases.

[2] And he sent them to preach the kingdom of God, and to heal the sick.

[3] And he said unto them, Take nothing for your journey, neither staves, nor scrip, neither bread, neither money; neither have two coats apiece.

[4] And whatsoever house ye enter into, there abide, and thence depart.

[5] And whosoever will not receive you, when ye go out of that city, shake off the very dust from your feet for a testimony against them.

[6] And they departed, and went through the towns, preaching the gospel, and healing every where.

[7] Now Herod the tetrarch heard of all that was done by him: and he was perplexed, because that it was said of some, that John was risen from the dead;

[8] And of some, that Elias had appeared; and of others, that one of the old prophets was risen again.

[9] And Herod said, John have I beheaded: but who is this, of whom I hear such things? And he desired to see him.

[10] And the apostles, when they were returned, told him all that they had done. And he took them, and went aside privately into a desert place belonging to the city called Bethsaida.

[11] And the people, when they knew it, followed him: and he received them, and spake unto them of the kingdom of God, and healed them that had need of healing.

[12] And when the day began to wear away, then came the twelve, and said unto him, Send the multitude away, that they may go into the towns and country round about, and lodge, and get victuals: for we are here in a desert place.

[13] But he said unto them, Give ye them to eat. And they said, We have no more but five loaves and two fishes; except we should go and buy meat for all this people.

[14] For they were about five thousand men. And he said to his disciples, Make them sit down by fifties in a company.

[15] And they did so, and made them all sit down.

[16] Then he took the five loaves and the two fishes, and looking up to heaven, he blessed them, and brake, and gave to the disciples to set before the multitude.

[17] And they did eat, and were all filled: and there was taken up of fragments that remained to them twelve baskets.

[18] And it came to pass, as he was alone praying, his disciples were with him: and he asked them, saying, Whom say the people that I am?

[19] They answering said, John the Baptist; but some say, Elias; and others say, that one of the old prophets is risen again.

[20] He said unto them, But whom say ye that I am? Peter answering said, The Christ of God.

[21] And he straitly charged them, and commanded them to tell no man that thing;

[22] Saying, The Son of man must suffer many things, and be rejected of the elders and chief priests and scribes, and be slain, and be raised the third day.

[23] And he said to them all, If any man will come after me, let him deny himself, and take up his cross daily, and follow me.

[24] For whosoever will save his life shall lose it: but whosoever will lose his life for my sake, the same shall save it.

[25] For what is a man advantaged, if he gain the whole world, and lose himself, or be cast away?

[26] For whosoever shall be ashamed of me and of my words, of him shall the Son of man be ashamed, when he shall come in his own glory, and in his Father's, and of the holy angels.

[27] But I tell you of a truth, there be some standing here, which shall not taste of death, till they see the kingdom of God.

[28] And it came to pass about an eight days after these sayings, he took Peter and John and James, and went up into a mountain to pray.

[29] And as he prayed, the fashion of his countenance was altered, and his raiment was white and glistering.

[30] And, behold, there talked with him two men, which were Moses and Elias:

[31] Who appeared in glory, and spake of his decease which he should accomplish at Jerusalem.

[32] But Peter and they that were with him were heavy with sleep: and when they were awake, they saw his glory, and the two men that stood with him.

[33] And it came to pass, as they departed from him, Peter said unto Jesus, Master, it is good for us to be here: and let us make three tabernacles; one for thee, and one for Moses, and one for Elias: not knowing what he said.

[34] While he thus spake, there came a cloud, and overshadowed them: and they feared as they entered into the cloud.

[35] And there came a voice out of the cloud, saying, This is my beloved Son: hear him.

[36] And when the voice was past, Jesus was found alone. And they kept it close, and told no man in those days any of those things which they had seen.

[37] And it came to pass, that on the next day, when they were come down from the hill, much people met him.

[38] And, behold, a man of the company cried out, saying, Master, I beseech thee, look upon my son: for he is mine only child.

[39] And, lo, a spirit taketh him, and he suddenly crieth out; and it teareth him that he foameth again, and bruising him hardly departeth from him.

[40] And I besought thy disciples to cast him out; and they could not.

[41] And Jesus answering said, O faithless and perverse generation, how long shall I be with you, and suffer you? Bring thy son hither.

[42] And as he was yet a coming, the devil threw him down, and tare him. And Jesus rebuked the unclean spirit, and healed the child, and delivered him again to his father.

[43] And they were all amazed at the mighty power of God. But while they wondered every one at all things which Jesus did, he said unto his disciples,

[44] Let these sayings sink down into your ears: for the Son of man shall be delivered into the hands of men.

[45] But they understood not this saying, and it was hid from them, that they perceived it not: and they feared to ask him of that saying.

[46] Then there arose a reasoning among them, which of them should be greatest.

[47] And Jesus, perceiving the thought of their heart, took a child, and set him by him,

[48] And said unto them, Whosoever shall receive this child in my name receiveth me: and whosoever shall receive me receiveth him that sent me: for he that is least among you all, the same shall be great.

[49] And John answered and said, Master, we saw one casting out devils in thy name; and we forbad him, because he followeth not with us.

[50] And Jesus said unto him, Forbid him not: for he that is not against us is for us.

[51] And it came to pass, when the time was come that he should be received up, he stedfastly set his face to go to Jerusalem,

[52] And sent messengers before his face: and they went, and entered into a village of the Samaritans, to make ready for him.

[53] And they did not receive him, because his face was as though he would go to Jerusalem.

[54] And when his disciples James and John saw this, they said, Lord, wilt thou that we command fire to come down from heaven, and consume them, even as Elias did?

[55] But he turned, and rebuked them, and said, Ye know not what manner of spirit ye are of.

[56] For the Son of man is not come to destroy men's lives, but to save them. And they went to another village.

[57] And it came to pass, that, as they went in the way, a certain man said unto him, Lord, I will follow thee whithersoever thou goest.

[58] And Jesus said unto him, Foxes have holes, and birds of the air have nests; but the Son of man hath not where to lay his head.

[59] And he said unto another, Follow me. But he said, Lord, suffer me first to go and bury my father.

[60] Jesus said unto him, Let the dead bury their dead: but go thou and preach the kingdom of God.

[61] And another also said, Lord, I will follow thee; but let me first go bid them farewell, which are at home at my house.

[62] And Jesus said unto him, No man, having put his hand to the plough, and looking back, is fit for the kingdom of God.

Luke.10

[1] After these things the Lord appointed other seventy also, and sent them two and two before his face into every city and place, whither he himself would come.

[2] Therefore said he unto them, The harvest truly is great, but the labourers are few: pray ye therefore the Lord of the harvest, that he would send forth labourers into his harvest.

[3] Go your ways: behold, I send you forth as lambs among wolves.

[4] Carry neither purse, nor scrip, nor shoes: and salute no man by the way.

[5] And into whatsoever house ye enter, first say, Peace be to this house.

[6] And if the son of peace be there, your peace shall rest upon it: if not, it shall turn to you again.

[7] And in the same house remain, eating and drinking such things as they give: for the labourer is worthy of his hire. Go not from house to house.

[8] And into whatsoever city ye enter, and they receive you, eat such things as are set before you:

[9] And heal the sick that are therein, and say unto them, The kingdom of God is come nigh unto you.

[10] But into whatsoever city ye enter, and they receive you not, go your ways out into the streets of the same, and say,

[11] Even the very dust of your city, which cleaveth on us, we do wipe off against you: notwithstanding be ye sure of this, that the kingdom of God is come nigh unto you.

[12] But I say unto you, that it shall be more tolerable in that day for Sodom, than for that city.

[13] Woe unto thee, Chorazin! woe unto thee, Bethsaida! for if the mighty works had been done in Tyre and Sidon, which have been done in you, they had a great while ago repented, sitting in sackcloth and ashes.

[14] But it shall be more tolerable for Tyre and Sidon at the judgment, than for you.

[15] And thou, Capernaum, which art exalted to heaven, shalt be thrust down to hell.

[16] He that heareth you heareth me; and he that despiseth you despiseth me; and he that despiseth me despiseth him that sent me.

[17] And the seventy returned again with joy, saying, Lord, even the devils are subject unto us through thy name.

[18] And he said unto them, I beheld Satan as lightning fall from heaven.

[19] Behold, I give unto you power to tread on serpents and scorpions, and over all the power of the enemy: and nothing shall by any means hurt you.

[20] Notwithstanding in this rejoice not, that the spirits are subject unto you; but rather rejoice, because your names are written in heaven.

[21] In that hour Jesus rejoiced in spirit, and said, I thank thee, O Father, Lord of heaven and earth, that thou hast hid these things from the wise and prudent, and hast revealed them unto babes: even so, Father; for so it seemed good in thy sight.

[22] All things are delivered to me of my Father: and no man knoweth who the Son is, but the Father; and who the Father is, but the Son, and he to whom the Son will reveal him.

[23] And he turned him unto his disciples, and said privately, Blessed are the eyes

which see the things that ye see:

[24] For I tell you, that many prophets and kings have desired to see those things which ye see, and have not seen them; and to hear those things which ye hear, and have not heard them.

[25] And, behold, a certain lawyer stood up, and tempted him, saying, Master, what shall I do to inherit eternal life?

[26] He said unto him, What is written in the law? how readest thou?

[27] And he answering said, Thou shalt love the Lord thy God with all thy heart, and with all thy soul, and with all thy strength, and with all thy mind; and thy neighbour as thyself.

[28] And he said unto him, Thou hast answered right: this do, and thou shalt live.

[29] But he, willing to justify himself, said unto Jesus, And who is my neighbour?

[30] And Jesus answering said, A certain man went down from Jerusalem to Jericho, and fell among thieves, which stripped him of his raiment, and wounded him, and departed, leaving him half dead.

[31] And by chance there came down a certain priest that way: and when he saw him, he passed by on the other side.

[32] And likewise a Levite, when he was at the place, came and looked on him, and passed by on the other side.

[33] But a certain Samaritan, as he journeyed, came where he was: and when he saw him, he had compassion on him,

[34] And went to him, and bound up his wounds, pouring in oil and wine, and set him on his own beast, and brought him to an inn, and took care of him.

[35] And on the morrow when he departed, he took out two pence, and gave them to the host, and said unto him, Take care of him; and whatsoever thou spendest more, when I come again, I will repay thee.

[36] Which now of these three, thinkest thou, was neighbour unto him that fell among the thieves?

[37] And he said, He that shewed mercy on him. Then said Jesus unto him, Go, and do thou likewise.

[38] Now it came to pass, as they went, that he entered into a certain village: and a certain woman named Martha received him into her house.

[39] And she had a sister called Mary, which also sat at Jesus' feet, and heard his word.

[40] But Martha was cumbered about much serving, and came to him, and said, Lord, dost thou not care that my sister hath left me to serve alone? bid her therefore that she help me.

[41] And Jesus answered and said unto her, Martha, Martha, thou art careful and troubled about many things:

[42] But one thing is needful: and Mary hath chosen that good part, which shall not be taken away from her.

Luke.11

[1] And it came to pass, that, as he was praying in a certain place, when he ceased, one of his disciples said unto him, Lord, teach us to pray, as John also taught his disciples.

[2] And he said unto them, When ye pray, say, Our Father which art in heaven, Hallowed be thy name. Thy kingdom come. Thy will be done, as in heaven, so in earth.

[3] Give us day by day our daily bread.

[4] And forgive us our sins; for we also forgive every one that is indebted to us. And lead us not into temptation; but deliver us from evil.

[5] And he said unto them, Which of you shall have a friend, and shall go unto him at midnight, and say unto him, Friend, lend me three loaves;

[6] For a friend of mine in his journey is come to me, and I have nothing to set before him?

[7] And he from within shall answer and say, Trouble me not: the door is now shut, and my children are with me in bed; I cannot rise and give thee.

[8] I say unto you, Though he will not rise and give him, because he is his friend, yet because of his importunity he will rise and give him as many as he needeth.

[9] And I say unto you, Ask, and it shall be given you; seek, and ye shall find; knock, and it shall be opened unto you.

[10] For every one that asketh receiveth; and he that seeketh findeth; and to him that knocketh it shall be opened.

[11] If a son shall ask bread of any of you that is a father, will he give him a stone? or if he ask a fish, will he for a fish give him a serpent?

[12] Or if he shall ask an egg, will he offer him a scorpion?

[13] If ye then, being evil, know how to give good gifts unto your children: how much more shall your heavenly Father give the Holy Spirit to them that ask him?

[14] And he was casting out a devil, and it was dumb. And it came to pass, when the devil was gone out, the dumb spake; and the people wondered.

[15] But some of them said, He casteth out devils through Beelzebub the chief of the devils.

[16] And others, tempting him, sought of him a sign from heaven.

[17] But he, knowing their thoughts, said unto them, Every kingdom divided against itself is brought to desolation; and a house divided against a house falleth.

[18] If Satan also be divided against himself, how shall his kingdom stand? because ye say that I cast out devils through Beelzebub.

[19] And if I by Beelzebub cast out devils, by whom do your sons cast them out? therefore shall they be your judges.

[20] But if I with the finger of God cast out devils, no doubt the kingdom of God is come upon you.

[21] When a strong man armed keepeth his palace, his goods are in peace:

[22] But when a stronger than he shall come upon him, and overcome him, he taketh from him all his armour wherein he trusted, and divideth his spoils.

[23] He that is not with me is against me: and he that gathereth not with me scattereth.

[24] When the unclean spirit is gone out of a man, he walketh through dry places, seeking rest; and finding none, he saith, I will return unto my house whence I came out.

[25] And when he cometh, he findeth it swept and garnished.

[26] Then goeth he, and taketh to him seven other spirits more wicked than himself; and they enter in, and dwell there: and the last state of that man is worse than the first.

[27] And it came to pass, as he spake these things, a certain woman of the company

lifted up her voice, and said unto him, Blessed is the womb that bare thee, and the paps which thou hast sucked.

[28] But he said, Yea rather, blessed are they that hear the word of God, and keep it.

[29] And when the people were gathered thick together, he began to say, This is an evil generation: they seek a sign; and there shall no sign be given it, but the sign of Jonas the prophet.

[30] For as Jonas was a sign unto the Ninevites, so shall also the Son of man be to this generation.

[31] The queen of the south shall rise up in the judgment with the men of this generation, and condemn them: for she came from the utmost parts of the earth to hear the wisdom of Solomon; and, behold, a greater than Solomon is here.

[32] The men of Nineve shall rise up in the judgment with this generation, and shall condemn it: for they repented at the preaching of Jonas; and, behold, a greater than Jonas is here.

[33] No man, when he hath lighted a candle, putteth it in a secret place, neither under a bushel, but on a candlestick, that they which come in may see the light.

[34] The light of the body is the eye: therefore when thine eye is single, thy whole body also is full of light; but when thine eye is evil, thy body also is full of darkness.

[35] Take heed therefore that the light which is in thee be not darkness.

[36] If thy whole body therefore be full of light, having no part dark, the whole shall be full of light, as when the bright shining of a candle doth give thee light.

[37] And as he spake, a certain Pharisee besought him to dine with him: and he went in, and sat down to meat.

[38] And when the Pharisee saw it, he marvelled that he had not first washed before dinner.

[39] And the Lord said unto him, Now do ye Pharisees make clean the outside of the cup and the platter; but your inward part is full of ravening and wickedness.

[40] Ye fools, did not he that made that which is without make that which is within also?

[41] But rather give alms of such things as ye have; and, behold, all things are clean unto you.

[42] But woe unto you, Pharisees! for ye tithe mint and rue and all manner of herbs, and pass over judgment and the love of God: these ought ye to have done, and not to leave the other undone.

[43] Woe unto you, Pharisees! for ye love the uppermost seats in the synagogues, and greetings in the markets.

[44] Woe unto you, scribes and Pharisees, hypocrites! for ye are as graves which appear not, and the men that walk over them are not aware of them.

[45] Then answered one of the lawyers, and said unto him, Master, thus saying thou reproachest us also.

[46] And he said, Woe unto you also, ye lawyers! for ye lade men with burdens grievous to be borne, and ye yourselves touch not the burdens with one of your fingers.

[47] Woe unto you! for ye build the sepulchres of the prophets, and your fathers killed them.

[48] Truly ye bear witness that ye allow the deeds of your fathers: for they indeed killed them, and ye build their sepulchres.

[49] Therefore also said the wisdom of God, I will send them prophets and apostles, and some of them they shall slay and persecute:

[50] That the blood of all the prophets, which was shed from the foundation of the world, may be required of this generation;

[51] From the blood of Abel unto the blood of Zacharias, which perished between the altar and the temple: verily I say unto you, It shall be required of this generation.

[52] Woe unto you, lawyers! for ye have taken away the key of knowledge: ye entered not in yourselves, and them that were entering in ye hindered.

[53] And as he said these things unto them, the scribes and the Pharisees began to urge him vehemently, and to provoke him to speak of many things:

[54] Laying wait for him, and seeking to catch something out of his mouth, that they might accuse him.

Luke.12

[1] In the mean time, when there were gathered together an innumerable multitude of people, insomuch that they trode one upon another, he began to say unto his disciples first of all, Beware ye of the leaven of the Pharisees, which is hypocrisy.

[2] For there is nothing covered, that shall not be revealed; neither hid, that shall not be known.

[3] Therefore whatsoever ye have spoken in darkness shall be heard in the light; and that which ye have spoken in the ear in closets shall be proclaimed upon the housetops.

[4] And I say unto you my friends, Be not afraid of them that kill the body, and after that have no more that they can do.

[5] But I will forewarn you whom ye shall fear: Fear him, which after he hath killed hath power to cast into hell; yea, I say unto you, Fear him.

[6] Are not five sparrows sold for two farthings, and not one of them is forgotten before God?

[7] But even the very hairs of your head are all numbered. Fear not therefore: ye are of more value than many sparrows.

[8] Also I say unto you, Whosoever shall confess me before men, him shall the Son of man also confess before the angels of God:

[9] But he that denieth me before men shall be denied before the angels of God.

[10] And whosoever shall speak a word against the Son of man, it shall be forgiven him: but unto him that blasphemeth against the Holy Ghost it shall not be forgiven.

[11] And when they bring you unto the synagogues, and unto magistrates, and powers, take ye no thought how or what thing ye shall answer, or what ye shall say:

[12] For the Holy Ghost shall teach you in the same hour what ye ought to say.

[13] And one of the company said unto him, Master, speak to my brother, that he divide the inheritance with me.

[14] And he said unto him, Man, who made me a judge or a divider over you?

[15] And he said unto them, Take heed, and beware of covetousness: for a man's life consisteth not in the abundance of the things which he possesseth.

[16] And he spake a parable unto them, saying, The ground of a certain rich man brought forth plentifully:

[17] And he thought within himself, saying, What shall I do, because I have no room where to bestow my fruits?

[18] And he said, This will I do: I will pull down my barns, and build greater; and

there will I bestow all my fruits and my goods.

[19] And I will say to my soul, Soul, thou hast much goods laid up for many years; take thine ease, eat, drink, and be merry.

[20] But God said unto him, Thou fool, this night thy soul shall be required of thee: then whose shall those things be, which thou hast provided?

[21] So is he that layeth up treasure for himself, and is not rich toward God.

[22] And he said unto his disciples, Therefore I say unto you, Take no thought for your life, what ye shall eat; neither for the body, what ye shall put on.

[23] The life is more than meat, and the body is more than raiment.

[24] Consider the ravens: for they neither sow nor reap; which neither have storehouse nor barn; and God feedeth them: how much more are ye better than the fowls?

[25] And which of you with taking thought can add to his stature one cubit?

[26] If ye then be not able to do that thing which is least, why take ye thought for the rest?

[27] Consider the lilies how they grow: they toil not, they spin not; and yet I say unto you, that Solomon in all his glory was not arrayed like one of these.

[28] If then God so clothe the grass, which is to day in the field, and to morrow is cast into the oven; how much more will he clothe you, O ye of little faith?

[29] And seek not ye what ye shall eat, or what ye shall drink, neither be ye of doubtful mind.

[30] For all these things do the nations of the world seek after: and your Father knoweth that ye have need of these things.

[31] But rather seek ye the kingdom of God; and all these things shall be added unto you.

[32] Fear not, little flock; for it is your Father's good pleasure to give you the kingdom.

[33] Sell that ye have, and give alms; provide yourselves bags which wax not old, a treasure in the heavens that faileth not, where no thief approacheth, neither moth corrupteth.

[34] For where your treasure is, there will your heart be also.

[35] Let your loins be girded about, and your lights burning;

[36] And ye yourselves like unto men that wait for their lord, when he will return from the wedding; that when he cometh and knocketh, they may open unto him immediately.

[37] Blessed are those servants, whom the lord when he cometh shall find watching: verily I say unto you, that he shall gird himself, and make them to sit down to meat, and will come forth and serve them.

[38] And if he shall come in the second watch, or come in the third watch, and find them so, blessed are those servants.

[39] And this know, that if the goodman of the house had known what hour the thief would come, he would have watched, and not have suffered his house to be broken through.

[40] Be ye therefore ready also: for the Son of man cometh at an hour when ye think not.

[41] Then Peter said unto him, Lord, speakest thou this parable unto us, or even to all?

[42] And the Lord said, Who then is that faithful and wise steward, whom his lord shall make ruler over his household, to give them their portion of meat in due

season?

[43] Blessed is that servant, whom his lord when he cometh shall find so doing.

[44] Of a truth I say unto you, that he will make him ruler over all that he hath.

[45] But and if that servant say in his heart, My lord delayeth his coming; and shall begin to beat the menservants and maidens, and to eat and drink, and to be drunken;

[46] The lord of that servant will come in a day when he looketh not for him, and at an hour when he is not aware, and will cut him in sunder, and will appoint him his portion with the unbelievers.

[47] And that servant, which knew his lord's will, and prepared not himself, neither did according to his will, shall be beaten with many stripes.

[48] But he that knew not, and did commit things worthy of stripes, shall be beaten with few stripes. For unto whomsoever much is given, of him shall be much required: and to whom men have committed much, of him they will ask the more.

[49] I am come to send fire on the earth; and what will I if it be already kindled?

[50] But I have a baptism to be baptized with; and how am I straitened till it be accomplished!

[51] Suppose ye that I am come to give peace on earth? I tell you, Nay; but rather division:

[52] For from henceforth there shall be five in one house divided, three against two, and two against three.

[53] The father shall be divided against the son, and the son against the father; the mother against the daughter, and the daughter against the mother; the mother in law against her daughter in law, and the daughter in law against her mother in law.

[54] And he said also to the people, When ye see a cloud rise out of the west, straightway ye say, There cometh a shower; and so it is.

[55] And when ye see the south wind blow, ye say, There will be heat; and it cometh to pass.

[56] Ye hypocrites, ye can discern the face of the sky and of the earth; but how is it that ye do not discern this time?

[57] Yea, and why even of yourselves judge ye not what is right?

[58] When thou goest with thine adversary to the magistrate, as thou art in the way, give diligence that thou mayest be delivered from him; lest he hale thee to the judge, and the judge deliver thee to the officer, and the officer cast thee into prison

[59] I tell thee, thou shalt not depart thence, till thou hast paid the very last mite.

Luke.13

[1] There were present at that season some that told him of the Galilaeans, whose blood Pilate had mingled with their sacrifices.

[2] And Jesus answering said unto them, Suppose ye that these Galilaeans were sinners above all the Galilaeans, because they suffered such things?

[3] I tell you, Nay: but, except ye repent, ye shall all likewise perish.

[4] Or those eighteen, upon whom the tower in Siloam fell, and slew them, think ye that they were sinners above all men that dwelt in Jerusalem?

[5] I tell you, Nay: but, except ye repent, ye shall all likewise perish.

[6] He spake also this parable; A certain man had a fig tree planted in his vineyard; and he came and sought fruit thereon, and found none.

[7] Then said he unto the dresser of his vineyard, Behold, these three years I come seeking fruit on this fig tree, and find none: cut it down; why cumbereth it the ground?

[8] And he answering said unto him, Lord, let it alone this year also, till I shall dig about it, and dung it:

[9] And if it bear fruit, well: and if not, then after that thou shalt cut it down.

[10] And he was teaching in one of the synagogues on the sabbath.

[11] And, behold, there was a woman which had a spirit of infirmity eighteen years, and was bowed together, and could in no wise lift up herself.

[12] And when Jesus saw her, he called her to him, and said unto her, Woman, thou art loosed from thine infirmity.

[13] And he laid his hands on her: and immediately she was made straight, and glorified God.

[14] And the ruler of the synagogue answered with indignation, because that Jesus had healed on the sabbath day, and said unto the people, There are six days in which men ought to work: in them therefore come and be healed, and not on the sabbath day.

[15] The Lord then answered him, and said, Thou hypocrite, doth not each one of you on the sabbath loose his ox or his ass from the stall, and lead him away to watering?

[16] And ought not this woman, being a daughter of Abraham, whom Satan hath bound, lo, these eighteen years, be loosed from this bond on the sabbath day?

[17] And when he had said these things, all his adversaries were ashamed: and all the people rejoiced for all the glorious things that were done by him.

[18] Then said he, Unto what is the kingdom of God like? and whereunto shall I resemble it?

[19] It is like a grain of mustard seed, which a man took, and cast into his garden; and it grew, and waxed a great tree; and the fowls of the air lodged in the branches of it.

[20] And again he said, Whereunto shall I liken the kingdom of God?

[21] It is like leaven, which a woman took and hid in three measures of meal, till the whole was leavened.

[22] And he went through the cities and villages, teaching, and journeying toward Jerusalem.

[23] Then said one unto him, Lord, are there few that be saved? And he said unto them,

[24] Strive to enter in at the strait gate: for many, I say unto you, will seek to enter in, and shall not be able.

[25] When once the master of the house is risen up, and hath shut to the door, and ye begin to stand without, and to knock at the door, saying, Lord, Lord, open unto us; and he shall answer and say unto you, I know you not whence ye are:

[26] Then shall ye begin to say, We have eaten and drunk in thy presence, and thou hast taught in our streets.

[27] But he shall say, I tell you, I know you not whence ye are; depart from me, all ye workers of iniquity.

[28] There shall be weeping and gnashing of teeth, when ye shall see Abraham, and Isaac, and Jacob, and all the prophets, in the kingdom of God, and you yourselves thrust out.

[29] And they shall come from the east, and from the west, and from the north, and

from the south, and shall sit down in the kingdom of God.

[30] And, behold, there are last which shall be first, and there are first which shall be last.

[31] The same day there came certain of the Pharisees, saying unto him, Get thee out, and depart hence: for Herod will kill thee.

[32] And he said unto them, Go ye, and tell that fox, Behold, I cast out devils, and I do cures to day and to morrow, and the third day I shall be perfected.

[33] Nevertheless I must walk to day, and to morrow, and the day following: for it cannot be that a prophet perish out of Jerusalem.

[34] O Jerusalem, Jerusalem, which killest the prophets, and stonest them that are sent unto thee; how often would I have gathered thy children together, as a hen doth gather her brood under her wings, and ye would not!

[35] Behold, your house is left unto you desolate: and verily I say unto you, Ye shall not see me, until the time come when ye shall say, Blessed is he that cometh in the name of the Lord.

Luke.14

[1] And it came to pass, as he went into the house of one of the chief Pharisees to eat bread on the sabbath day, that they watched him.

[2] And, behold, there was a certain man before him which had the dropsy.

[3] And Jesus answering spake unto the lawyers and Pharisees, saying, Is it lawful to heal on the sabbath day?

[4] And they held their peace. And he took him, and healed him, and let him go;

[5] And answered them, saying, Which of you shall have an ass or an ox fallen into a pit, and will not straightway pull him out on the sabbath day?

[6] And they could not answer him again to these things.

[7] And he put forth a parable to those which were bidden, when he marked how they chose out the chief rooms; saying unto them,

[8] When thou art bidden of any man to a wedding, sit not down in the highest room; lest a more honourable man than thou be bidden of him;

[9] And he that bade thee and him come and say to thee, Give this man place; and thou begin with shame to take the lowest room.

[10] But when thou art bidden, go and sit down in the lowest room; that when he that bade thee cometh, he may say unto thee, Friend, go up higher: then shalt thou have worship in the presence of them that sit at meat with thee.

[11] For whosoever exalteth himself shall be abased; and he that humbleth himself shall be exalted.

[12] Then said he also to him that bade him, When thou makest a dinner or a supper, call not thy friends, nor thy brethren, neither thy kinsmen, nor thy rich neighbours; lest they also bid thee again, and a recompence be made thee.

[13] But when thou makest a feast, call the poor, the maimed, the lame, the blind:

[14] And thou shalt be blessed; for they cannot recompense thee: for thou shalt be recompensed at the resurrection of the just.

[15] And when one of them that sat at meat with him heard these things, he said unto him, Blessed is he that shall eat bread in the kingdom of God.

[16] Then said he unto him, A certain man made a great supper, and bade many:

[17] And sent his servant at supper time to say to them that were bidden, Come; for all things are now ready.

[18] And they all with one consent began to make excuse. The first said unto him, I have bought a piece of ground, and I must needs go and see it: I pray thee have me excused.

[19] And another said, I have bought five yoke of oxen, and I go to prove them: I pray thee have me excused.

[20] And another said, I have married a wife, and therefore I cannot come.

[21] So that servant came, and shewed his lord these things. Then the master of the house being angry said to his servant, Go out quickly into the streets and lanes of the city, and bring in hither the poor, and the maimed, and the halt, and the blind.

[22] And the servant said, Lord, it is done as thou hast commanded, and yet there is room.

[23] And the lord said unto the servant, Go out into the highways and hedges, and compel them to come in, that my house may be filled.

[24] For I say unto you, That none of those men which were bidden shall taste of my supper.

[25] And there went great multitudes with him: and he turned, and said unto them,

[26] If any man come to me, and hate not his father, and mother, and wife, and children, and brethren, and sisters, yea, and his own life also, he cannot be my disciple.

[27] And whosoever doth not bear his cross, and come after me, cannot be my disciple.

[28] For which of you, intending to build a tower, sitteth not down first, and counteth the cost, whether he have sufficient to finish it?

[29] Lest haply, after he hath laid the foundation, and is not able to finish it, all that behold it begin to mock him,

[30] Saying, This man began to build, and was not able to finish.

[31] Or what king, going to make war against another king, sitteth not down first, and consulteth whether he be able with ten thousand to meet him that cometh against him with twenty thousand?

[32] Or else, while the other is yet a great way off, he sendeth an ambassage, and desireth conditions of peace.

[33] So likewise, whosoever he be of you that forsaketh not all that he hath, he cannot be my disciple.

[34] Salt is good: but if the salt have lost his savour, wherewith shall it be seasoned?

[35] It is neither fit for the land, nor yet for the dunghill; but men cast it out. He that hath ears to hear, let him hear.

Luke.15

[1] Then drew near unto him all the publicans and sinners for to hear him.

[2] And the Pharisees and scribes murmured, saying, This man receiveth sinners, and eateth with them.

[3] And he spake this parable unto them, saying,

[4] What man of you, having an hundred sheep, if he lose one of them, doth not leave the ninety and nine in the wilderness, and go after that which is lost, until he

find it?

[5] And when he hath found it, he layeth it on his shoulders, rejoicing.

[6] And when he cometh home, he calleth together his friends and neighbours, saying unto them, Rejoice with me; for I have found my sheep which was lost.

[7] I say unto you, that likewise joy shall be in heaven over one sinner that repenteth, more than over ninety and nine just persons, which need no repentance.

[8] Either what woman having ten pieces of silver, if she lose one piece, doth not light a candle, and sweep the house, and seek diligently till she find it?

[9] And when she hath found it, she calleth her friends and her neighbours together, saying, Rejoice with me; for I have found the piece which I had lost.

[10] Likewise, I say unto you, there is joy in the presence of the angels of God over one sinner that repenteth.

[11] And he said, A certain man had two sons:

[12] And the younger of them said to his father, Father, give me the portion of goods that falleth to me. And he divided unto them his living.

[13] And not many days after the younger son gathered all together, and took his journey into a far country, and there wasted his substance with riotous living.

[14] And when he had spent all, there arose a mighty famine in that land; and he began to be in want.

[15] And he went and joined himself to a citizen of that country; and he sent him into his fields to feed swine.

[16] And he would fain have filled his belly with the husks that the swine did eat: and no man gave unto him.

[17] And when he came to himself, he said, How many hired servants of my father's have bread enough and to spare, and I perish with hunger!

[18] I will arise and go to my father, and will say unto him, Father, I have sinned against heaven, and before thee,

[19] And am no more worthy to be called thy son: make me as one of thy hired servants.

[20] And he arose, and came to his father. But when he was yet a great way off, his father saw him, and had compassion, and ran, and fell on his neck, and kissed him.

[21] And the son said unto him, Father, I have sinned against heaven, and in thy sight, and am no more worthy to be called thy son.

[22] But the father said to his servants, Bring forth the best robe, and put it on him; and put a ring on his hand, and shoes on his feet:

[23] And bring hither the fatted calf, and kill it; and let us eat, and be merry:

[24] For this my son was dead, and is alive again; he was lost, and is found. And they began to be merry.

[25] Now his elder son was in the field: and as he came and drew nigh to the house, he heard musick and dancing.

[26] And he called one of the servants, and asked what these things meant.

[27] And he said unto him, Thy brother is come; and thy father hath killed the fatted calf, because he hath received him safe and sound.

[28] And he was angry, and would not go in: therefore came his father out, and intreated him.

[29] And he answering said to his father, Lo, these many years do I serve thee, neither transgressed I at any time thy commandment: and yet thou never gavest me a kid, that I might make merry with my friends:

[30] But as soon as this thy son was come, which hath devoured thy living with

harlots, thou hast killed for him the fatted calf.

[31] And he said unto him, Son, thou art ever with me, and all that I have is thine.

[32] It was meet that we should make merry, and be glad: for this thy brother was dead, and is alive again; and was lost, and is found.

Luke.16

[1] And he said also unto his disciples, There was a certain rich man, which had a steward; and the same was accused unto him that he had wasted his goods.

[2] And he called him, and said unto him, How is it that I hear this of thee? give an account of thy stewardship; for thou mayest be no longer steward.

[3] Then the steward said within himself, What shall I do? for my lord taketh away from me the stewardship: I cannot dig; to beg I am ashamed.

[4] I am resolved what to do, that, when I am put out of the stewardship, they may receive me into their houses.

[5] So he called every one of his lord's debtors unto him, and said unto the first, How much owest thou unto my lord?

[6] And he said, An hundred measures of oil. And he said unto him, Take thy bill, and sit down quickly, and write fifty.

[7] Then said he to another, And how much owest thou? And he said, An hundred measures of wheat. And he said unto him, Take thy bill, and write fourscore.

[8] And the lord commended the unjust steward, because he had done wisely: for the children of this world are in their generation wiser than the children of light.

[9] And I say unto you, Make to yourselves friends of the mammon of unrighteousness; that, when ye fail, they may receive you into everlasting habitations.

[10] He that is faithful in that which is least is faithful also in much: and he that is unjust in the least is unjust also in much.

[11] If therefore ye have not been faithful in the unrighteous mammon, who will commit to your trust the true riches?

[12] And if ye have not been faithful in that which is another man's, who shall give you that which is your own?

[13] No servant can serve two masters: for either he will hate the one, and love the other; or else he will hold to the one, and despise the other. Ye cannot serve God and mammon.

[14] And the Pharisees also, who were covetous, heard all these things: and they derided him.

[15] And he said unto them, Ye are they which justify yourselves before men; but God knoweth your hearts: for that which is highly esteemed among men is abomination in the sight of God.

[16] The law and the prophets were until John: since that time the kingdom of God is preached, and every man presseth into it.

[17] And it is easier for heaven and earth to pass, than one tittle of the law to fail.

[18] Whosoever putteth away his wife, and marrieth another, committeth adultery: and whosoever marrieth her that is put away from her husband committeth adultery.

[19] There was a certain rich man, which was clothed in purple and fine linen, and fared sumptuously every day:

[20] And there was a certain beggar named Lazarus, which was laid at his gate, full of sores,

[21] And desiring to be fed with the crumbs which fell from the rich man's table: moreover the dogs came and licked his sores.

[22] And it came to pass, that the beggar died, and was carried by the angels into Abraham's bosom: the rich man also died, and was buried;

[23] And in hell he lift up his eyes, being in torments, and seeth Abraham afar off, and Lazarus in his bosom.

[24] And he cried and said, Father Abraham, have mercy on me, and send Lazarus, that he may dip the tip of his finger in water, and cool my tongue; for I am tormented in this flame.

[25] But Abraham said, Son, remember that thou in thy lifetime receivedst thy good things, and likewise Lazarus evil things: but now he is comforted, and thou art tormented.

[26] And beside all this, between us and you there is a great gulf fixed: so that they which would pass from hence to you cannot; neither can they pass to us, that would come from thence.

[27] Then he said, I pray thee therefore, father, that thou wouldest send him to my father's house:

[28] For I have five brethren; that he may testify unto them, lest they also come into this place of torment.

[29] Abraham saith unto him, They have Moses and the prophets; let them hear them.

[30] And he said, Nay, father Abraham: but if one went unto them from the dead, they will repent.

[31] And he said unto him, If they hear not Moses and the prophets, neither will they be persuaded, though one rose from the dead.

Luke.17

[1] Then said he unto the disciples, It is impossible but that offences will come: but woe unto him, through whom they come!

[2] It were better for him that a millstone were hanged about his neck, and he cast into the sea, than that he should offend one of these little ones.

[3] Take heed to yourselves: If thy brother trespass against thee, rebuke him; and if he repent, forgive him.

[4] And if he trespass against thee seven times in a day, and seven times in a day turn again to thee, saying, I repent; thou shalt forgive him.

[5] And the apostles said unto the Lord, Increase our faith.

[6] And the Lord said, If ye had faith as a grain of mustard seed, ye might say unto this sycamine tree, Be thou plucked up by the root, and be thou planted in the sea; and it should obey you.

[7] But which of you, having a servant plowing or feeding cattle, will say unto him by and by, when he is come from the field, Go and sit down to meat?

[8] And will not rather say unto him, Make ready wherewith I may sup, and gird thyself, and serve me, till I have eaten and drunken; and afterward thou shalt eat and drink?

[9] Doth he thank that servant because he did the things that were commanded him? I trow not.

[10] So likewise ye, when ye shall have done all those things which are commanded you, say, We are unprofitable servants: we have done that which was our duty to do.

[11] And it came to pass, as he went to Jerusalem, that he passed through the midst of Samaria and Galilee.

[12] And as he entered into a certain village, there met him ten men that were lepers, which stood afar off:

[13] And they lifted up their voices, and said, Jesus, Master, have mercy on us.

[14] And when he saw them, he said unto them, Go shew yourselves unto the priests. And it came to pass, that, as they went, they were cleansed.

[15] And one of them, when he saw that he was healed, turned back, and with a loud voice glorified God,

[16] And fell down on his face at his feet, giving him thanks: and he was a Samaritan.

[17] And Jesus answering said, Were there not ten cleansed? but where are the nine?

[18] There are not found that returned to give glory to God, save this stranger.

[19] And he said unto him, Arise, go thy way: thy faith hath made thee whole.

[20] And when he was demanded of the Pharisees, when the kingdom of God should come, he answered them and said, The kingdom of God cometh not with observation:

[21] Neither shall they say, Lo here! or, lo there! for, behold, the kingdom of God is within you.

[22] And he said unto the disciples, The days will come, when ye shall desire to see one of the days of the Son of man, and ye shall not see it.

[23] And they shall say to you, See here; or, see there: go not after them, nor follow them.

[24] For as the lightning, that lighteneth out of the one part under heaven, shineth unto the other part under heaven; so shall also the Son of man be in his day.

[25] But first must he suffer many things, and be rejected of this generation.

[26] And as it was in the days of Noe, so shall it be also in the days of the Son of man.

[27] They did eat, they drank, they married wives, they were given in marriage, until the day that Noe entered into the ark, and the flood came, and destroyed them all.

[28] Likewise also as it was in the days of Lot; they did eat, they drank, they bought, they sold, they planted, they builded;

[29] But the same day that Lot went out of Sodom it rained fire and brimstone from heaven, and destroyed them all.

[30] Even thus shall it be in the day when the Son of man is revealed.

[31] In that day, he which shall be upon the housetop, and his stuff in the house, let him not come down to take it away: and he that is in the field, let him likewise not return back.

[32] Remember Lot's wife.

[33] Whosoever shall seek to save his life shall lose it; and whosoever shall lose his life shall preserve it.

[34] I tell you, in that night there shall be two men in one bed; the one shall be taken, and the other shall be left.

[35] Two women shall be grinding together; the one shall be taken, and the other left.

[36] Two men shall be in the field; the one shall be taken, and the other left.
[37] And they answered and said unto him, Where, Lord? And he said unto them, Wheresoever the body is, thither will the eagles be gathered together.

Luke.18

[1] And he spake a parable unto them to this end, that men ought always to pray, and not to faint;
[2] Saying, There was in a city a judge, which feared not God, neither regarded man:
[3] And there was a widow in that city; and she came unto him, saying, Avenge me of mine adversary.
[4] And he would not for a while: but afterward he said within himself, Though I fear not God, nor regard man;
[5] Yet because this widow troubleth me, I will avenge her, lest by her continual coming she weary me.
[6] And the Lord said, Hear what the unjust judge saith.
[7] And shall not God avenge his own elect, which cry day and night unto him, though he bear long with them?
[8] I tell you that he will avenge them speedily. Nevertheless when the Son of man cometh, shall he find faith on the earth?
[9] And he spake this parable unto certain which trusted in themselves that they were righteous, and despised others:
[10] Two men went up into the temple to pray; the one a Pharisee, and the other a publican.
[11] The Pharisee stood and prayed thus with himself, God, I thank thee, that I am not as other men are, extortioners, unjust, adulterers, or even as this publican.
[12] I fast twice in the week, I give tithes of all that I possess.
[13] And the publican, standing afar off, would not lift up so much as his eyes unto heaven, but smote upon his breast, saying, God be merciful to me a sinner.
[14] I tell you, this man went down to his house justified rather than the other: for every one that exalteth himself shall be abased; and he that humbleth himself shall be exalted.
[15] And they brought unto him also infants, that he would touch them: but when his disciples saw it, they rebuked them.
[16] But Jesus called them unto him, and said, Suffer little children to come unto me, and forbid them not: for of such is the kingdom of God.
[17] Verily I say unto you, Whosoever shall not receive the kingdom of God as a little child shall in no wise enter therein.
[18] And a certain ruler asked him, saying, Good Master, what shall I do to inherit eternal life?
[19] And Jesus said unto him, Why callest thou me good? none is good, save one, that is, God.
[20] Thou knowest the commandments, Do not commit adultery, Do not kill, Do not steal, Do not bear false witness, Honour thy father and thy mother.
[21] And he said, All these have I kept from my youth up.
[22] Now when Jesus heard these things, he said unto him, Yet lackest thou one thing: sell all that thou hast, and distribute unto the poor, and thou shalt have

treasure in heaven: and come, follow me.

[23] And when he heard this, he was very sorrowful: for he was very rich.

[24] And when Jesus saw that he was very sorrowful, he said, How hardly shall they that have riches enter into the kingdom of God!

[25] For it is easier for a camel to go through a needle's eye, than for a rich man to enter into the kingdom of God.

[26] And they that heard it said, Who then can be saved?

[27] And he said, The things which are impossible with men are possible with God.

[28] Then Peter said, Lo, we have left all, and followed thee.

[29] And he said unto them, Verily I say unto you, There is no man that hath left house, or parents, or brethren, or wife, or children, for the kingdom of God's sake,

[30] Who shall not receive manifold more in this present time, and in the world to come life everlasting.

[31] Then he took unto him the twelve, and said unto them, Behold, we go up to Jerusalem, and all things that are written by the prophets concerning the Son of man shall be accomplished.

[32] For he shall be delivered unto the Gentiles, and shall be mocked, and spitefully entreated, and spitted on:

[33] And they shall scourge him, and put him to death: and the third day he shall rise again.

[34] And they understood none of these things: and this saying was hid from them, neither knew they the things which were spoken.

[35] And it came to pass, that as he was come nigh unto Jericho, a certain blind man sat by the way side begging:

[36] And hearing the multitude pass by, he asked what it meant.

[37] And they told him, that Jesus of Nazareth passeth by.

[38] And he cried, saying, Jesus, thou Son of David, have mercy on me.

[39] And they which went before rebuked him, that he should hold his peace: but he cried so much the more, Thou Son of David, have mercy on me.

[40] And Jesus stood, and commanded him to be brought unto him: and when he was come near, he asked him,

[41] Saying, What wilt thou that I shall do unto thee? And he said, Lord, that I may receive my sight.

[42] And Jesus said unto him, Receive thy sight: thy faith hath saved thee.

[43] And immediately he received his sight, and followed him, glorifying God: and all the people, when they saw it, gave praise unto God.

Luke.19

[1] And Jesus entered and passed through Jericho.

[2] And, behold, there was a man named Zacchaeus, which was the chief among the publicans, and he was rich.

[3] And he sought to see Jesus who he was; and could not for the press, because he was little of stature.

[4] And he ran before, and climbed up into a sycomore tree to see him: for he was to pass that way.

[5] And when Jesus came to the place, he looked up, and saw him, and said unto

him, Zacchaeus, make haste, and come down; for to day I must abide at thy house.

[6] And he made haste, and came down, and received him joyfully.

[7] And when they saw it, they all murmured, saying, That he was gone to be guest with a man that is a sinner.

[8] And Zacchaeus stood, and said unto the Lord; Behold, Lord, the half of my goods I give to the poor; and if I have taken any thing from any man by false accusation, I restore him fourfold.

[9] And Jesus said unto him, This day is salvation come to this house, forsomuch as he also is a son of Abraham.

[10] For the Son of man is come to seek and to save that which was lost.

[11] And as they heard these things, he added and spake a parable, because he was nigh to Jerusalem, and because they thought that the kingdom of God should immediately appear.

[12] He said therefore, A certain nobleman went into a far country to receive for himself a kingdom, and to return.

[13] And he called his ten servants, and delivered them ten pounds, and said unto them, Occupy till I come.

[14] But his citizens hated him, and sent a message after him, saying, We will not have this man to reign over us.

[15] And it came to pass, that when he was returned, having received the kingdom, then he commanded these servants to be called unto him, to whom he had given the money, that he might know how much every man had gained by trading.

[16] Then came the first, saying, Lord, thy pound hath gained ten pounds.

[17] And he said unto him, Well, thou good servant: because thou hast been faithful in a very little, have thou authority over ten cities.

[18] And the second came, saying, Lord, thy pound hath gained five pounds.

[19] And he said likewise to him, Be thou also over five cities.

[20] And another came, saying, Lord, behold, here is thy pound, which I have kept laid up in a napkin:

[21] For I feared thee, because thou art an austere man: thou takest up that thou layedst not down, and reapest that thou didst not sow.

[22] And he saith unto him, Out of thine own mouth will I judge thee, thou wicked servant. Thou knewest that I was an austere man, taking up that I laid not down, and reaping that I did not sow:

[23] Wherefore then gavest not thou my money into the bank, that at my coming I might have required mine own with usury?

[24] And he said unto them that stood by, Take from him the pound, and give it to him that hath ten pounds.

[25] (And they said unto him, Lord, he hath ten pounds.)

[26] For I say unto you, That unto every one which hath shall be given; and from him that hath not, even that he hath shall be taken away from him.

[27] But those mine enemies, which would not that I should reign over them, bring hither, and slay them before me.

[28] And when he had thus spoken, he went before, ascending up to Jerusalem.

[29] And it came to pass, when he was come nigh to Bethphage and Bethany, at the mount called the mount of Olives, he sent two of his disciples,

[30] Saying, Go ye into the village over against you; in the which at your entering ye shall find a colt tied, whereon yet never man sat: loose him, and bring him hither.

[31] And if any man ask you, Why do ye loose him? thus shall ye say unto him,

Because the Lord hath need of him.

[32] And they that were sent went their way, and found even as he had said unto them.

[33] And as they were loosing the colt, the owners thereof said unto them, Why loose ye the colt?

[34] And they said, The Lord hath need of him.

[35] And they brought him to Jesus: and they cast their garments upon the colt, and they set Jesus thereon.

[36] And as he went, they spread their clothes in the way.

[37] And when he was come nigh, even now at the descent of the mount of Olives, the whole multitude of the disciples began to rejoice and praise God with a loud voice for all the mighty works that they had seen;

[38] Saying, Blessed be the King that cometh in the name of the Lord: peace in heaven, and glory in the highest.

[39] And some of the Pharisees from among the multitude said unto him, Master, rebuke thy disciples.

[40] And he answered and said unto them, I tell you that, if these should hold their peace, the stones would immediately cry out.

[41] And when he was come near, he beheld the city, and wept over it,

[42] Saying, If thou hadst known, even thou, at least in this thy day, the things which belong unto thy peace! but now they are hid from thine eyes.

[43] For the days shall come upon thee, that thine enemies shall cast a trench about thee, and compass thee round, and keep thee in on every side,

[44] And shall lay thee even with the ground, and thy children within thee; and they shall not leave in thee one stone upon another; because thou knewest not the time of thy visitation.

[45] And he went into the temple, and began to cast out them that sold therein, and them that bought;

[46] Saying unto them, It is written, My house is the house of prayer: but ye have made it a den of thieves.

[47] And he taught daily in the temple. But the chief priests and the scribes and the chief of the people sought to destroy him,

[48] And could not find what they might do: for all the people were very attentive to hear him.

Luke.20

[1] And it came to pass, that on one of those days, as he taught the people in the temple, and preached the gospel, the chief priests and the scribes came upon him with the elders,

[2] And spake unto him, saying, Tell us, by what authority doest thou these things? or who is he that gave thee this authority?

[3] And he answered and said unto them, I will also ask you one thing; and answer me:

[4] The baptism of John, was it from heaven, or of men?

[5] And they reasoned with themselves, saying, If we shall say, From heaven; he will say, Why then believed ye him not?

[6] But and if we say, Of men; all the people will stone us: for they be persuaded that John was a prophet.

[7] And they answered, that they could not tell whence it was.

[8] And Jesus said unto them, Neither tell I you by what authority I do these things.

[9] Then began he to speak to the people this parable; A certain man planted a vineyard, and let it forth to husbandmen, and went into a far country for a long time.

[10] And at the season he sent a servant to the husbandmen, that they should give him of the fruit of the vineyard: but the husbandmen beat him, and sent him away empty.

[11] And again he sent another servant: and they beat him also, and entreated him shamefully, and sent him away empty.

[12] And again he sent a third: and they wounded him also, and cast him out.

[13] Then said the lord of the vineyard, What shall I do? I will send my beloved son: it may be they will reverence him when they see him.

[14] But when the husbandmen saw him, they reasoned among themselves, saying, This is the heir: come, let us kill him, that the inheritance may be ours.

[15] So they cast him out of the vineyard, and killed him. What therefore shall the lord of the vineyard do unto them?

[16] He shall come and destroy these husbandmen, and shall give the vineyard to others. And when they heard it, they said, God forbid.

[17] And he beheld them, and said, What is this then that is written, The stone which the builders rejected, the same is become the head of the corner?

[18] Whosoever shall fall upon that stone shall be broken; but on whomsoever it shall fall, it will grind him to powder.

[19] And the chief priests and the scribes the same hour sought to lay hands on him; and they feared the people: for they perceived that he had spoken this parable against them.

[20] And they watched him, and sent forth spies, which should feign themselves just men, that they might take hold of his words, that so they might deliver him unto the power and authority of the governor.

[21] And they asked him, saying, Master, we know that thou sayest and teachest rightly, neither acceptest thou the person of any, but teachest the way of God truly:

[22] Is it lawful for us to give tribute unto Caesar, or no?

[23] But he perceived their craftiness, and said unto them, Why tempt ye me?

[24] Shew me a penny. Whose image and superscription hath it? They answered and said, Caesar's.

[25] And he said unto them, Render therefore unto Caesar the things which be Caesar's, and unto God the things which be God's.

[26] And they could not take hold of his words before the people: and they marvelled at his answer, and held their peace.

[27] Then came to him certain of the Sadducees, which deny that there is any resurrection; and they asked him,

[28] Saying, Master, Moses wrote unto us, If any man's brother die, having a wife, and he die without children, that his brother should take his wife, and raise up seed unto his brother.

[29] There were therefore seven brethren: and the first took a wife, and died without children.

[30] And the second took her to wife, and he died childless.

[31] And the third took her; and in like manner the seven also: and they left no

children, and died.

[32] Last of all the woman died also.

[33] Therefore in the resurrection whose wife of them is she? for seven had her to wife.

[34] And Jesus answering said unto them, The children of this world marry, and are given in marriage:

[35] But they which shall be accounted worthy to obtain that world, and the resurrection from the dead, neither marry, nor are given in marriage:

[36] Neither can they die any more: for they are equal unto the angels; and are the children of God, being the children of the resurrection.

[37] Now that the dead are raised, even Moses shewed at the bush, when he calleth the Lord the God of Abraham, and the God of Isaac, and the God of Jacob.

[38] For he is not a God of the dead, but of the living: for all live unto him.

[39] Then certain of the scribes answering said, Master, thou hast well said.

[40] And after that they durst not ask him any question at all.

[41] And he said unto them, How say they that Christ is David's son?

[42] And David himself saith in the book of Psalms, The LORD said unto my Lord, Sit thou on my right hand,

[43] Till I make thine enemies thy footstool.

[44] David therefore calleth him Lord, how is he then his son?

[45] Then in the audience of all the people he said unto his disciples,

[46] Beware of the scribes, which desire to walk in long robes, and love greetings in the markets, and the highest seats in the synagogues, and the chief rooms at feasts;

[47] Which devour widows' houses, and for a shew make long prayers: the same shall receive greater damnation.

Luke.21

[1] And he looked up, and saw the rich men casting their gifts into the treasury.

[2] And he saw also a certain poor widow casting in thither two mites.

[3] And he said, Of a truth I say unto you, that this poor widow hath cast in more than they all:

[4] For all these have of their abundance cast in unto the offerings of God: but she of her penury hath cast in all the living that she had.

[5] And as some spake of the temple, how it was adorned with goodly stones and gifts, he said,

[6] As for these things which ye behold, the days will come, in the which there shall not be left one stone upon another, that shall not be thrown down.

[7] And they asked him, saying, Master, but when shall these things be? and what sign will there be when these things shall come to pass?

[8] And he said, Take heed that ye be not deceived: for many shall come in my name, saying, I am Christ; and the time draweth near: go ye not therefore after them.

[9] But when ye shall hear of wars and commotions, be not terrified: for these things must first come to pass; but the end is not by and by.

[10] Then said he unto them, Nation shall rise against nation, and kingdom against kingdom:

[11] And great earthquakes shall be in divers places, and famines, and pestilences;

and fearful sights and great signs shall there be from heaven.

[12] But before all these, they shall lay their hands on you, and persecute you, delivering you up to the synagogues, and into prisons, being brought before kings and rulers for my name's sake.

[13] And it shall turn to you for a testimony.

[14] Settle it therefore in your hearts, not to meditate before what ye shall answer:

[15] For I will give you a mouth and wisdom, which all your adversaries shall not be able to gainsay nor resist.

[16] And ye shall be betrayed both by parents, and brethren, and kinsfolks, and friends; and some of you shall they cause to be put to death.

[17] And ye shall be hated of all men for my name's sake.

[18] But there shall not an hair of your head perish.

[19] In your patience possess ye your souls.

[20] And when ye shall see Jerusalem compassed with armies, then know that the desolation thereof is nigh.

[21] Then let them which are in Judaea flee to the mountains; and let them which are in the midst of it depart out; and let not them that are in the countries enter thereinto.

[22] For these be the days of vengeance, that all things which are written may be fulfilled.

[23] But woe unto them that are with child, and to them that give suck, in those days! for there shall be great distress in the land, and wrath upon this people.

[24] And they shall fall by the edge of the sword, and shall be led away captive into all nations: and Jerusalem shall be trodden down of the Gentiles, until the times of the Gentiles be fulfilled.

[25] And there shall be signs in the sun, and in the moon, and in the stars; and upon the earth distress of nations, with perplexity; the sea and the waves roaring;

[26] Men's hearts failing them for fear, and for looking after those things which are coming on the earth: for the powers of heaven shall be shaken.

[27] And then shall they see the Son of man coming in a cloud with power and great glory.

[28] And when these things begin to come to pass, then look up, and lift up your heads; for your redemption draweth nigh.

[29] And he spake to them a parable; Behold the fig tree, and all the trees;

[30] When they now shoot forth, ye see and know of your own selves that summer is now nigh at hand.

[31] So likewise ye, when ye see these things come to pass, know ye that the kingdom of God is nigh at hand.

[32] Verily I say unto you, This generation shall not pass away, till all be fulfilled.

[33] Heaven and earth shall pass away: but my words shall not pass away.

[34] And take heed to yourselves, lest at any time your hearts be overcharged with surfeiting, and drunkenness, and cares of this life, and so that day come upon you unawares.

[35] For as a snare shall it come on all them that dwell on the face of the whole earth.

[36] Watch ye therefore, and pray always, that ye may be accounted worthy to escape all these things that shall come to pass, and to stand before the Son of man.

[37] And in the day time he was teaching in the temple; and at night he went out, and abode in the mount that is called the mount of Olives.

[38] And all the people came early in the morning to him in the temple, for to hear him.

Luke.22

[1] Now the feast of unleavened bread drew nigh, which is called the Passover.

[2] And the chief priests and scribes sought how they might kill him; for they feared the people.

[3] Then entered Satan into Judas surnamed Iscariot, being of the number of the twelve.

[4] And he went his way, and communed with the chief priests and captains, how he might betray him unto them.

[5] And they were glad, and covenanted to give him money.

[6] And he promised, and sought opportunity to betray him unto them in the absence of the multitude.

[7] Then came the day of unleavened bread, when the passover must be killed.

[8] And he sent Peter and John, saying, Go and prepare us the passover, that we may eat.

[9] And they said unto him, Where wilt thou that we prepare?

[10] And he said unto them, Behold, when ye are entered into the city, there shall a man meet you, bearing a pitcher of water; follow him into the house where he entereth in.

[11] And ye shall say unto the goodman of the house, The Master saith unto thee, Where is the guestchamber, where I shall eat the passover with my disciples?

[12] And he shall shew you a large upper room furnished: there make ready.

[13] And they went, and found as he had said unto them: and they made ready the passover.

[14] And when the hour was come, he sat down, and the twelve apostles with him.

[15] And he said unto them, With desire I have desired to eat this passover with you before I suffer:

[16] For I say unto you, I will not any more eat thereof, until it be fulfilled in the kingdom of God.

[17] And he took the cup, and gave thanks, and said, Take this, and divide it among yourselves:

[18] For I say unto you, I will not drink of the fruit of the vine, until the kingdom of God shall come.

[19] And he took bread, and gave thanks, and brake it, and gave unto them, saying, This is my body which is given for you: this do in remembrance of me.

[20] Likewise also the cup after supper, saying, This cup is the new testament in my blood, which is shed for you.

[21] But, behold, the hand of him that betrayeth me is with me on the table.

[22] And truly the Son of man goeth, as it was determined: but woe unto that man by whom he is betrayed!

[23] And they began to inquire among themselves, which of them it was that should do this thing.

[24] And there was also a strife among them, which of them should be accounted the greatest.

[25] And he said unto them, The kings of the Gentiles exercise lordship over them; and they that exercise authority upon them are called benefactors.

[26] But ye shall not be so: but he that is greatest among you, let him be as the younger; and he that is chief, as he that doth serve.

[27] For whether is greater, he that sitteth at meat, or he that serveth? is not he that sitteth at meat? but I am among you as he that serveth.

[28] Ye are they which have continued with me in my temptations.

[29] And I appoint unto you a kingdom, as my Father hath appointed unto me;

[30] That ye may eat and drink at my table in my kingdom, and sit on thrones judging the twelve tribes of Israel.

[31] And the Lord said, Simon, Simon, behold, Satan hath desired to have you, that he may sift you as wheat:

[32] But I have prayed for thee, that thy faith fail not: and when thou art converted, strengthen thy brethren.

[33] And he said unto him, Lord, I am ready to go with thee, both into prison, and to death.

[34] And he said, I tell thee, Peter, the cock shall not crow this day, before that thou shalt thrice deny that thou knowest me.

[35] And he said unto them, When I sent you without purse, and scrip, and shoes, lacked ye any thing? And they said, Nothing.

[36] Then said he unto them, But now, he that hath a purse, let him take it, and likewise his scrip: and he that hath no sword, let him sell his garment, and buy one.

[37] For I say unto you, that this that is written must yet be accomplished in me, And he was reckoned among the transgressors: for the things concerning me have an end.

[38] And they said, Lord, behold, here are two swords. And he said unto them, It is enough.

[39] And he came out, and went, as he was wont, to the mount of Olives; and his disciples also followed him.

[40] And when he was at the place, he said unto them, Pray that ye enter not into temptation.

[41] And he was withdrawn from them about a stone's cast, and kneeled down, and prayed,

[42] Saying, Father, if thou be willing, remove this cup from me: nevertheless not my will, but thine, be done.

[43] And there appeared an angel unto him from heaven, strengthening him.

[44] And being in an agony he prayed more earnestly: and his sweat was as it were great drops of blood falling down to the ground.

[45] And when he rose up from prayer, and was come to his disciples, he found them sleeping for sorrow,

[46] And said unto them, Why sleep ye? rise and pray, lest ye enter into temptation.

[47] And while he yet spake, behold a multitude, and he that was called Judas, one of the twelve, went before them, and drew near unto Jesus to kiss him.

[48] But Jesus said unto him, Judas, betrayest thou the Son of man with a kiss?

[49] When they which were about him saw what would follow, they said unto him, Lord, shall we smite with the sword?

[50] And one of them smote the servant of the high priest, and cut off his right ear.

[51] And Jesus answered and said, Suffer ye thus far. And he touched his ear, and healed him.

[52] Then Jesus said unto the chief priests, and captains of the temple, and the elders, which were come to him, Be ye come out, as against a thief, with swords and staves?

[53] When I was daily with you in the temple, ye stretched forth no hands against me: but this is your hour, and the power of darkness.

[54] Then took they him, and led him, and brought him into the high priest's house. And Peter followed afar off.

[55] And when they had kindled a fire in the midst of the hall, and were set down together, Peter sat down among them.

[56] But a certain maid beheld him as he sat by the fire, and earnestly looked upon him, and said, This man was also with him.

[57] And he denied him, saying, Woman, I know him not.

[58] And after a little while another saw him, and said, Thou art also of them. And Peter said, Man, I am not.

[59] And about the space of one hour after another confidently affirmed, saying, Of a truth this fellow also was with him: for he is a Galilaean.

[60] And Peter said, Man, I know not what thou sayest. And immediately, while he yet spake, the cock crew.

[61] And the Lord turned, and looked upon Peter. And Peter remembered the word of the Lord, how he had said unto him, Before the cock crow, thou shalt deny me thrice.

[62] And Peter went out, and wept bitterly.

[63] And the men that held Jesus mocked him, and smote him.

[64] And when they had blindfolded him, they struck him on the face, and asked him, saying, Prophesy, who is it that smote thee?

[65] And many other things blasphemously spake they against him.

[66] And as soon as it was day, the elders of the people and the chief priests and the scribes came together, and led him into their council, saying,

[67] Art thou the Christ? tell us. And he said unto them, If I tell you, ye will not believe:

[68] And if I also ask you, ye will not answer me, nor let me go.

[69] Hereafter shall the Son of man sit on the right hand of the power of God.

[70] Then said they all, Art thou then the Son of God? And he said unto them, Ye say that I am.

[71] And they said, What need we any further witness? for we ourselves have heard of his own mouth.

Luke.23

[1] And the whole multitude of them arose, and led him unto Pilate.

[2] And they began to accuse him, saying, We found this fellow perverting the nation, and forbidding to give tribute to Caesar, saying that he himself is Christ a King.

[3] And Pilate asked him, saying, Art thou the King of the Jews? And he answered him and said, Thou sayest it.

[4] Then said Pilate to the chief priests and to the people, I find no fault in this man.

[5] And they were the more fierce, saying, He stirreth up the people, teaching

throughout all Jewry, beginning from Galilee to this place.

[6] When Pilate heard of Galilee, he asked whether the man were a Galilaean.

[7] And as soon as he knew that he belonged unto Herod's jurisdiction, he sent him to Herod, who himself also was at Jerusalem at that time.

[8] And when Herod saw Jesus, he was exceeding glad: for he was desirous to see him of a long season, because he had heard many things of him; and he hoped to have seen some miracle done by him.

[9] Then he questioned with him in many words; but he answered him nothing.

[10] And the chief priests and scribes stood and vehemently accused him.

[11] And Herod with his men of war set him at nought, and mocked him, and arrayed him in a gorgeous robe, and sent him again to Pilate.

[12] And the same day Pilate and Herod were made friends together: for before they were at enmity between themselves.

[13] And Pilate, when he had called together the chief priests and the rulers and the people,

[14] Said unto them, Ye have brought this man unto me, as one that perverteth the people: and, behold, I, having examined him before you, have found no fault in this man touching those things whereof ye accuse him:

[15] No, nor yet Herod: for I sent you to him; and, lo, nothing worthy of death is done unto him.

[16] I will therefore chastise him, and release him.

[17] (For of necessity he must release one unto them at the feast.)

[18] And they cried out all at once, saying, Away with this man, and release unto us Barabbas:

[19] (Who for a certain sedition made in the city, and for murder, was cast into prison.)

[20] Pilate therefore, willing to release Jesus, spake again to them.

[21] But they cried, saying, Crucify him, crucify him.

[22] And he said unto them the third time, Why, what evil hath he done? I have found no cause of death in him: I will therefore chastise him, and let him go.

[23] And they were instant with loud voices, requiring that he might be crucified. And the voices of them and of the chief priests prevailed.

[24] And Pilate gave sentence that it should be as they required.

[25] And he released unto them him that for sedition and murder was cast into prison, whom they had desired; but he delivered Jesus to their will.

[26] And as they led him away, they laid hold upon one Simon, a Cyrenian, coming out of the country, and on him they laid the cross, that he might bear it after Jesus.

[27] And there followed him a great company of people, and of women, which also bewailed and lamented him.

[28] But Jesus turning unto them said, Daughters of Jerusalem, weep not for me, but weep for yourselves, and for your children.

[29] For, behold, the days are coming, in the which they shall say, Blessed are the barren, and the wombs that never bare, and the paps which never gave suck.

[30] Then shall they begin to say to the mountains, Fall on us; and to the hills, Cover us.

[31] For if they do these things in a green tree, what shall be done in the dry?

[32] And there were also two other, malefactors, led with him to be put to death.

[33] And when they were come to the place, which is called Calvary, there they crucified him, and the malefactors, one on the right hand, and the other on the left.

[34] Then said Jesus, Father, forgive them; for they know not what they do. And they parted his raiment, and cast lots.

[35] And the people stood beholding. And the rulers also with them derided him, saying, He saved others; let him save himself, if he be Christ, the chosen of God.

[36] And the soldiers also mocked him, coming to him, and offering him vinegar,

[37] And saying, If thou be the king of the Jews, save thyself.

[38] And a superscription also was written over him in letters of Greek, and Latin, and Hebrew, THIS IS THE KING OF THE JEWS.

[39] And one of the malefactors which were hanged railed on him, saying, If thou be Christ, save thyself and us.

[40] But the other answering rebuked him, saying, Dost not thou fear God, seeing thou art in the same condemnation?

[41] And we indeed justly; for we receive the due reward of our deeds: but this man hath done nothing amiss.

[42] And he said unto Jesus, Lord, remember me when thou comest into thy kingdom.

[43] And Jesus said unto him, Verily I say unto thee, To day shalt thou be with me in paradise.

[44] And it was about the sixth hour, and there was a darkness over all the earth until the ninth hour.

[45] And the sun was darkened, and the veil of the temple was rent in the midst.

[46] And when Jesus had cried with a loud voice, he said, Father, into thy hands I commend my spirit: and having said thus, he gave up the ghost.

[47] Now when the centurion saw what was done, he glorified God, saying, Certainly this was a righteous man.

[48] And all the people that came together to that sight, beholding the things which were done, smote their breasts, and returned.

[49] And all his acquaintance, and the women that followed him from Galilee, stood afar off, beholding these things.

[50] And, behold, there was a man named Joseph, a counseller; and he was a good man, and a just:

[51] (The same had not consented to the counsel and deed of them;) he was of Arimathaea, a city of the Jews: who also himself waited for the kingdom of God.

[52] This man went unto Pilate, and begged the body of Jesus.

[53] And he took it down, and wrapped it in linen, and laid it in a sepulchre that was hewn in stone, wherein never man before was laid.

[54] And that day was the preparation, and the sabbath drew on.

[55] And the women also, which came with him from Galilee, followed after, and beheld the sepulchre, and how his body was laid.

[56] And they returned, and prepared spices and ointments; and rested the sabbath day according to the commandment.

Luke.24

[1] Now upon the first day of the week, very early in the morning, they came unto the sepulchre, bringing the spices which they had prepared, and certain others with them.

[2] And they found the stone rolled away from the sepulchre.

[3] And they entered in, and found not the body of the Lord Jesus.

[4] And it came to pass, as they were much perplexed thereabout, behold, two men stood by them in shining garments:

[5] And as they were afraid, and bowed down their faces to the earth, they said unto them, Why seek ye the living among the dead?

[6] He is not here, but is risen: remember how he spake unto you when he was yet in Galilee,

[7] Saying, The Son of man must be delivered into the hands of sinful men, and be crucified, and the third day rise again.

[8] And they remembered his words,

[9] And returned from the sepulchre, and told all these things unto the eleven, and to all the rest.

[10] It was Mary Magdalene, and Joanna, and Mary the mother of James, and other women that were with them, which told these things unto the apostles.

[11] And their words seemed to them as idle tales, and they believed them not.

[12] Then arose Peter, and ran unto the sepulchre; and stooping down, he beheld the linen clothes laid by themselves, and departed, wondering in himself at that which was come to pass.

[13] And, behold, two of them went that same day to a village called Emmaus, which was from Jerusalem about threescore furlongs.

[14] And they talked together of all these things which had happened.

[15] And it came to pass, that, while they communed together and reasoned, Jesus himself drew near, and went with them.

[16] But their eyes were holden that they should not know him.

[17] And he said unto them, What manner of communications are these that ye have one to another, as ye walk, and are sad?

[18] And the one of them, whose name was Cleopas, answering said unto him, Art thou only a stranger in Jerusalem, and hast not known the things which are come to pass therein these days?

[19] And he said unto them, What things? And they said unto him, Concerning Jesus of Nazareth, which was a prophet mighty in deed and word before God and all the people:

[20] And how the chief priests and our rulers delivered him to be condemned to death, and have crucified him.

[21] But we trusted that it had been he which should have redeemed Israel: and beside all this, to day is the third day since these things were done.

[22] Yea, and certain women also of our company made us astonished, which were early at the sepulchre;

[23] And when they found not his body, they came, saying, that they had also seen a vision of angels, which said that he was alive.

[24] And certain of them which were with us went to the sepulchre, and found it even so as the women had said: but him they saw not.

[25] Then he said unto them, O fools, and slow of heart to believe all that the prophets have spoken:

[26] Ought not Christ to have suffered these things, and to enter into his glory?

[27] And beginning at Moses and all the prophets, he expounded unto them in all the scriptures the things concerning himself.

[28] And they drew nigh unto the village, whither they went: and he made as though

he would have gone further.

[29] But they constrained him, saying, Abide with us: for it is toward evening, and the day is far spent. And he went in to tarry with them.

[30] And it came to pass, as he sat at meat with them, he took bread, and blessed it, and brake, and gave to them.

[31] And their eyes were opened, and they knew him; and he vanished out of their sight.

[32] And they said one to another, Did not our heart burn within us, while he talked with us by the way, and while he opened to us the scriptures?

[33] And they rose up the same hour, and returned to Jerusalem, and found the eleven gathered together, and them that were with them,

[34] Saying, The Lord is risen indeed, and hath appeared to Simon.

[35] And they told what things were done in the way, and how he was known of them in breaking of bread.

[36] And as they thus spake, Jesus himself stood in the midst of them, and saith unto them, Peace be unto you.

[37] But they were terrified and affrighted, and supposed that they had seen a spirit.

[38] And he said unto them, Why are ye troubled? and why do thoughts arise in your hearts?

[39] Behold my hands and my feet, that it is I myself: handle me, and see; for a spirit hath not flesh and bones, as ye see me have.

[40] And when he had thus spoken, he shewed them his hands and his feet.

[41] And while they yet believed not for joy, and wondered, he said unto them, Have ye here any meat?

[42] And they gave him a piece of a broiled fish, and of an honeycomb.

[43] And he took it, and did eat before them.

[44] And he said unto them, These are the words which I spake unto you, while I was yet with you, that all things must be fulfilled, which were written in the law of Moses, and in the prophets, and in the psalms, concerning me.

[45] Then opened he their understanding, that they might understand the scriptures,

[46] And said unto them, Thus it is written, and thus it behoved Christ to suffer, and to rise from the dead the third day:

[47] And that repentance and remission of sins should be preached in his name among all nations, beginning at Jerusalem.

[48] And ye are witnesses of these things.

[49] And, behold, I send the promise of my Father upon you: but tarry ye in the city of Jerusalem, until ye be endued with power from on high.

[50] And he led them out as far as to Bethany, and he lifted up his hands, and blessed them.

[51] And it came to pass, while he blessed them, he was parted from them, and carried up into heaven.

[52] And they worshipped him, and returned to Jerusalem with great joy:

[53] And were continually in the temple, praising and blessing God. Amen.

CHRISTADELPHIAN STATEMENT OF FAITH- THIS STATEMENT OF FAITH HAS BEEN UPLOADED FROM THE INTERNET AND IS NOT MY OWN COMPOSITION.

Who are the Christadelphians? Are they new?

The Christadelphians are a small religious body who have deliberately attempted to get back to the faith and character of the early Christian church. We have been in existence for over 150 years. The name "Christadelphian" means "Brother in Christ" or "in brotherhood with Christ".

Where are Christadelphians found?

We are located throughout the world. Like the early Christians, we meet in homes, rented rooms, and in some cases, our own halls. (Acts 1:13; 2:46; 18:7; 19:9; 28:30) For more information on how to find us, please click here.

How are Christadelphians organized?

We are a lay community patterned after first century Christianity. Members of each congregation are addressed as "Brother" and "Sister", and all have an equal joint responsibility for the welfare of the church. A strong common belief binds our Brotherhood together. (Mt. 23:8-12; Rom. 12:4-6; Rom. 16:1; 1 Cor. 12:4-27; Gal. 3:28)

What kind of life do Christadelphians lead?

God's way of salvation gives effective direction to our lives. We try to rely fully upon God and develop a faith which is active in prayer and good works. At the same time, however, we recognize that salvation is by grace. (Col. 1:3-11; 1 Pet. 2:1-5; 2 Pet. 1:5-11; James 2:17; 5:16; Eph. 2:5-10)

With God's help, we seek to please and obey Him every day, striving to imitate Christ who faithfully obeyed his Father and unselfishly gave himself for mankind. (Phil. 2:13; 4:13; Eph. 3:20; Phil. 2:1-5; Rom. 12:1-2; Eph. 5:1-2)

We therefore endeavor to be enthusiastic in work, loyal in marriage, generous in giving, dedicated in preaching, cheerful in living, and happy in our God. (Eph. 5:5; 6; 2 Cor. 9; 2 Tim. 4:1-5; Jn. 16:33; Mt. 5:1-16; Phil. 4:4-7)

What do Christadelphians believe and teach?

We believe that the Bible is God's only revealed message to mankind, given to bring responsive individuals to the obedience of faith. The Bible is our only authority, and we teach that is should be read prayerfully and with care at every opportunity. (Rom. 16:26; Jn. 17:17; Acts 17:11)

Certain key teachings stand out:

God

There is only one eternal, immortal God. Jesus Christ is His only begotten Son, and the Holy Spirit is His power. (Isa. 45:5; 1 Tim. 1:17; Eph. 4:6; Lk. 1:35; Acts 1:8; Lk. 24:49)

Man

Man is mortal and a sinner before God. His whole being is prone to sin, and the punishment for sin is death - real death, the end of all life. (Job 4:17; Rom. 3:23; Jer. 17:9; Mk. 7:21-23; Rom. 6:23; Ecc. 9:1-6; Psa. 146:4)

Jesus

In His love, God sent the man Jesus into the world to save men from their sins. Those who believe on him will not perish, but have everlasting life. (Mt. 1:21; Jn. 3:16)

Hope

The only hope of life after death is the resurrection of the body and everlasting life in God's Kingdom on earth. (Psa. 49:12-20; 1 Cor. 15:12-50; Rom. 8:23-35; Acts 24:15; Jn. 11:25; Rev. 5:10; 20:4)

Sacrifice of Christ

Jesus was sinless. He died to show the righteousness of God and to redeem those who receive this sacrifice by faith. God raised him from the dead, gave him immortality, granted him all authority in heaven and on earth, and set him as the mediator in heaven between God and man. (Acts 2:23-36; Eph. 1:19-23; 1 Tim. 2:5; Heb. 4:14-16; Rom. 3:21-26)

Return of Christ

Jesus will return to the earth soon. At that time he will raise many of the dead, judge them with the living, and give his faithful followers everlasting life in the Kingdom of God. (Rev. 22:12; Lk. 21:20-32; Jn. 5:28-29; Dan. 12:2; 2 Tim. 4:1; Mt. 25:34)

Kingdom of God

The Kingdom of God will be established on earth with Jesus as King. His capital will be Jerusalem, his dominion will be worldwide, and his government will bring righteousness and peace without end. (Dan. 2:44; 7:27; Acts 3:21; Jer. 3:17; Isa. 2:2-4; Psa. 72; Dan. 7:14; Isa. 9:6-9; 11:1-9; 61:1-11)

The Promises

The Gospel is inseparable from the promises which God made to Abraham and David in Old Testament times. These promises find their fulfillment in Jesus Christ. (Gal. 3:6-9, 16, 25-29; 2 Pet. 1:2-4; Gen. 14:14-17; 22:15-18; 2 Sam. 7:12-16; Lk. 1:31-33)

The Way of Salvation

The way to enter the Kingdom of God is by faith. This involves belief in His Word - the Bible - and obedience to its requirements that men and women confess their sins, repent, be baptized, and follow Jesus faithfully. (Heb. 11:6; 1 Thess. 2:13; 2 Tim. 3:15; Acts 2:37; Mk. 16:16; Jn. 3:3-5; Mt. 16:24-27)

This book is a new commentary on Luke not related to earlier ones from me being 146 pages long on Times New Roman 9 Font, 89598 words and 492352 characters.

ORIGINAL MANUSCRIPTS FOR LUKE REINTERPRETED. I usually write by hand first and then type up so I can listen to music while I'm typing. There may be an empty page here for notes due to reformatting.

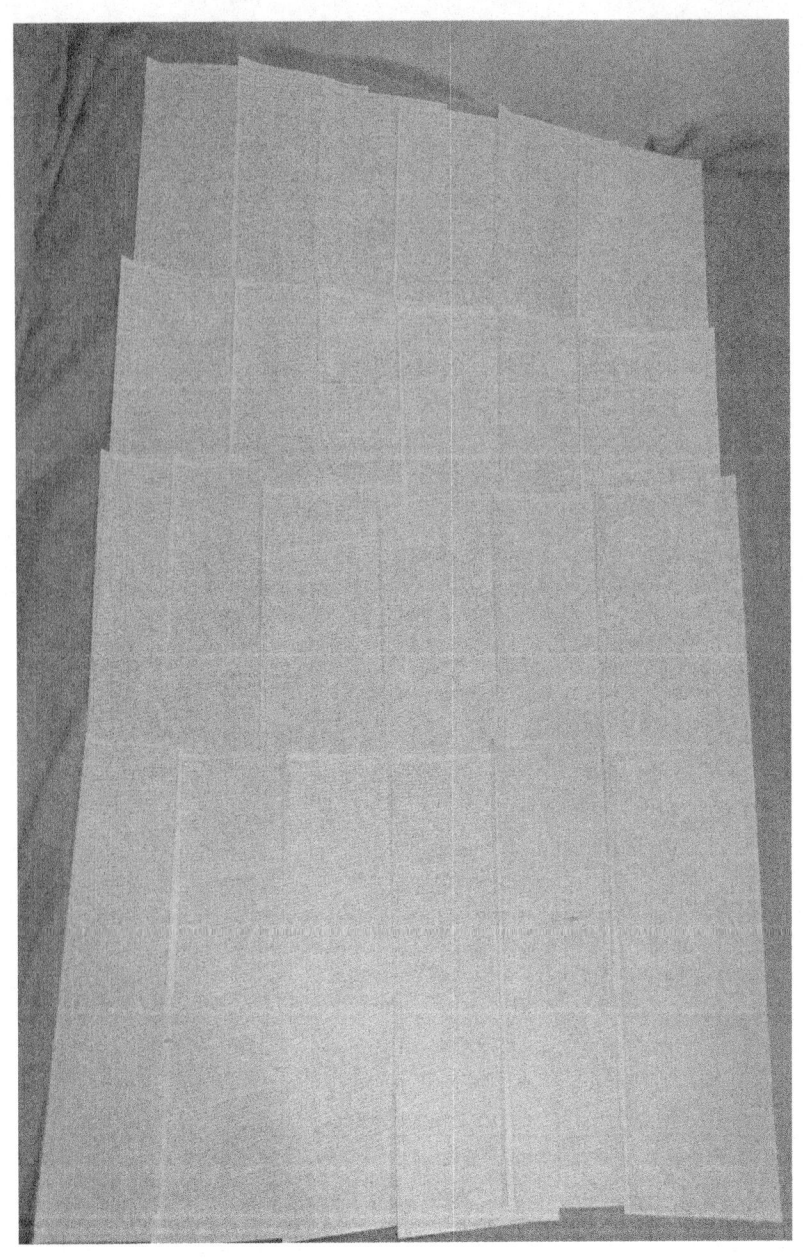

Printed in Dunstable, United Kingdom

63800251R00087